A DICTIONARY OF THE EUROPEAN ECONOMIC COMMUNITY

A DICTIONARY OF THE EUROPEAN ECONOMIC COMMUNITY

John Paxton

M

First published 1977 by

THE MACMILLAN PRESS LIMITED

London and Basingstoke
Associated companies in New York Dublin Melbourne and Madras

Printed in Great Britain by
Lowe & Brydone (Printers) Ltd., Thetford, Norfolk

British Library Cataloguing in Publication Data

Paxton, John
A dictionary of the European Economic Community.
1. European Economic Community-Dictionaries
I. Title
382′.9142′03   HC241.2

ISBN 0-333-21381-5

VICTOR BEUTTELL

Acknowledgements

I should like to thank the Commission of the European Communities in London for considerable help. Also Stephen Brooks, Judith Eversley, Sheila Fairfield and Richard Haig-Brown for advice and help with some entries. Penny White did her usual stint at typing and her eye for error came to my rescue on many occasions. Eve Beadle and Sheila Bryant read the whole manuscript and made valuable suggestions.

Preface

Twenty years have gone by since the signing of the Treaty of Rome, twenty five years since the European Coal and Steel Community started work in Luxembourg under its President, Jean Monnet, and thirty years since General Marshall made his speech at Harvard which led to the recovery of Europe after the war. Many of us have followed the drama since 1947 but there is now a generation of young people studying modern history and European studies at universities and polytechnics, or starting on the first stages of a business career, born after the signing of the Rome Treaty in 1957. I therefore felt that there was a need for definitions and statements about the European Economic Community to be compiled in a dictionary giving all information in a succinct and accurate form. I have not limited myself to the E.E.C. but have included other related organisations where I felt this appropriate.

I've tried to avoid compiling an 'encyclopaedia' and this has been achieved by breaking up large entries, such as the Rome Treaty, into a large number of entries of small wordage. I have also tried to avoid the other extreme of producing a 'directory'. Also I've tried to make each entry complete in itself rather than cause the reader to go on a wild goose chase through the dictionary. (I rather like 'reference book wild goose chases' but few people have sufficient leisure for this sort of activity.)

There will be omissions and I shall be grateful to have suggestions from readers for inclusion in the next edition. Sadly, as with any reference book, some error could creep in. Such errors will be my own and I shall be happy to be alerted so that these can be corrected in subsequent editions.

JOHN PAXTON

Bruton, Somerset
April, 1977

A

A.A.S.M.
The Associated African States and Madagascar. These were the eighteen states associated with the E.E.C. under the Yaoundé Convention of 1964.

A/B
Aktiebolaget, joint stock company in Sweden.

Accession, Treaty of
The Treaty of Accession was signed in Brussels on 22 Jan. 1972 by the Six and Denmark, the Irish Republic, Norway and the United Kingdom.

The declaration of the Council of the Communities in favour of the admission of the new members required no further ratification because the Treaty of Rome empowers the Council acting by unanimous vote to admit other European states. On the other hand the new members had to submit the Treaty to their Parliaments for ratification. Denmark, Norway and the Irish Republic were obliged, by their Constitutions, to hold referenda as well. The instruments of ratification had to be deposited by the new member states by 31 Dec. 1972 for the Treaty to enter into force on 1 Jan. 1973.

The Treaty consists essentially of two parts:

(i) The Treaty concerning the accession of the new members to the European Economic Community and the European Atomic Energy Community; and the Decision of the Council of the Communities concerning the accession of the new members to the European Coal and Steel Community. (The need for a separate procedure lay in legalistic differences between the Treaty of Rome, which established the European Economic Community and Euratom, and the Treaty of Paris, which established the European Coal and Steel Community.)

(ii) The 'Act' concerning the conditions of accession and the adjustments

1

and amendments to the treaties.

The Treaty set out all the amendments to and derogations from the Treaty of Rome and its subsequent legislative instruments made necessary by the agreements on the terms of entry of the new members. For summarised details *see* United Kingdom, Terms of Entry to the E.E.C.

The Act provided, *inter alia*, for an increase in the number of delegates to the Assembly from 142 to 208 to provide seats for the new members, of the size of the Council from six to ten and of the Commission from nine to fourteen. It also provides an increase in the number of Judges in the Court of Justice and changes their rota.

The 161 Articles included details of the transitional period for new members, adjustments to the Statute of the European Investment Bank to the rights of the Channel Islands and the Isle of Man. It includes, as Protocols, a full list of the Community treaties and related instruments as at the date of the signature of the Treaty of Accession, by which the new members are bound.

One important Protocol provides for an interim committee for consultation between the Four and the Six on matters which involved the Four after membership, including trade negotiations with the rump of Efta.

Although ratification was not legally necessary each member state decided on this course. In France ratification of the Treaty of Accession by the French President was approved in a referendum held throughout metropolitan France and the French overseas territories and departments on 23 April 1972.

The Treaty was approved in Belgium by the Senate on 30 June 1972, and by the Chamber of Deputies on 8 Dec.; in the Federal German Republic by the *Bundestag* on 21 June and by the *Bundesrat* on 7 July; in Italy by the Chamber of Deputies on 5 Dec. and by the Senate on 19 Dec.; in Luxembourg by the Parliament on 20 Dec.; and in the Netherlands by the Second Chamber of the States-General on 14 Sept. and by the First Chamber on 14 Nov. 1972.

Denmark, the Irish Republic and the United Kingdom became members of the European Communities on 1 Jan. 1973, in accordance with the provisions of the Treaty of Accession. Norway decided, in a referendum in Sept. 1972, against joining by 53·49 % to 46·51 %.

Accords of Luxembourg
see Luxembourg Agreement

A.C.P.
A.C.P. countries are those located in Africa, the Caribbean and the Pacific and consist of the forty-three (later forty-six) countries that signed the Lomé agreement (Bahamas, Barbados, Benin, Botswana, Burundi, Cameroon, Central African Republic, Chad, Congo, Equatorial Guinea, Ethiopia, Fiji, Gabon, Gambia, Ghana, Grenada, Guinea, Guinea-Bissau, Guyana, Ivory Coast, Jamaica, Kenya, Lesotho, Liberia, Madagascar, Malawi, Mali, Mauritania, Mauritius, Niger, Nigeria, Rwanda, Senegal, Sierra Leone, Somalia, Sudan, Swaziland, Tanzania, Togo, Tonga, Trinidad and Tobago, Uganda, Upper Volta, Western Samoa, Zaïre and Zambia).

Adenauer, Konrad
Born Cologne, Germany, 1876, died 1967. Chief Burgomeister of Cologne, Germany from 1917–33. Dismissed in March 1933 he was reinstated to that position in June 1945 but removed from the post by the British Military Government in Oct. of the same year for 'obstruction and non-co-operation'. Dr Adenauer was the founder of the Christian Democratic Union in 1945. He was the first Chancellor of the German Federal Republic 1949–63 and its Foreign Minister 1951–5.

In 1950 he advocated a Franco-German union as the first step towards bringing the Federal German Republic into a united Europe and in 1963 he signed the Franco-German Treaty of Co-operation.

A.D.R.
The European *Agreement* on the International Carriage of *Dangerous* Goods by *Road* came into force in 1968. Fourteen countries are signatories to the agreement, including all E.E.C. countries except Denmark and the Irish Republic, together with Austria, German Democratic Republic, Portugal, Spain, Switzerland and Yugoslavia. The Agreement ensures that dangerous goods being conveyed by road can cross international frontiers without hindrance provided that goods are packed

3

and labelled in accordance with the Agreement. Tanker vehicles carrying inflammable substances are subject to technical inspection.

A.E.L.E.
Association européenne de libre-échange, see European Free Trade Association.

AG
Aktiengesellschaft, joint stock company in Austria and the Federal German Republic.

agriculture

The basic aim of the E.E.C. agricultural policy is to provide reliable supplies of foodstuffs at stable prices, giving a fair return to those who work on the land. Each year the Council of Ministers agrees the E.E.C. farm support prices. These fix lowest levels at which imported foodstuffs can reach the Community market, the floor price for home-produced commodities and the direct aid which may be given to farmers in some sectors such as beef. These official prices aim to provide the framework for market prices.

Some products, like grains, sugar, beef, butter and skimmed milk powder can be sold to the intervention agencies in the member states when market prices fall to the intervention levels. For grains and sugar this system is a welcome safeguard against shortage, as they are products which keep well and where the world cannot be sure of adequate supply even twelve months ahead. Stocks which build up in a good year can be used in times of scarcity. For products like skimmed milk powder and wine, where there is a serious over-production, the European Commission is pressing for reforms which will better match supply to demand. To put surpluses back on the market too quickly would depress prices, and so jeopardise future supplies. Methods used to give consumers more benefits from abundant supplies have been: (*a*) the butter subsidy, which helps to maintain consumption and keep down prices; (*b*) beef tokens, which provided temporary help to pensioners to buy more beef; (*c*) direct payments to beef producers, which mean that less beef goes into store and more to the consumer if prices drop, but *see* Common Agricultural Policy.

Agriculture 1980
see Mansholt Plan

A.I.F.T.A.
Anglo-Irish Free Trade Agreement came into force on 1 July 1966.

aircraft, civil, produced in the E.E.C.

aircraft	country	engines	no.	seats	in service
BAC One-Eleven	U.K.	Rolls-Royce Spey	2	79–119	1965
Hawker Siddeley Trident	U.K.	Rolls-Royce Spey	3	up to 171	1964
Hawker Siddeley 125	U.K.	Rolls-Royce Viper	2	7–12	1964
Hawker Siddeley 748	U.K.	Rolls-Royce Dart	2	45–60	1961
BAC/Aerospatiale Concorde	U.K./F	Rolls-Royce/ Snecma Olympus	4	128	1976
Short Skyvan	U.K.	Garrett (U.S.A.)	2	20	1966
Fokker-VFW F 27	N/F.G.R.	Rolls-Royce Dart	2	48–56	1958
Fokker-VFW F 28	N/F.G.R./U.K.	Rolls-Royce Spey	2	50–79	1969
Fokker-VFW 614	F.G.R./N	Rolls-Royce M45H	2	44	1975
Dassault Mercure	F	Pratt and Whitney (U.S.A.) JT8D-15	2	155	1973
Dassault Fan Jet Falcon	F	General Electric (U.S.A.) CF700	2	10	1966
Airbus Industrie A300B	U.K./F/F.G.R./N	General Electric (U.S.A.) CF-6-50A	2	250–306	1974
Scottish Aviation Jetstream	U.K.	Azatou	2	12–18	1974
Britten Norman Islander	U.K./B	Lycoming (U.S.A.)	2	12	1967
Britten Norman Trilander	U.K./B	Lycoming (U.S.A.)	3	12–18	1971

Algeria
Negotiations were concluded on 17–18 Jan. 1976 for a trade and co-operation agreement between the E.E.C. and Algeria.

Alliance Européenne des Agences de Presse
see Press Agencies, European Alliance of

anti-dumping policy of the E.E.C.
The Regulation, which covers not only dumping but the granting of bounties or subsidies by countries which are not members of the E.E.C., was introduced as part of the Treaty obligations to ensure fair competition policy in the Community.

A product is considered to have been dumped 'if the price of the product when exported to the Community is less than the comparable price, in the ordinary course of trade of the like product . . . when destined for consumption in the exporting country of origin'.

Both the Gatt Anti-dumping Code and the E.E.C. Regulation provide for anti-dumping measures to be taken if there is injury to a Community industry, either the entire industry or a major proportion of it. Furthermore, both measures expressly recognise that, in certain circumstances, it may be necessary to act in defence of the industry in a region of the Community, thus ensuring considerable flexibility to deal with all problems.

A determination of injury must be based on fact and not on allegations, but industries suffering from dumping have the option either of approaching member states directly or of making their problems known to the Commission in the first place, which will give all possible advice and assistance.

If a preliminary examination provides sufficient evidence of injury from dumping, the Commission, on its own initiative, can impose a provisional but compulsory anti-dumping duty on the product, which must later be confirmed or amended by the Council.

anti-trust policy
see competition policy

Argentina
A non-preferential trade agreement between the E.E.C. and Argentina came into force on 1 Jan. 1972 for a period of three years under Article 113

6

of the Treaty of Rome. The agreement was extended twice; first, for one year to 31 Dec. 1975 and again until 31 Dec. 1976. The United Kingdom was not party to the 1972 agreement but was bound by the provisions of the agreement under Article 4 (1) of the Treaty of Accession.

Article xxxv
Article xxxv, when invoked, is the Article in the General Agreement on Tariffs and Trade whereby, at the time of accession, the acceding country may elect not to apply the General Agreement in its relations with any other contracting party. Similarly any contracting party may invoke this Article against any newly acceding country.

Arusha, Tanzania
Capital of Arusha region in the north of the country situated to the south-west of Mount Meru. Centre of a coffee-growing region and headquarters of the East African Community. The Arusha E.E.C. Convention was signed there in 1969. Population at 1967 census 32,452.

Arusha Convention
The Arusha Convention, a four-year agreement of association between the E.E.C. and Kenya, Uganda and Tanzania was signed on 24 Sept. 1969. An earlier agreement signed on 26 July 1968 had not been ratified by all the E.E.C. members before the expiry date. The provisions were similar to those in the Yaoundé agreements except that there is no arrangement for development and the preferential agreement for E.E.C. goods is more limited. The agreement ended in 1975 and was replaced by the Lomé Convention.

A/S
Aktjeselskap, Norwegian, and *Aktieselskab*, Danish, for joint stock company.

Assembly
see Parliament, European

A.S.S.U.C.
Association des organisations professionnelles de commerce des sucres pour les pays de la C.E.E., Association of Sugar Trade Organisations for the E.E.C. Countries.

A.T.A. carnet
An A.T.A. carnet is an international customs temporary importation document and can be used for exhibits for international trade fairs, samples and professional equipment. It can be used in all E.E.C. member countries and many other countries of Europe.

Austria
Austria was a founder-member of Efta. A preferential agreement establishing a free-trade area between the E.E.C. and Austria came into force on 1 Jan. 1973 for an unlimited period under Article 113 of the Treaty of Rome. An interim agreement of 1 Oct. 1972 was superseded by the definitive agreement of Jan. 1973.

Economic profile: Area 83,900 sq. km. Population (1973) 7,520,000 (male (1971) 3,502,000) density 90 per sq. km. Births (per 1,000 of pop. 1973) 13·9; marriages, 7·7; deaths, 12·7. Infant mortality, 25·2.
   Labour force (1972) 3,054,000; percentage in agriculture, 16·4; industry, 41; services, 42·6.

International trade (in millions of U.A.):

	1965	*1970*	*1973*
Imports	2,100	3,549	5,415
Exports	1,600	2,857	4,013

	per 1,000 of population
Standard of living:	
Motor vehicles (1973)	195
Televisions (1972)	213
Telephones (1972)	207

awards

Bech Prize (Federal Republic of Germany), created in 1977 to be awarded annually as a distinction for signal services and personal engagements in the cause of Europe, to commemorate Dr Joseph Bech, the Luxembourg statesman. Awarded by the Freiherr von Stein Foundation in Hamburg. Value 20,000 Deutsche Marks. First winners Shirley Williams and Prof. Henri Rieben.

Bentinck Prize (France), awarded annually since 1973 in memory of Adolphe Bentinck, former French ambassador to the Netherlands, for work contributing to solidarity and co-operation in Europe, the development of European institutions and promotion of European relations with the rest of the world. Value: 15,000 French francs.

1973 Karl Kaiser
1974 Giovanni Magnifico
1975 Hendryck Brugmans
1976 Jean Monnet

Charlemagne Prize (Federal German Republic), created in 1949 to be awarded annually by the West German city of Aachen, for outstanding contributions to European unity and the encouragement of international co-operation. Value: 5,000 Deutsche Marks.

1950 Count Richard Coudenhove-Kalergi
1951 Hendryck Brugmans
1952 Alcide de Gasperi
1953 Jean Monnet
1954 Konrad Adenauer
1955 No award
1956 Winston Churchill
1957 Paul-Henri Spaak
1958 Robert Schuman

1959 Gen. George C. Marshall
1960 Joseph Bech
1961 Walter Hallstein
1962 No award
1963 Edward Heath
1964 Antonio Segni
1965 No award
1966 Jens-Otto Krag
1967 Joseph Luns
1968
1969 All 14 members of the E.E.C. Commission
1970 François Seydoux
1971 No award
1972 Roy Jenkins
1973 Salvador de Madariaga
1974 No award
1975 Cardinal Mindszenty (posthumously)
1976 Leo Tindemans
1977 Walter Scheel

Deutsch Foundation European Prize (Switzerland), founded by Austrian publisher Dr Hans Deutsch in 1963 when it was awarded to Salvador de Madariaga. Awarded for work promoting the idea of Europe as a single cultural and political community. Value: 50,000 Swiss Francs.

Erasmus Prize (The Netherlands), awarded by the European Cultural Foundation annually. Created by Prince Bernhard of the Netherlands and funded by the Dutch Government. Awarded to a person or institution for activity in the cultural, social or scientific field contributing to or reflecting European unity. Created in 1958. Value: 100,000 Guilders (each prize).

1958 Adolf Schaerf and the Austrian people
1959 Karl Jaspers and Robert Schuman
1960 Oskar Kokoschka and Marc Chagall
1961
1962 Romano Guardini
1963 Martin Buber
1964 Union Académique Internationale
1965 Charlie Chaplin and Ingmar Bergman
1966 Sir Herbert Read and René Huyghe
1967 Jan Tinbergen

1968 Henry Moore
1969 Gabriel Marcel and Carl-Friedrich von Weizsäcker
1970 Hans Scharoun
1971 Olivier Messiaen
1972 Jean Piaget
1973 Claude Lévi-Strauss
1974 Ninette de valois and Maurice Béjart
1975 Ernst Gombrich and William Sandberg
1976 Amnesty International and René David
1977 Werner Kaegi

Europa Prize, awarded annually 1967—71 for contribution to the European economic and financial field, by the 'Top Five' financial publications: *Handelsblatt, La Vie Française, La Métropole, Elseviers* and *Il Sole/24 Ore*, with the Union of European Economic and Financial Press.

1967 Sicco Mansholt	1970 City of Brussels
1968 Walter Hallstein	1971 Credit Lyonnais, Commerzbank
1969 Emilio Colombo	and Banco di Roma

Europe Prize, awarded from 1956—60 by the Consultative Assembly of the Council of Europe for work contributing to European co-operation and unity. Funded by the Hamburg F.V.S. (Freiherr von Stein) Foundation endowed by Alfred Töpfer. Value: 18,000 French francs.
1956 Jean Durivau
1957 Anna Kethly
1958 Georg Eckert
1959
1960 Prince Bernhard of the Netherlands

Europe Prize, awarded annually to towns which have furthered the cause of European integration and fostered links between the people of Europe by the Committee on Local Authorities of the Council of Europe in Strasbourg. First awarded 1955. Value: 2,500 French francs (until 1970), 20,000 French francs (from 1973). To be spent on encouraging youth exchanges.
1955 Coventry
1956 Puteaux and Offenbach
1957 Bordeaux and Turin
1958 The Hague and Vienna
1959 Istanbul
1960 Aarhus and Bruges

11

1961 Rhodes and Schwarzenbeck (Denmark)
1962 Palermo
1963 Aubenas (France)
1964 Innsbruck
1965 Tübingen and Saint-Savin
1966 Kristiansand
1967 Strasbourg
1968 Faenza (Italy)
1969 Nancy and Karlsruhe
1970 Sierre
1971 Udine
1972 Zeigate (Belgium)
1973 Würzburg
1974 Cesenatico and Macon
1975 Darmstadt
1976 Devon County Council

Paul Finet Foundation was created in 1965 by the High Authority of the European Coal and Steel Community in honour of its former President. Its purpose is to provide financial assistance to the orphans of workers in the coal, iron ore mining and steel industries of the E.C.S.C. who died after 30 June 1965 (for citizens of the United Kingdom, Irish Republic and Denmark, after 1 Jan. 1973) of industrial accidents or occupational diseases. The object of this assistance is to provide or assist such children with their education or vocational training. The children must be at least fourteen years of age or be ahead of the normal curriculum. They must be following courses of vocational training, general secondary education, or higher education at a university or establishment of university level. They must have the capacities required for the studies they wish to pursue and show good educational results.

The Foundation does not assist all orphans, but reserves the available funds for those who really need them and who deserve it most because of their skills, zeal and success in their studies.

The financial aids are awarded annually; they are renewable so that the beneficiary has a certain guarantee of continuity. He will know that he can rely on the help of the Foundation for the whole period of the studies he wants to undertake if he shows evidence of good results. Application for grants must be sent to the Secretariat of the Paul Finet Foundation, Batiment Jean Monnet—A 2, rue Alcide de Gasperi, Luxembourg: directly by those concerned or by their legal representative; through their father's former employer; via trade unions, social security organisations, regional scholarship committees, schools or universities.

Schuman Prize (Federal German Republic), awarded annually from 1966 by Bonn University to honour eminent Europeans who have promoted the cause of European unity. Funds provided by F.V.S. Foundation (Freiherr von Stein) endowed by Alfred Töpfer. Value: 25,000 Deutsche Marks.

1966 Jean Monnet
1967 Joseph Bech
1968 Sicco Mansholt
1969 Walter Hallstein
1970 Denis de Rougemont
1971 Silvio Magnago
1972 Roy Jenkins
1973 Jens-Otto Krag
1974 Altiero Spinelli
1975 Pierre Pflimlin
1976 Sir Christopher Soames
1977 Gaston Thorn

Schuman Prize (France), awarded annually by the Foundation and Association of the Friends of Robert Schuman, for contributions to European unity. Gold Medal.

1967 Walter Hallstein and René Mayer
1968 Emilio Colombo
1969 Paul-Henri Spaak
1970
1971 Pierre Werner
1972
1973 Jack Lynch
1974 Olivier Reverdin
1975
1976

Sonning Prize (Denmark), awarded for contributions to European Culture. Value: 200,000 Danish kroners.

1973 Sir Karl Popper

Stresemann Prize (Federal German Republic), awarded for contributions to European Politics. Gold Medal. Presented by the Gustav

Stresemann Society, Mainz.
Laureates include Joseph Luns and
Amintore Fanfani (1971)

B

Baccalaureate, European
The European Baccalaureate examination is taken at the end of a seven
year secondary course, the final four years being divided between a course
common to all candidates and concentration on one of the five sections:
(*i*) Latin-Greek; (*ii*) Latin-Modern Languages; (*iii*) Latin-Mathematics-
Science; (*iv*) Modern Languages-Mathematics-Science; (*v*) Economics-
Social Science.

The examinations for each section follow a similar pattern: Written
examinations are taken in six subjects which together give a maximum of
120/300 marks. Papers in the mother tongue, mathematics, philosophy and
a foreign language are taken in each section, in addition to the specialist
subjects, though the awards for each subject are not necessarily given the
same weighting in each section of the Baccalaureate.

Oral examinations (80/300 marks) are given in four subjects, the mother
tongue, a modern foreign language and two others. The others are chosen,
by lot a week before the examination, from amongst the subjects studied by
the pupil during his last year in school: one must be of a literary, and the
other of a scientific, kind; and neither subject must have been included in
the written examination.

Classwork assessment forms the third element of the examinations
(100/300 marks) and is based on gradings in all subjects studied (13 or
more) during the last two terms of the final year in school.

Bahamas
The Commonwealth of the Bahamas was a signatory of the Lomé
Convention in Feb. 1975.

Bank for International Settlements
The B.I.S. is an international institution founded in Basle, Switzerland in 1930.

Barbados
Barbados was a signatory of the Lomé Convention in Feb. 1975.

Barre Plan
The Barre Plan was one of the steps towards economic and monetary union within the E.E.C. and the Plan was presented to the Council of Ministers in Feb. 1969 by Raymond Barre, then vice-president of the E.E.C. Commission. The Plan advocated that each member country should undertake to place part of its reserves at the disposal of the other members so that, in the event of difficulties, any member would be able to call on its partners for assistance up to a limited figure. Then joint consultations would be held to re-establish equilibrium. If no agreement could be reached the indebted country would have to repay the borrowed funds within a three-month period, but if agreement was reached this could lead to medium-term assistance. There would, at the same time, have to be a move towards greater alignment of economic policies of the member countries concerned. It was further advocated that negotiations and arrangements were to be between the central banks rather than with governments. The Barre Plan received the approval of the Council of Ministers in July 1969.

Barre, Raymond
Born Réunion, 1924. *Directeur du Cabinet* and Minister of Industry, 1959–62. He was a member of the Committee of Experts, *Comité Lorain*, on financing investments in France, 1963–4; Vice-President of Commission of European Communities with responsibility for economic and financial affairs, 1967–72, and became Prime Minister of France in 1976.

basket unit of account
see unit of account

basic price
Basic price methods apply to fruit, vegetables and pigmeat. Once the average market price is below the basic, or cost of production price, action can be taken to support the market by buying in surplus output.

Basle credits
European and certain other Central Bankers gather regularly at Basle for the meetings of the Bank for International Settlements. Basle credits is the description sometimes given to the *ad hoc* mutual arrangements between Central Banks for rendering each other foreign exchange assistance.

B.E.C.
Bureau Européen du Café, European Coffee Bureau.

Bech, Joseph
Born Diekirch, Luxembourg, 1887. He entered Luxembourg Parliament as a Deputy in 1914; held the posts of Minister of Justice and Home Affairs, 1921–5, Minister of Foreign Affairs, 1926–44 and 1953–8, and for the latter period was also Prime Minister. He was a signatory to the Statute setting up the Council of Europe in 1949; he presided over the Messina conference in 1955, and was a member of the E.E.C. Council of Ministers, 1958.

Bech Prize
see awards

beef 'mountain'
see 'mountain'

B.E.E.P.
Bureau européen de l'éducation populaire, European Bureau of Adult Education.

B.E.I.
Banque européenne d'investissement, see European Investments Bank.

Belgium
Belgium signed the Treaty of Paris (E.C.S.C.) in 1951, the Treaties of Rome (E.E.C. and Euratom) in 1957 and the Treaty of Brussels (Treaty of Accession) in 1972.

Economic profile: Area 30,500 sq. km. Population (1973) 9,742,000 (male 4,760,000) density 319 per sq. km. Births (per 1,000 of pop. 1973) 13·3; marriages, 7·5; deaths, 12·1. Infant mortality, 17.

Labour force (1972) 3,875,000; percentage in agriculture, 4·2; industry, 43·3; services, 52·5.

International trade (together with Luxembourg in millions of U.A.):

	1965	1970	1973	1976
Imports	6,374	11,362	17,492	28,022
Exports	6,382	11,609	17,854	25,994

	per 1,000 of population
Standard of living:	
Motor vehicles (1973)	235
Televisions (1972)	227
Telephones (1972)	224

Benelux
A portmanteau word, formed from the first syllables of *Be*lgium, the *Ne*therlands and *Lux*embourg, which was first used to describe the customs union of these three countries and was subsequently applied to any of their concerted actions.

A customs union between the Kingdom of Belgium and the Grand Duchy of Luxembourg was concluded at Brussels on 25 July 1921 and ratified on 5 March 1922, and the customs frontier between the two countries was abolished on 1 May 1922. The union was dissolved in 1940 but re-established on 1 May 1945.

Benin

On 14 March 1947 a customs union was concluded between Belgium and Luxembourg on the one hand, and the Netherlands on the other. The union came into force on 1 Jan. 1948 and is now known as the Benelux Economic Union. A joint tariff has been adopted and import duties are no longer levied at the Netherlands frontier, but import licences may still be required. A full economic union of the three countries came into operation on 1 Nov. 1960.

Although it maintains its identity its aims have been, in part, absorbed by the larger organisations which developed in Europe in later years.

Benin
Benin, *formerly* Dahomey, signed the Yaoundé Conventions of 1963 and 1969 and the Lomé Convention of 1975.

Bentinck Prize
see awards

Berne Union
The Berne Union is an International Convention dealing with copyright, first drawn up in Berne in 1886. Under the terms of the Convention, literary or artistic works published in a country which is a signatory to the Convention enjoy copyright in the territories of the other signatories.

B.E.U.C.
Bureau Européen des Unions de Consommateurs, European Bureau of Consumers' Unions.

Bevin, Ernest
Born Winsford, England, 1881, died 1951. General Secretary of the National Transport and General Workers' Union, which he helped to found, 1921–40. Minister of Labour and National Service, 1940–5. Foreign Secretary, 1945–51.

In 1948 negotiated the implementation of Marshall Aid and signed the

Convention setting up the O.E.E.C. In 1949 he presided over the meeting of Foreign Secretaries which produced the statute setting up the Council of Europe. On 13 June 1947 Ernest Bevin said, in the course of an address to the Foreign Press Association: 'We welcome the inspiring lead given to us and the peoples of Europe by Mr. Marshall. His speech at Harvard will rank, I think, as one of the greatest speeches made in world history. It seemed to me to focus a need, and to have behind it the conception of a great co-operation between Europe and the Western Hemisphere. I can only say to other nations that when the U.S.A. throws a bridge to link east and west, it would be disastrous for ideological reasons to frustrate her in that great endeavour . . . So far as the British Government is concerned, I think the initiative devolves upon us in trying to lead Europe back to a healthy state. We are glad to know that misunderstanding has been removed by including Russia in the proposals, removing any idea that there was anything ideological in them.' That last sentence refers to the fact that, after the American Secretary of State's Harvard speech, some people in Europe and elsewhere felt uncertain as to where the frontiers of Mr. Marshall's 'Europe' began and ended. At a press conference a week later Mr. Marshall elucidated: in his Harvard speech, the word 'Europe' had been intended to include the Soviet Union and Britain, and, indeed 'everything west of Asia'.

Beyen, Johan Willem

Born 1897. Minister of Foreign Affairs, 1952–6. Government Commissioner for Netherlands-German relations; Netherlands Ambassador to France, 1958–63; Executive Director of the International Monetary Fund, 1948. Executive Director of the Bank for Reconstruction and Development, Washington, 1964.

B.I.A.C.

Business and Industry Advisory Committee, advisory body on management and trade union sides of industry, in association with O.E.C.D.

B.I.E.

see Britain in Europe.

birth rate (1974)

country	live births per 1,000 inhabitants
Belgium	12·7
Denmark	14·2
France	15·2
Federal German Republic	10·1
Irish Republic	22·3
Italy	15·7
Luxembourg	11·0
Netherlands	13·8
United Kingdom	13·2
E.E.C.	13·5

B.I.S.
Bank for International Settlements.

B.L.E.U.
Belgo-Luxembourg Economic Union.

B.L.I.C.
Bureau de liaison des industries du caoutchouc de la C.E.E., Rubber Industries Liaison Bureau of the E.E.C.

block exemptions
The E.E.C. Commission, acting under the Council of Ministers, has identified certain broad categories of agreement which it has laid down as exempt from the ban on restrictive trade agreements. Such agreements are said to fall under the heading of block exemptions.

B.N.
Brussels nomenclature *see* B.T.N.

B.O.T.B.
British Overseas Trade Board.

Botswana
Botswana was a signatory of the Lomé Convention in Feb. 1975. In March 1976 the E.E.C. agreed to provide Botswana with about 90m. Rand in aid over four years. An agreement set out a wide-ranging programme covering a tribal land grazing scheme, road tarring and the construction of integrated office accommodation for district councils.

Brandt, Willy
Born Lübeck, Germany, 1913. Member of the *Bundestag* of the Federal German Republic, 1949–57; President of the *Bundesrat*, 1957–8; Minister of Foreign Affairs and Vice-Chancellor, 1966–9; Chancellor of the Federal German Republic, 1969–74. In 1968 he advocated widening the membership of the E.E.C. to include the countries then applying for membership, including the United Kingdom. He put forward two plans for increased co-operation between the Six and the applicant countries to ease entry into full membership.

Bratteli, Trygvi Martin
Born Norway, 1910. Norwegian newspaper editor and labour politician, Prime Minister, 1971–2 and again, 1973–6, when he resigned following the vote (53%–47%) against membership of the European Communities in the referendum after his Government had negotiated the terms of entry.

Brazil
On 19 Dec. 1973 Brazil signed a three-year non-preferential trade agreement with the E.E.C. under Article 113 of the Treaty of Rome.

Bretton Woods
Bretton Woods is a resort in the White Mountains of New Hampshire,

U.S.A., where the United Nations Monetary and Financial Conference met in 1944. This Conference agreed to set up the International Monetary Fund and the International Bank for Reconstruction and Development, also known as the World Bank.

Britain in Europe
Britain in Europe was the pro-Common Market 'umbrella' organisation active in the United Kingdom referendum campaign.

British dependent territories
Under the Treaty of Accession all British dependent territories except Gibraltar and Hong Kong can be offered association with the E.E.C. under Part IV of the Treaty of Rome.

Brussels
Capital of Belgium in the province of Brabant, situated on the Senne river. A cultural and commercial centre. Industries include textiles, chemicals, manufacture of paper, furniture, clothing and lace. Administrative centre of the European Economic Community. Population, with suburbs, in 1975 estimated at 1,050,787.

Brussels Treaty
see Accession, Treaty of

B.S.I.
The British Standards Institution is the official organisation for the preparation of national standards in the United Kingdom and co-operates with other national organisations in drawing up recommendations for common standards.

B.T.N.
Brussels Tariff Nomenclature is the standard classification of goods for

customs tariff purposes now used by the majority of countries, but *see* Nimexe.

budget

The European Parliament and the Council of Ministers jointly control the E.E.C.'s budget. For each calendar year the Commission draws up a preliminary budget, which the Council and Parliament then consider in two 'readings'.

All Community expenditure is classified as either 'compulsory' or 'non-compulsory'. In the words of the Treaty, compulsory expenditure is 'expenditure necessarily resulting from this Treaty or from acts adopted in accordance therewith'; all other expenditure is non-compulsory.

The European Parliament now has the power to reject the budget as a whole. Within the budget, it has the last word on non-compulsory expenditure, while the Council has the last word on compulsory items. However, in the exercise of these powers a wide measure of agreement is required between the two.

For example, Parliament cannot increase non-compulsory expenditure beyond a certain limit without the Council's consent. This limit is fixed on the basis of a maximum rate of increase over the previous year, which is calculated each year by the Commission and can be altered subsequently by agreement between Council and Parliament.

In addition to being responsible for the final adoption of the budget as a whole, Parliament gives the Commission the ultimate authority to spend money.

Each year the Community's budget goes through the following stages:
(i) By 1 May the Commission anounces the maximum rate fixed for the coming budgetary discussions.
(ii) By 1 July each of the Community's institutions submits to the Commission an estimate of its expenditure.
(iii) The Commission consolidates these into a preliminary draft budget, which it submits to the Council by 1 Sept.
(iv) The Council adopts the draft budget, voting by qualified majority, and forwards it to the Parliament by 5 Oct.
(v) Within forty-five days of receiving the Council's draft budget, Parliament must complete the first 'reading' of the budget. It can 'amend' the non-compulsory expenditure by a majority of all members and the

Five Year Revenues and Expenses and 1976 Budget

Revenues   *Years ended 31st Dec.*

Amounts collected by the member states and paid to the EEC regarding the title 'Own Resources'	*1971*[1]	*1972*[1]	*1973*[1]	*1974*[1]	*1975*[2]	*Budget 1976*[3]
		(millions of units of account[4]				
Belgium	121·9	153·4	175·7	215·4	293·4	266·9
Denmark	—	—	38·6	52·6	84·0	74·4
France	254·2	368·5	448·7	562·0	691·3	640·2
German Federal Republic	458·9	621·7	731·6	861·4	988·6	997·2
Irish Republic	—	—	12·7	17·3	26·5	38·6
Italy	271·2	375·3	403·5	508·0	627·6	637·4
Luxembourg	2·1	2·8	3·0	4·4	4·1	4·1
Netherlands	187·8	235·1	280·6	297·9	374·3	409·5
United Kingdom	—	—	402·5	548·7	841·0	1,223·5
Total Own Resources	1,296·1	1,756·8	2,496·5	3,067·7	3,930·8	4,291·8
ECSC contributions to administrative expenses	18·0	18·0	18·0	18·0	18·0	18·0
Taxation on Staff salaries	13·1	15·5	19·7	24·7	—	—
Financial Contributions						
Belgium	63·2	94·1	161·6	137·5	126·4	214·5
Denmark	—	—	12·6	17·3	23·1	76·0
France	365·8	462·3	686·8	630·2	734·0	997·8
German Federal Republic	244·8	336·6	600·2	554·7	751·5	1,073·3
Irish Republic	—	—	—	—	—	—
Italy	206·7	263·9	468·7	405·7	462·5	614·3
Luxembourg	2·3	3·2	5·2	4·1	6·1	7·6
Netherlands	41·0	76·5	152·2	154·3	163·6	230·5
United Kingdom	—	—	—	—	—	—
Total Contributions	923·8	1,236·6	2,087·3	1,903·8	2,267·2	3,214·0
Miscellaneous Revenues	38·4	47·5	19·5	22·5	52·3[5]	53·0[5]
Total Revenues	2,289·4	3,074·4	4,641·0	5,036·7	6,268·3	7,576·9

[1] Final.

[2] Preliminary.

[3] The figures contained in the 1976 budget are estimates of future revenues and expenditures.

[4] 1 unit of account =

Danish kroners	7·50
Deutsche Mark	3·66
Belgian/Luxembourg francs	50·00
Dutch guilders	3·62
French Francs	5·55419
Italian Lira	625·00
Pound sterling	0·41667

[5] The taxation on staff salaries is included.

Years ended 31st Dec.

Expenses	1971[1]	1972[1]	1973[1]	1974[1]	1975[2]	Budget 1976[3]
	(millions of units of account)					
Parliament	11·0	14·9	22·8	32·0	41·6	52·1
Council	16·7	23·1	27·9	36·6	50·5	64·5
Commission						
Administrative expenses	240·9	313·0	447·3	612·3	710·7	881·0
Research and investment	65·0	75·1	69·1	82·8	101·2	135·2
European Social Fund and Regional Fund	56·5	97·5	269·2	290·7	516·2	741·0
European Agricultural Guidance and Guarantee Fund—Gurantee Section	1,883·6	2,302·7	3,593·8	3,389·9	4,336·3	5,160·3
European Agricultural Guidance and Guarantee Fund—Guidance Section	–	174·9	175·1	261·4	262·5	325·0
Cooperation with the Developing Countries	13·2	69·7	30·1	324·1	249·0	206·6
Total Commission	2,259·2	3,032·9	4,584·6	4,961·2	6,166·9	7,449·1
Court of Justice	2·5	3·5	5·7	6·9	9·3	11·2
Total Expenses	2,289·4	3,074·4	4,641·0	5,036·7	6,268·3	7,576·9

[1] Final.
[2] Preliminary.
[3] The figures contained in the 1976 budget are estimates of future revenues and expenditures.

compulsory expenditure by a majority of votes cast.

If the draft budget has not been changed in any way within forty-five days, it is considered formally adopted. If any amendments have been made, it is returned to the Council.

(vi) Within fifteen days of receiving the amended draft budget, the Council considers it for the second time. It can re-amend Parliament's amendments to non-compulsory expenditure and finally adopt or reject Parliament's changes in compulsory expenditure.

If the draft received from Parliament has not been altered in any way within the fifteen days, the budget is considered formally adopted. If any

25

changes have been made, the draft is re-submitted to Parliament.

(vii) Within fifteen days of receiving back the draft budget, Parliament must complete the second and final 'reading'. Parliament has no power at this stage to reject the changes made by the Council in the field of compulsory expenditure. It can, however, reject the Council's changes in the field of non-compulsory expenditure, acting by a majority of members (over ninety-nine positive votes) and three-fifths of the votes cast. Parliament may also, acting by a majority of members and two-thirds of the votes cast, reject the draft budget as a whole and ask for a new draft to be submitted.

If no such majority against the draft budget is obtained, or if Parliament does not take any decision within the fifteen days, the budget is considered finally adopted.

At several stages during this budgetary procedure, formal consultations may take place between Parliament and the Council to reconcile differences. These consultations may be initiated by either Parliament or the Council, and take place in a 'conciliation committee' consisting of the members of the Council and a delegation from Parliament, with the Commission participating.

In addition a Council representative takes part in the meetings of Parliament's Committee on budgets during the budgetary procedure; and the President of the Council takes part in Parliament's budget debates.

budget of the European Coal and Steel Community

In addition to 702m. U.A. new loans granted out of funds borrowed on the world's capital markets and redemptions of 56m. U.A., the E.C.S.C. had the following income and expenditure in 1975:

Income	*Millions of European Monetary Units of Account*
Product of levy	70
Interest from loans made	151
Other	43
	264

Expenditure	*Millions of European Monetary Units of Account*
Servicing borrowed funds	146
Administrative fee payable to the General Budget	17
Rehabilitation of workers	28
Research	20
Other	11
	222

Excess of income over expenditure 42m. U.A.

Budgetary Policy Committee of the E.E.C.
The committee was founded in 1964 and is attended by senior officials of member countries. Information on each country's forthcoming budget is exchanged at meetings.

Burundi
Burundi signed the Yaoundé Conventions of 1963 and 1969 and the Lomé Convention of 1975.

butter
see dairy produce

butter 'mountain'
see 'mountain'

C

Cameroon

Cameroon signed the Yaoundé Conventions of 1963 and 1969 and the Lomé Convention of 1975.

Canada

In 1975 the E.E.C. Commission recommended to the Council of Ministers that negotiations should be opened with Canada on the framework for an economic and commercial co-operation agreement. This would be the first such agreement between the E.E.C. and an advanced industrial nation. This matter was still being pursued in 1977.

Economic profile: Area 9,976,100 sq. km. Population (1973) 22,130,000 (male (1971) 10,795,000) density 2 per sq. km. Births (per 1,000 of pop. 1973) 16·8; marriages, 8·9; deaths, 7·3. Infant mortality, 17·6.

Labour force (1972) 8,891,000; percentage in agriculture, 6·9; industry, 30·9; services, 62·2.

International trade (in millions of U.A.):

	1965	1970	1973
Imports	7,986	13,308	18,643
Exports	8,107	16,134	20,160

	per 1,000 of population
Standard of living:	
Motor vehicles (1973)	337
Televisions (1972)	349
Telephones (1972)	468

C.A.P.
Common Agricultural Policy of the E.E.C. the aims of which are laid down in Articles 38–47 of the Rome Treaty.

C.A.P.C.
Civil Aviation Planning Committee of Nato.

Cape Verde Islands
The Cape Verde Islands became a member of the Lomé Convention in 1977.

Capital, free movement of
Under Articles 67–73 of the Rome Treaty member states shall, in the course of the transitional period and to the extent necessary for the proper functioning of the Common Market, progressively abolish as between themselves restrictions on the movement of capital belonging to persons resident in member states and also any discriminatory treatment based on the nationality or place of residence of the parties or on the place in which such capital is invested.

Current payments connected with movements of capital between member states shall be freed from all restrictions not later than at the end of the first stage.

Member states shall grant in the most liberal manner possible such exchange authorisations as are still necessary after the date of the entry into force of the Treaty.

Where a member state applies its domestic provisions in respect of the capital market and credit system to the movements of capital freed in accordance with the provisions of the Treaty, it shall do so in a non-discriminatory manner.

Loans intended for the direct or indirect financing of a member state or of its territorial sub-divisions may not be issued or placed in other member states save when the states concerned have reached agreement in this respect . . .

The Council, acting on a proposal of the Commission which shall consult the Monetary Committee provided for in Article 105, shall, in the course of the first two stages by means of a unanimous vote and subsequently by means of a qualified majority vote, issue the directives necessary for the progressive implementation of the provisions of Article 67.

The Commission shall propose to the Council measures for the progressive co-ordination of the exchange policies of member states in respect of the movement of capital between those states and third countries. The Council, acting by means of a unanimous vote, shall issue directives in this connection. It shall endeavour to achieve the highest possible degree of liberalisation.

Where the action taken in application of the preceding paragraph does not permit the abolition of discrepancies between the exchange rules of member states and where such discrepancies should lead persons resident in one of the member states to make use of the transfer facilities within the Community, as provided for under Article 67, in order to evade the rules of one of the member states in regard to third countries, that state may, after consulting the other member states and the Commission, take appropriate measures to overcome these difficulties . . .

Member states shall keep the Commission informed of any movements of capital to and from third countries as are known to them. The Commission may address to member states any opinion which it deems appropriate on this subject.

In the event of movements of capital leading to disturbances in the functioning of the capital market in any member state, the Commission shall, after consulting the Monetary Committee, authorise such state to take, in regard to such movements of capital, protective measures of which the Commission shall determine the conditions and particulars . . .

The member state which is in difficulty may, however, on the ground of their secret or urgent character, itself take the above-mentioned measures if they should become necessary. The Commission and the other member states shall be informed of such measures not later than at the date of their entry into force. In this case, the Commission may, after consulting the Monetary Committee, decide that the state concerned shall modify or abolish such measures.

Caribbean Community
The Treaty establishing the Caribbean Community, including the Caribbean Common Market and the Agreement establishing the Common External Tariff for the Caribbean Common Market, was signed by the

Prime Ministers of Barbados, Guyana, Jamaica, and Trinidad and Tobago at Chaguaramas, Trinidad, on 4 July 1973, and came into force on 1 Aug. 1973. This organisation replaced Carifta. Six less-developed countries signed the Treaty of Chaguaramas on 17 April 1974. They were Belize, Dominica, Grenada, St Lucia, St Vincent and Montserrat, and the Treaty came into effect for those countries on 1 May 1974. Antigua acceded to membership on 4 July 1974 and on 26 July the Associated State of St Kitts-Nevis-Anguilla signed the Treaty of Chaguaramas in Kingston, Jamaica, and became a member of the Caribbean Community.

The Caribbean Community has three areas of activity; economic integration (that is, the Caribbean Common Market); co-operation in non-economic areas and the operation of certain common services; and co-ordination of foreign policies of independent member states.

The Caribbean Common Market provides for the establishment of a Common External Tariff and a common protective policy and the progressive co-ordination of external trade policies; the adoption of a scheme for the harmonisation of fiscal incentives to industry; double taxation arrangements among member countries; the co-ordination of economic policies and development planning; and a special regime for the less developed countries of the community.

Caricom
formerly Carifta *see* Caribbean Community

Carifta
Caribbean Free Trade Association *now* Caribbean Community, Caricom

cartels
see competition policy

C.B.N.M.
Central Bureau of Nuclear Measurements, belonging to Euratom.

C.C.C.
Customs Co-operation Council.

C.C.E.
Conseil des communes d'Europe, Council of European Municipalities.

C.C.N.R.
Consultative Committee for Nuclear Research of the Council of Europe.

C.C.P.F.
Comité central de la propriété forestière de la C.E.E., Central Committee on Forest Property for the E.E.C.

C.C.T.
Common customs tariff of the E.E.C., often less accurately referred to as C.E.T. and even C.X.T.

C.E.A.
Comité européen des assurances, European Insurance Committee and *Confédération européenne de l'agriculture*, European Confederation of Agriculture.

C.E.A.C.
Commission européenne de l'aviation civile, European Civil Aviation Commission

C.E.C.A.
Communauté Européenne du Charbon et de l'Acier, *see* European Coal and Steel Community.

C.E.D.I.
Centre Européen de Documentation et d'Information, European Documentation and Information Centre.

C.E.E.
Commission économique pour l'Europe, Economic Commission for Europe, *Communauté économique européenne*, European Economic Community and *Comunidade Económica Europeia*, European Economic Community (Portuguese).

C.E.E.A.
Communauté européenne de l'énergie atomique, see European Atomic Energy Community, (*also* Euratom.)

C.E.E.P.
Centre Européene de l'Enterprise Publique, European Centre for Public Enterprises.

C.E.F.I.C.
Conseil Européen des Fédérations de l'Industrie Chimique, European Council of Chemical Industry Federations.

C.E.F.S.
Comité européen des fabricants de sucre, European Committee of Sugar Manufacturers.

C.E.I.
Centre d'Etudes Industrielles, Centre for Industrial Studies based on Geneva.

C.E.I.F.

C.E.I.F.
Council of European Industrial Federations *also* R.E.I.

C.E.M.T.
Conférence européenne des ministres des transport, European Conference of Ministers of Transport.

C.E.N.
Comité Européen de Normalisation, European Committee for Standardisation.

C.E.N.E.L.
Comité Européen de Coordination des Normes Electriques, European Electrical Standards Co-ordinating Committee.

census
A census of population will take place in 1981 in all member countries of the E.E.C. and will conform to a directive of the Council of Ministers.

Central African Republic
The Central African Republic signed the Yaoundé Conventions of 1963 and 1969 and the Lomé Convention of 1975.

Central Banks, The Committee of Governors of
The Committee of Governors of the Central Banks was established with advisory status by the Council of Ministers on 8 May 1964 in order to facilitate co-operation among the Central Banks of the member states. The Committee of Governors has developed into an organ of permanent consultation and co-operation among the Central Banks of the member states, even outside the scope of the E.E.C. It is composed of Central Bank Governors; the Commission, though not a member, is regularly invited to send a representative. Unlike the Monetary Committee its secretariat is not

responsible to the Commission but is responsible directly to the Committee of Governors. Although it does not have any decision-making power within the E.E.C., the Committee of Governors is involved in the preparation of all decisions and resolutions of the Council of Ministers concerning monetary policy and the proper functioning of the E.E.C. exchange system. Acting in parallel with the Monetary Committee, it has established a method of surveying the economic condition of each member state, with particular reference to its balance of payments position.

C.E.P.T.
Conférence européenne des administrations des postes et des télécommunications, European Conference of Postal and Telecommunications Administrations.

C.E.R.N.
Centre Européen de Recherches Nucléaires, European Organisation, formerly Council, for Nuclear Research, based on Geneva.

C.E.S.
Comité economique et social, Economic and Social Committee.

C.E.T.
common external tariff *but see* C.C.T.

Chad
Chad signed the Yaoundé Conventions of 1963 and 1969 and the Lomé Convention of 1975.

Channel Islands
Free trade in agriculture and industrial goods between the Channel Islands and members of the E.E.C. was agreed under the Treaty of Accession but the islands are exempt from other E.E.C. rules and regulations, including

V.A.T., free movement of labour, freedom of establishment and competition policy.

channel tunnel
There have been plans for a channel tunnel since 1802, and in 1973, following completion of financial and technical feasibility studies, the decision to begin the first phase of a bored rail tunnel under the Channel was agreed by the British and French Governments. It was intended that the 50 km. tunnel would provide ferry train services for road vehicles in addition to through rail services. However, on 20 Jan. 1975 the British Government decided to abandon the project. On 22 Jan. the French Cabinet expressed 'regret over the unilateral decision of the British Government to suspend the execution of the agreement signed between the two Governments in 1973 on the continuation of the great European undertaking the Channel Tunnel'.

Charlemagne (c. 742–814)
When the Pope crowned Charlemagne (or Charles I) as Holy Roman Emperor on Christmas Day 800 A.D. it did not signify the recreation of the Roman Empire. Europe was feudal, a patchwork of complex tribal and regional customs with few towns and little learning. Charles, King of the Franks, was a great warrior, whose small army marched victoriously from the Pyrenees to central Germany, and whose fame reached to Byzantium and the Grand Caliph in Baghdad. If there was a central factor in ninth century Europe it was the Church, whose language and rites alone remained as a living survival from the Roman Empire. Charles' military fame and prowess were useful to the Church in its struggle with Byzantium and Islam; hence the Church honoured Charles with a universalist title. Charlemagne had neither the desire nor the capacity to recreate a true unitary state, nor was Europe in a fit state to return to its former glory. At the Treaty of Verdun in 843 A.D. Charlemagne's Empire, according to feudal custom, was split into three parts and given to his three heirs.

Charlemagne Prize
see awards

Charles V
Charles V (1500–58) was Emperor of the Holy Roman Empire and, (as Charles I) King of Spain. The centre of Charlemagne's Empire, the point from which it sprang, was France. As the Middle Ages proceeded, France became a unitary and self-conscious nation and the universalist, Imperial idea shifted to Germany and Italy. The Holy Roman Empire, which disappeared so swiftly after Charlemagne, was recreated by a German dynasty and became an elective office of great prestige but little actual power. From the fourteenth century the office became the preserve of a single family, the Habsburgs. Unyielding loyalty to the Papacy, successful dynastic marriages and diplomatic skill gave the Habsburgs, by the sixteenth century, an unrivalled position in Europe. Their possessions included Spain and Spanish America, the empire on which the sun never set, and much of Eastern Europe. Their holdings outside Germany gave the Habsburgs a power base inside it. Under Charles V it seemed to some people, especially clerics and mystics, that a Universal Empire would soon be reborn, with a single head, the Emperor, and a single heart, the Church. But two things ensured that the mystics' dreams were not to be; the rising power of France, and the appearance of Protestantism, which challenged both head and heart. Charles V did see himself as a universal Emperor but was never more than a constitutional figurehead in those parts of Germany of which he was not actually direct ruler. After his death Spain, with the Low Countries and the overseas possessions, became a separate Habsburg monarchy.

China
In Sept. 1976 China established formal relations with the E.E.C. and was the second Communist country (after Yugoslavia) to have an ambassador accredited to the Community.

Christian Democratic Parties, Federation of
In April 1976, at a meeting held in Brussels, delegates of seven of the nine E.E.C. countries, representing thirteen Christian Democratic and centerist parties, agreed to establish the 'European People's Party—Federation of Christian Democratic Parties of the European Community'. The main aim

Chronology

of the new Federation is to prepare for direct elections to the European
Parliament.

Chronology

19 Sept.	1946	Winston Churchill, in a speech at Zurich, urges Franco-German reconciliation with 'a kind of United States of Europe'.
5 June	1947	General Marshall proposes American aid to stimulate recovery in Europe.
29 Oct.		Creation of Benelux—economic union of Belguim, Luxembourg and the Netherlands.
16 April	1948	Convention for European Economic Co-operation signed—the birth of O.E.E.C.
5 May	1949	Statute of the Council of Europe signed.
9 May	1950	Robert Schuman makes his historic proposal to place French and German coal and steel under a common Authority.
18 April	1951	The Treaty setting up the European Coal and Steel Community (E.C.S.C.) is signed in Paris.
10 Feb.	1953	E.C.S.C. common market for coal, iron ore, and scrap is opened.
1 May		E.C.S.C. common market for steel is opened.
1–3 June	1955	Messina Conference: the Foreign Ministers of the Community's member states propose further steps towards full integration in Europe.
25 March	1957	Signature of the Rome Treaties setting up the Common Market and Euratom.
1 Jan.	1958	The Rome Treaties come into force: the Common Market and Euratom are established.
19–21 March		First session of the European Parliament — Robert Schuman elected president.
1 Jan.	1959	First tariff reductions and quota enlargements in the Common Market. Establishment of common market for nuclear materials.
20 Nov.		European Free Trade Association convention signed between Austria, Denmark, Norway, Portugal, Sweden, Switzerland and the United Kingdom.
9 July	1961	Greece signs association agreement with E.E.C.

		(comes into force 1 Nov. 1962).
1 Aug.		The Republic of Ireland applies for membership of the Common Market.
10 Aug.		The United Kingdom and Denmark request negotiations aiming at membership of the Common Market.
8 Nov.		Negotiations with the United Kingdom open in Brussels.
15 Dec.		The three neutrals, Austria, Sweden and Switzerland, apply for association with the Common Market.
30 April	1962	Norway requests negotiations for membership of the Common Market.
14 Jan.	1963	President de Gaulle declares that the United Kingdom is not ready for Community membership.
29 Jan.		United Kingdom negotiations with Six broken off.
1 July		Signature of Yaoundé Convention, associating eighteen independent states in Africa and Madagascar with the Community for five years from 1 June 1964.
12 Sept.		Turkey signs association agreement with Community (comes into force 1 Dec. 1964).
9 Dec.	1964	First meeting of the Parliamentary Conference of members of European Parliament and parliamentarians from Yaoundé associated states.
15 Dec.		Council adopts the Mansholt Plan for common prices for grains.
31 March	1965	Common Market Commission proposes that, as from 1 July 1967, all Community countries' import duties and levies be paid into Community budget and that powers of European Parliament be increased.
8 April		Six sign treaty merging the Community Executives.
31 May		Common Market Commission publishes first memorandum proposing lines of Community policy for regional development.
1 July		Council fails to reach agreement by agreed deadline on financing common farm policy; French boycott of Community Institutions begins seven-month-long crisis.
26 July		Council meets and conducts business without French

39

		representative present.
17 Jan.	1966	Six foreign ministers meet in Luxembourg without Commission present and agree to resume full Community activity.
10 Nov.		United Kingdom Prime Minister Harold Wilson announces plans for 'a high-level approach' to the Six with intention of entering E.E.C.
11 May	1967	The United Kingdom lodges formal application for membership of the European Economic Community.
	1968	The United Kingdom's application for membership of the European Economic Community remains on the table with the Community.
25 April	1969	General de Gaulle resigns as President of France.
16 June		M. Georges Pompidou elected President.
2 Dec.		At a Summit Conference at The Hague the Community formally agree to open membership negotiations with the United Kingdom, Norway, Denmark and the Republic of Ireland on their applications of 1967.
29 June	1970	Talks begin in Luxembourg between the Six and the United Kingdom, Norway, Denmark and the Republic of Ireland.
23 June	1971	The Council of Ministers of the Community announces that agreement has been reached with the United Kingdom for the basis of the accession of the United Kingdom to the Communities.
11–13 July		At a Ministerial-level negotiating session, agreement is reached on major outstanding issues: the transitional period for the United Kingdom; Commonwealth Sugar; Capital Movements; and the common commercial policy.
28 Oct.		Vote in the House of Commons on the motion 'That this House approves her Majesty's Government's decision of principle to join the European Communities on the basis of the arrangements which have been negotiated.' The voting figures in the House of Commons were 356 For, 244 Against, majority of 112; and in the House of Lords 451 For,

		58 Against, majority of 393.
22 Jan.	1972	Treaty of Accession was signed in Brussels between the European Communities (France, Belgium, Germany, Italy, Luxembourg and the Netherlands) on the one side and the United Kingdom, Denmark, Norway and the Republic of Ireland on the other side.
22 July		E.E.C. signs free trade agreements with Austria, Iceland, Portugal, Sweden and Switzerland.
26 Sept.		Rejection by Norway of full membership of E.E.C. following a referendum.
31 Dec.		The United Kingdom and Denmark withdraw from Efta.
1 Jan.	1973	The United Kingdom, Irish Republic and Denmark join the Community.
21 Feb.		Court upholds Continental Can's appeal against Commission ruling that it abused its 'dominant position' in Common Market, but supports Commission's contention that E.E.C. Treaty empowers it to control mergers and monopolies.
1 April		First 20% cut in industrial tariffs between the original Six and the new member states.
14 May		E.E.C. signs free trade agreement with Norway.
1 Jan.	1974	Second 20% cut in tariffs on imports between the United Kingdom, Irish Republic and Denmark and the original Six is made. The United Kingdom adopts the Common Customs Nomenclature.
4 June		The United Kingdom gives detailed plans for renegotiation, on budget, C.A.P. State aid and imports. Council approves in principle increased budgetary powers for Parliament.
28 Feb.	1975	The Lomé Convention establishing an overall trading and economic co-operation relationship between the E.E.C. and forty-six developing African, Caribbean and Pacific countries, is signed in Togo.
5 June		The United Kingdom holds first referendum and the electorate votes by a two-to-one majority to remain in the E.E.C.

41

Churchill, Sir Winston
Born Blenheim, England, 1874, died 1965. Member of the British Parliament from 1900; Home Secretary, 1910; Minister of Munitions, 1917; Secretary of State for War and Air, 1919–21; Chancellor of the Exchequer, 1924–9. Leader of a coalition Government, 1940–5. Sponsor of the United Europe Movement, 1946. Delegate to, and active participant in, the Congress of Europe at the Hague, 1948.

'From Stettin in the Baltic to Trieste in the Adriatic, an iron curtain has descended across the Continent. Behind that line lie all the capitals of the ancient states of Central and Eastern Europe. Warsaw, Berlin, Prague, Vienna, Budapest, Belgrade, Bucharest and Sofia, all these famous cities and the populations around them lie in what I must call the Soviet sphere, and all are subject in one form or another, not only to Soviet influence but to a very high and, in many cases, increasing measure of control from Moscow. . . . Police Governments are prevailing in nearly every case, and so far, except in Czechoslovakia, there is no true democracy'. (In a speech at Fulton, Missouri, 5 March 1946.)

'What will be the fate of Europe? Here in this continent of superior climates dwell the parent breeds of western and modern civilisation. Here is the story, descending from the ancient Roman Empire, of Christendom, of the Renaissance, and of the French Revolution. It is from the hatreds and quarrels of Europe that the catastrophes of the whole world have sprung. Shall we establish again the glory of Europe, and thus consolidate the foundations of Peace?' (In a speech at Metz, 14 July 1946.)

'I am now going to say something that will astonish you. . . . The first step in the re-creation of the European family must be a partnership between France and Germany. In this way only can France recover the moral leadership of Europe. There can be no revival of Europe without a spiritually great Germany. The structure of the United States of Europe, if well and truly built, will be such as to make the material strength of a single state less important. Small nations will count as much as large ones, and gain their honour by their contribution'. (In a speech at Zurich, 19 Sept. 1946.)

'We hope to reach again a Europe purged of the slavery of ancient days, in which men will be as proud to say "I am a European" as once they were to say *Civis Romanus sum*'. (In a speech at an Albert Hall meeting to launch the United Europe Movement, 14 May 1947.)

C.I.M.E.
comité intergouvernemental pour les migrations européennes, Intergovernmental Committee for European Migration.

Civil Servants, European
see Eurocrat

C.M.E.A.
Council for Mutual Economic Assistance *also* Comecon

coal
Average output a manshift underground in coal mining in some countries in the E.E.C. was as follows: Federal German Republic (1975, 80 cwt.; 1976, 80·3 cwt.); France (54·4, 54·8); Belgium (47·8, 46·0); United Kingdom (68·8, 63·3).

Coal and Steel, Consultative Committee for
A Consultative Committee exists in the framework of the European Coal and Steel Community. It was set up in 1952 under Articles 18 and 19 of the E.C.S.C. treaty. It is a parallel body to the Economic and Social Committee for the two industrial sectors.

The Committee has eighty-one members who are appointed by the Council on the proposal of the different governments. Coal trade unions, coal employers and coal users are represented, and the steel sector similarly. The secretariat is located in Luxembourg.

C.O.C.C.E.E.
Comité des Organisations Commerciales des Pays de la C.E.E., Committee of Commercial Organisations in the E.E.C. Countries.

Comecon
see Council for Mutual Economic Assistance.

Comitextil
Comité de Coordination des Industries Textiles de la C.E.E., Co-ordinating Committee of the Textile Industry in the E.E.C.

Commission, The
The Commission consists of thirteen members; two each from France, the Federal German Republic, Italy and the United Kingdom, one each from Belgium, Denmark, Irish Republic, Luxembourg and the Netherlands. It is the executive and policy-proposing body of the Communities and its members must act, throughout their period in office, in full independence both of the member Governments and of the Council. The Council cannot remove any member from office; the European Parliament can, if it wishes, cause a vote of censure, which would compel the Commission to resign *en bloc*.

Members of the Commission were as follows at Jan. 1977:
President:

Roy Jenkins,   Secretariat-General, Legal Service, Information, Spokesman's Group

Vice-Presidents:

François-Xavier Ortoli,   Economic and Financial Affairs, Credits and Investments, Statistical Office

Wilhelm Haferkamp,   External Affairs

Finn Olav Gundelach,   Agriculture and Fisheries

Lorenzo Natali,   Special responsibilities for institutional questions pertaining to enlargement; environmental affairs, nuclear safety, preparations for direct elections to the European Parliament

Members:

Henk Vredeling   Employment and Social Affairs, Tripartite Conference

Claude Cheysson   Development aid

Guido Brunner   Energy, Research and Science, Education

Raymond Vouel   Competition policy

Antonio Gioletti	Co-ordination of Community Funds, Regional Policy
Richard Burke	Taxation, Transport, Consumer Affairs, Relations with the European Parliament
Viscount Etienne Davignon	Industrial Affairs, Internal Market
Christopher Tugendhat	Budget and Financial Control, Financial Institutions, Personnel and Administration.

committees

The Brussels administration is helped in its work by many Committees varying from, for example, the Advisory Committee on Raw Tobacco, set up by the Commission, or the Medium-term Economic Policy Committee, set up by the Council on the recommendation of the Commission, to the Monetary Committee, established by the E.E.C. Treaty itself. These Committees are composed of members, called experts, drawn from the member states and fulfil an advisory rôle.

Answering a parliamentary question in July 1976, the Council stated that there were at that time forty Committees set up by the Treaties or the Council, but this excluded those set up by the Commission, at least sixteen by 1972.

Working groups are sub-Committees set up to study more specialised subjects and normally reporting to a Committee.

Common Agricultural Policy

The basic features of a common policy in agriculture were first adopted in Jan. 1962. The aims are greater efficiency in production, stable market conditions, a fair return for farmers and reasonable prices for consumers. The two essential principles are common price levels and the replacement of national systems of protection by a Community system whose most characteristic feature is a system of variable levies on imports of certain farm products. The common marketing arrangements for all major items were operative by July 1968. Management committees of national experts advise the Commission on the various products. A European Guidance and Guarantee Fund has also been established to finance the common

45

policy. Various measures have been introduced at a Community level to help the modernisation of farms and to assist older farmers who wish to give up farming their land. Denmark, the Irish Republic and the United Kingdom will gradually be integrated into the C.A.P. during a five-year period ending on 31 Dec. 1977. In 1975, the Community completed a review of the C.A.P., concluding that, while it required adjustments, its basic principles remained sound.

Common Agricultural Policy, Accession of the Three to
The common agricultural policy was officially adopted by the three new member countries, Denmark, the Irish Republic and the United Kingdom, on 1 Feb. 1973.

Negotiations on their accession to the policy had been conducted in 1972 and final agreement was reached in Brussels on 24 Jan. 1973.

The terms under which Denmark, the Irish Republic and the United Kingdom had agreed to become members of the European Communities provided for the implementation of the common agricultural policy in six equal stages over a five-year period beginning on 1 Feb. 1973. The White Paper on the United Kingdom's proposed membership, published on 7 July 1972, had stated that the E.E.C. system would be adopted in the first year of membership, although actual price levels would be different from existing Community levels. Under the E.E.C. system: (i) imports were kept up to minimum, or threshold, prices by means of variable import levies; (ii) slightly lower intervention prices were set, at which the internal market was supported by the Community's Agricultural Fund; and (iii) Community exporters were compensated from the Fund when sales were made to outside countries at prices below Community levels.

The United Kingdom's initial threshold and intervention prices would be lower than those of the Community, the White Paper said, because of the difference between United Kingdom market prices and those of the original Community members, but they would be increased to full Community levels in six equal steps over a five-year transitional period, during which deficiency payments to United Kingdom farmers would be phased out. To enable free trade in agricultural products to take place immediately, compensatory amounts to cover the difference in price levels would be levied on exports to the Six from the new members and paid as subsidies on commodities moving the other way. These levies and subsidies, which were also to operate between the new members themselves, were to be reduced gradually over the five-year period as prices came into line. For those agricultural commodities for which the Community had a common external tariff instead of, or in addition to, levies, the transitional arrangements were to take the form of tariff adjustments similar to those agreed for industry.

The negotiations from July 1972 to Jan. 1973 centred on the problem of fixing intervention prices and 'accession compensatory amounts' on agricultural commodities in a situation where world prices were rising rapidly and where sterling had been floating since June 1972. On 20 July 1972 the Council of Ministers reached a first agreement on the compensatory amounts for cereals and also fixed the level of intervention prices for these commodities. However, the basis on which this agreement was reached soon dissolved with the sharp rise in world cereal prices and the consequent rise in United Kingdom prices, so that pressure arose among the original Community members for a renegotiation of the compensatory amounts.

In Nov. 1972 the Council agreed in principle to intervention price levels in the acceding countries for milk, dairy produce and oil-seeds, and also to compensatory amounts for milk and dairy produce. On fruit and vegetables, the United Kingdom accepted the decision taken by the Six in March 1972 and to this formula secured the addition of a further criterion, that the interests of consumers should be taken into account when fruit and vegetable prices were fixed in the future. This was the first time that consumers' interests had been mentioned in guidelines for price-fixing in the E.E.C. and on the proposal of Italy it was agreed by the Council of Ministers that the principle should be written into the criteria for all other agricultural prices.

The next round of talks, held in Dec. 1972, settled the question of the minimum prices and compensatory amounts for the United Kingdom imports of New Zealand butter and cheese on the basis of figures proposed by the Commission, the agreement ensuring that New Zealand would be able to maintain her exports of these products to the United Kingdom in accordance with the transitional arrangements established during the entry negotiations.

The main terms of the final agreement were as follows:
Cereals In view of the *de facto* devaluation of sterling against the U.A., the United Kingdom conceded that the sterling intervention prices for

cereals established in U.A. in July 1972 should be increased by a corresponding amount. She also agreed that the compensatory amounts fixed in July 1972 were no longer applicable in the light of the rapid rise in world prices and that these amounts should be reduced to approximately the level of the Community's levy on imports from third countries. This ensured that, if world cereal prices eased, prices in the United Kingdom would also go down.

Pigmeat A serious conflict of views developed betweeen Denmark and the United Kingdom, since the former sought the highest possible compensatory amounts for her large bacon exports to the United Kingdom in place of the high national subsidies for pig-farmers which Denmark was committed to abolishing upon accession, while the United Kingdom was concerned to balance the consumers' interests with the need for some measure of protection for United Kingdom pigmeat producers and therefore favoured lower compensatory amounts. The outcome was a compromise by which the compensatory amounts were to be progressively reduced over six months from the maximum level demanded by Denmark to the minimum figure proposed by the United Kingdom, during which period the United Kingdom bacon-curing subsidy, which the Danish Government had claimed contravened the Treaty of Rome, would be phased out. The compromise was regarded as being nearer the United Kingdom position than the Danish, and was only accepted by the Danish Minister of Agriculture with the proviso that he would have to refer it back to his Government.

Poultry and Eggs The compensatory amounts finally fixed were higher than those proposed by the United Kingdom negotiators, who had wanted lower rates to protect home producers and to facilitate United Kingdom egg exports.

Sugar The United Kingdom secured agreement on a higher refining margin than that applicable to the original members, to ensure that the full quantities of sugar cane from the Commonwealth, as specified in the entry terms, could continue to be refined and marketed in the United Kingdom. It was further agreed that the United Kingdom subsidy on sugar would be phased out by 1 July, and that cane-sugar refineries in the Six should receive a special subsidy from the Community's Agricultural Fund.

These agreements made it possible for the common agricultural policy to be officially adopted by the acceding countries on 1 Feb., although France subsequently requested and obtained a further meeting of the Community's Agriculture Ministers to clarify certain French difficulties, relating principally to the phasing out of the United Kingdom's deficiency payments to farmers, while the United Kingdom subsequently found the agreed terms for the sugar-refining margin to be unsatisfactory and therefore informed the Council of Ministers on 27 March that a subsidy would be granted on sugar and made retroactive to 1 Feb.

Although all the relevant administrative and legal regulations were not ready by the midnight deadline on 31 Jan., the policy was nevertheless officially adopted in the United Kingdom, the Irish Republic and Denmark on 1 Feb., as envisaged under the terms of the Treaty of Accession.

In Denmark the final terms of the agreements reached in Brussels were accepted by the minority Social Democratic Government as the best obtainable in the circumstances. They provoked strong criticism among the Opposition parties, however, and a motion of censure was brought against the Government in the *Folketing* which was defeated.

Common Market E.E.C.
see history

Community Patents Convention
see patents

Community resources
Originally the E.E.C. budget was financed entirely from direct contributions by member states. An independent revenue system for the Community is now being phased in which will ultimately comprise 90 % of all food-import levies, 90 % of import duties and a value-added tax levy of up to 1 % In 1975, in response to a British request for re-negotiation, machinery was established to compensate any member state paying an undue proportion of the budget.

Comoro Islands
The Comoro Islands became a member of the Lomé Convention in 1977.

company law, harmonisation programme on

first directive,   adopted by the Council of Ministers 9 March 1968, covers information to be published by companies and ways of disclosure. Also some technical company law subjects (*ultra vires*, nullity of a company) of particular interest to third parties. Implemented in all member states.

second directive,   proposed 9 March 1970, concerns formation requirements, the safeguarding of share capital and the increase and reduction of capital. Amended proposal of 1972 currently being discussed by the Council of Ministers. It could be adopted in 1977.

third directive,   proposed 16 June 1970, concerns mergers of public companies incorporated under the same national law, preliminary to the convention on international mergers.

         The amended proposal of 1972 (a second amendment was submitted by the Commission in 1976) has been discussed in a first reading by the Council of Ministers.

fourth directive,   proposed 16 Nov. 1971, concerns annual accounts of limited liability companies.

         The amended proposal of 1974 is being discussed in a second reading by the Council of Ministers and is making good progress.

fifth directive,   proposed 9 Oct. 1972, concerns the structure of public companies and the powers and obligations of their organs.

         In Nov. 1975 the Commission published a green paper on employee participation and company structure.

sixth directive,   on a prospectus to be published when securities are admitted to official Stock Exchange quotation.

seventh directive, proposals of harmonising national laws concerning group accounts.

Company Statute

Proposals for a European Company Statute now being discussed by the Council should not be confused with the proposals for harmonising company law in the member states. The European Company Statute provides for an entirely new legal instrument largely independent of the national jurisdictions and ultimately supervised by the European Court.

comparability of transactions

Comparability of transactions is a term used in the European Coal and Steel Community. It arises from the decision to sever the link which existed between the ban on discrimination and the obligation on enterprises to publish their price lists. All comparably placed consumers of coal and steel have equal access to the sources of production; unequal conditions favouring some buyers and not others are eliminated. The Commission has extended the concept of comparability of transactions to buyers who produce similar or identical goods or who exercise the same function. Price differentials will depend on quantities sold and period of delivery and supply.

competition policy

E.E.C. competition policy is intended to serve as an instrument to help to strike the right balance between those restrictions on competition which are permissible or even desirable as a means of creating an enlarged Common Market and the restrictive practices which actually impede the integration of markets and should, therefore, be eliminated.

The three basic objectives of the policy are:

(a) To help create and maintain a single common market for the benefit of business and the consumers. Simply removing frontier barriers is insufficient if goods and services are to be traded freely through the Community;

(b) To prevent large companies and groups from abusing their economic power;

(c) To induce firms to rationalise production and distribution and to strive towards greater technological and scientific achievement.

In practical terms the Treaties of Paris and Rome provide instruments for tackling these problems:

(i) Article 85 of the E.E.C. Treaty and Article 65 of the E.C.S.C. Treaty enable action to be taken against agreements and concerted practices which hinder the normal competitive process;

Congo

(ii) Article 86 of the E.E.C. Treaty enables direct action to be taken against firms which take advantage of a dominant market position *see* Zoja Laboratories;

(iii) Article 66 of the E.C.S.C. Treaty enables action to be taken against mergers which would prevent the maintenance of effective competition in the coal and steel industries.

Outside these sections the E.E.C. Treaty does not provide a systematic pre-merger control although discussion is taking place to bring this about.

The Treaty provisions have been put into effect by implementing Regulations. Some of these Regulations are procedural but others are more fundamental; the block exemption regulations, for instance, determine the E.E.C. Commission's policy on specified categories of agreement between firms.

Congo
Congo signed the Yaoundé Conventions of 1963 and 1969, and the Lomé Convention of 1975.

conscription
see military service

Continental Can Company
On 8 Jan. 1972 the Commission invoked Article 86 of the Rome Treaty against the Continental Can Company of America, the leading world producer of metal containers, on the grounds that it had abused a dominant position which it held in the E.E.C. by acquiring control of one of its leading Dutch competitors, Thomassen Drijver-Verblifa. The case against the company was based on its attempts to extend its operations in the Community, having already, through its subsidiary, Euroemballage of Belgium, gained control of the largest German producer of metal cans and closures for food packaging, Schalbach-Lubeca-Werke AG of Brunswick. The Commission alleged that having achieved a dominant position on the German market, with a share of 50–90 % of the trade according to the type of product, it misused this position by acquiring another company which might have competed in the German market, thus eliminating a large part

of the competition in a substantial part of the E.E.C.

The Commission first intervened in the proposal to acquire the Dutch company in 1971. The subsequent formal decision in Jan. 1972 required the American company to submit proposals ending the infringement. In addition, the Commission announced that it was investigating Continental Can Company's extensive licensing agreements which it had with companies in all the Community countries except Luxembourg, in addition to licensing agreements in most other European countries, including the United Kingdom.

On 9 Feb. 1972 Continental Can and Euroemballage requested the Court of Justice to annul the Commission's decision.

In Feb. 1973 the European Court of Justice upheld the Continental Can Company's appeal against the Commission, on the grounds that the Commission had failed to prove specifically which sections of the market had been abused to the detriment of consumers.

This ruling by the Court of Justice was held to be a landmark decision in the area of anti-trust policy. Article 86 of the Rome Treaty is a declaration of principle rather than a case of direct rules. Although, on technical grounds, the Commission lost the appeal to the Court of Justice, the ruling provides it with the kind of interpretation of Article 86 which it needed in order to proceed to the next stage in framing a policy for the future on competition in general, and on the abuse of a dominant position in particular.

The judgement gave the Commission ample latitude to proceed against monopolies and companies which strengthen their dominant position by any means at their disposal, but it leaves the definition of that position vague and undetermined. Nevertheless, the decision has opened the way for the Commission to introduce prior control of mergers in the Common Market. It will take the Commission several years to formulate its policy. In the meantime the Court has left open the question of whether an expansion prohibited by Article 86 is void in the same way as restrictive agreements are automatically banned by Article 85.

continental shelf

The 1958 Geneva Convention stipulated that coastal states would exercise 'sovereign rights' on the continental shelf for the purpose of exploration and of exploiting their natural resources. The problem arising from the

C.O.P.A.

introduction of the 200 mile economic zone is to decide what system is to be applied when the continental shelf of a coastal state, *i.e.* the land area under the sea before the sharp declivity into the 'continental slope', extends beyond the 200 mile limit. Forty-four coastal states have an extended continental shelf, of which sixteen, including the United Kingdom, France, the Irish Republic and Denmark within the E.E.C., are already exploiting or intending to exploit the shelf beyond the limit, mainly for oil. The Rockall Basin is an example.

C.O.P.A.
Comité des Organisations Professionnelles Agricoles de la C.E.E., Committee of Agricultural Organisations in the E.E.C.

Copmec
Comité des petites et moyennes entreprises commerciales des pays de la C.E.E., Committee of Small and Medium Sized Commercial Enterprises of the E.E.C. Countries.

Coreper
Comité des Représentants Permanents de la C.E.E. Committee of Permanent Representatives of the E.E.C. instituted by Article 3 of the Merger Treaty.

C.O.S.T.
Co-opération Européenne dans le Domaine de la Recherche Scientifique et Technique; the European Co-operation in Science and Technology was formed to pursue some fifty collaborative proposals in the fields of data processing, telecommunications, transport, oceanography, meteorology, metallurgy and pollution. Although it was initiated by the E.E.C., nineteen European countries are members.

Coudenhave-Kalergi, Count Richard
Born 1894, died 1972. Founder-President of the European Union, 1940.

54

Secretary-General of the European Parliamentary Union. First holder of the Charlemagne Prize, 1954. Edited *Paneuropa*, 1924–38.

Council for Mutual Economic Assistance (Comecon)
The Council was founded in 1949 to assist the economic development of its member states through joint utilisation and co-ordination of efforts, particularly industrial development. Development of trade between members has not progressed at the rate expected because of artificial exchange rates between member countries.

Founder members were U.S.S.R., Bulgaria, Czechoslovakia, Hungary, Poland and Romania. Later admissions were Albania (1949; ceased participation 1961), Cuba (1972), German Democratic Republic (1950), Mongolia (1962). Since 1964 Yugoslavia has enjoyed associate status with limited participation. Observers are China, North Korea, North Vietnam.

The supreme authority is the Session of the Council, usually held annually in members' capitals in rotation under the chairmanship of the head of the delegation of the host country; all members must be present and decisions must be unanimous.

The Executive Committee is made up of one representative of deputy premier rank from each member state. It meets at least once every three months and has a 'Bureau for Common Questions of Economic Planning' in which each member country is represented by a deputy chairman of its national planning body. The secretariat is based on Moscow.

C.M.E.A. is the official abbreviation. Other unofficial abbreviations are Comecon and Cema. Comecon is also current in French and German alongside vernacular formulations. The working language of the organisation is Russian. The Russian form is *Sovet Ekonomicheskoi Vzaimopomoshchi* (S.E.V.).

Council of Europe
In 1948 the 'Congress of Europe', bringing together at The Hague nearly 1,000 influential Europeans from twenty-six countries, called for the creation of a united Europe, including a European Assembly. This proposal, examined first by the Ministerial Council of the Brussels Treaty Organisation and then by a conference of ambassadors, was the origin of the Council of Europe. The Statute of the Council was signed at London on

5 May 1949 and came into force two months later. The founder members were Belgium, Denmark, France, the Irish Republic, Italy, Luxembourg, the Netherlands, Norway, Sweden and the United Kingdom. Turkey and Greece joined in 1949, Iceland in 1950, the Federal German Republic in 1951 (having been an associate since 1950), Austria in 1956, Cyprus in 1961, Switzerland in 1963, Malta in 1965.

Membership is limited to European States which 'accept the principles of the rule of law and of the enjoyment by all persons within [their] jurisdiction of human rights and fundamental freedoms'. The Statute provides for both withdrawal (Article 7) and suspension (Articles 8 and 9). Greece withdrew from the Council in Dec. 1969 and rejoined in Nov. 1974.

Under the Statute two organs were set up: an inter-governmental Committee of (Foreign) Ministers with powers of decision and of recommendation to governments, and an inter-Parliamentary deliberative body, the Consultative Assembly — both of which are served by the Secretariat. In addition a large number of committees of experts have been established, two of them, the Council for Cultural Co-operation and the Committee on Legal Co-operation, having a measure of autonomy; on municipal matters the Committee of Ministers receives recommendations from the European Local Authorities Conference.

The Committee of Ministers usually meets twice a year and the ministers' deputies meet ten times a year.

The Parliamentary Assembly normally consists of 147 parliamentarians elected or appointed by their national parliaments (Austria 6, Belgium 7, Cyprus 3, Denmark 5, France 18, Federal German Republic 18, Greece 7, Iceland 3, Irish Republic 4, Italy 18, Luxembourg 3, Malta 3, Netherlands 7, Norway 5, Sweden 6, Switzerland 6, Turkey 10, United Kingdom 18); it meets three times a year for approximately a week. For domestic reasons Cyprus is not at present represented in the Assembly. The work of the Assembly is prepared by parliamentary committees.

The Joint Committee, consisting of the Committee of Ministers and representatives of the Assembly, harmonises relations between the two organs.

The European Convention on Human Rights, signed in 1950, set up special machinery to guarantee internationally fundamental rights and freedoms. A European Commission investigates alleged violations of the Convention submitted to it either by States or, in most cases, by individuals. Its findings can then be examined by the European Court of

Human Rights (established in 1959), whose obligatory jurisdiction has been recognised by twelve states, or by the Committee of Ministers, empowered to take binding decisions by two-thirds majority vote.

For questions of national refugees and over-population a Special Representative has been appointed, responsible to the governments collectively.

The European Youth Centre was set up in 1970. The European Youth Foundation is administered by the Secretary-General of the Council of Europe.

Article 1 of the Statute states that the Council's aim is 'to achieve a greater unity between its members for the purpose of safeguarding and realising the ideals and principles which are their common heritage and facilitating their economic and social progress'; 'this aim shall be pursued . . . by discussion of questions of common concern and by agreements and common action'. The only limitation is provided by Article 1(d) which excludes 'matters relating to national defence'.

It has been the task of the Assembly to propose action to bring European countries closer together, to keep under constant review the progress made and to voice the views of European public opinion on the main political and economic questions of the day. The Ministers' role is to translate the Assembly's recommendations into action, particularly as regards lowering the barriers between the European countries, harmonising their legislation or introducing where possible common European laws, abolishing discrimination on grounds of nationality and undertaking certain tasks on a joint European basis.

The Committee of Ministers periodically reviews the programme of activities of the Council of Europe. It comprises projects for co-operation between member governments in economic, legal, social, public health, environmental, and educational and scientific matters.

About eighty conventions have been concluded, covering such matters as social security, patents, extradition, medical treatment, training of nurses, equivalence of degrees and diplomas, innkeepers' liability, compulsory motor insurance, the protection of television broadcasts, adoption of children, transportation of animals and *au pair* placement. A Social Charter sets out the social and economic rights which all member governments agree to guarantee to their citizens.

The official languages are English and French.

Council of Ministers

The Council of Ministers is the only Community institution whose members directly represent the member governments. Representatives of the national governments sit in the Council. The Foreign Ministers are generally present for major decisions, but the actual Minister of, say, Agriculture or Transport or Economic Affairs is generally present for the subject under discussion. The Council consists of one representative each from the governments of the member countries and it takes decisions in one of three ways: either unanimously, by simple majority, or by a weighted majority according to the various circumstances laid down in the Treaties. The unanimity requirement applied particularly in the early stages of the Community's existence.

Decisions requiring a simple or a qualified majority are in most cases taken only on a proposal made by the Commission and any such proposal would not generally be amended by the Council except by unanimous vote. (This provision was aimed at conferring great responsibility upon the Commission and at safeguarding the stability of its activities; the method was applied with some difficulty largely because France and the E.E.C. Commission clashed over the Common Agricultural Policy.)

The various means by which the Council of Ministers and the Commission guide the work of the Community are defined as follows:

(i) *regulations*, which are compulsory and directly applicable to any member state;

(ii) *directives*, which are binding on the recipient state in respect of the result to be attained, but allow it to choose ways and means of achieving that end;

(iii) *decisions*, which are obligatory on the parties concerned; and

(iv) *recommendations and opinions*, which have no binding force.

The Commission has nineteen Directorates-General (external relations, economic and financial affairs, industry and technology, competition, social affairs, agriculture, transport, development and co-operation, personnel and administration, information, internal market research, science and education, dissemination of technical and scientific information, financial institutions and taxation, regional policy, energy and Euratom safeguards and control, community budgets and financial control) and ten specialised services (secretariat-general, legal service, spokesman's group, statistical office, joint research establishments, administration of the customs union, environmental and consumer service,

Couve de Murville, Maurice

Euratom supply agency, security office and official publications office).

Court of Justice, The European

The Court of Justice is common to the three Communities and superseded the original Court of Justice of the European Coal and Steel Community. It consists of nine members, jointly appointed by the member governments, holding office for six years and eligible for reappointment. There are also two Advocates-General.

The functions of the Court are to safeguard the law in the interpretation and application of the Treaties, to decide on the legality of decisions of the Council of Ministers or the Commission, and to determine violations of the Treaties. Actions can be brought before the Court either by a member country, or by the Council of Ministers, or by the E.E.C. Commission, or by any person or legal entity affected by a decision of the Community. Action is based on the contention that the Council or the Commission were not empowered to take a decision, have violated essential rules of procedure, have violated a treaty or any rule implementing it, or have abused their discretionary powers.

European Court judges (1977):

Hans Kutscher (Federal German Republic) President – elected 7 Oct. 1976
Josse Mertens de Wilmars (Belgium)
Max Sørensen (Denmark)
Adolphe Touffait (France)
Aindrias O'Keeffe (Irish Republic)
Giancinto Bosco (Italy)
Pierre Pescatore (Luxembourg)
Andreas Donner (Netherlands)
Lord Mackenzie Stuart (United Kingdom)

Couve de Murville, Maurice

Born France, 1907. Director General of Political Affairs at the French Foreign Office, 1945–50. Minister for Foreign Affairs, 1958–68. Prime Minister, 1968–9. He was opposed to widening the membership of the

59

C.R.E.S.T.

E.E.C. to include those countries applying for membership in 1967, especially the United Kingdom.

C.R.E.S.T.
Comité de Recherche Scientifique et Technique; the Committee of Scientific and Technological Research is a specialist committee of the Commission of the E.E.C.

currencies of E.E.C. and Efta countries

Belgium	Belgian *franc.*
Denmark	*krone* divided into 100 *øre.*
France	French *franc.*
German Federal Republic	*Deutsche Mark.*
Irish Republic	Irish *pound* divided into 100 *pence.*
Italy	*lira.*
Luxembourg	Luxembourg *franc* (at part with Belgian *franc* which is legal tender in Luxembourg).
Netherlands	*gulden* divided into 100 cents.
United Kingdom	*pound* sterling divided into 100 *pence.*
Greece	*drachmai* divided into 100 *lepta.*
Turkey	Turkish *Lira* divided into 100 *kuruş* (*piastres*).
Austria	*Schilling* divided into 100 *groschen.*
Iceland	*króna.*
Norway	*krone* divided into 100 *øre.*
Portugal	*escudo* divided into 100 *centavos.* 1000 *escudos* is a *conto.*
Switzerland	Swiss *franc* divided into 100 *Rappen/centimes.*
Finland	Finnish *mark* divided into 100 *pennis.*

customs duties, elimination of

The first aim of the Treaty of Rome was to set up a customs union and for the original Six this was achieved as follows:

		Moves in Internal Tariffs for Common Market Countries trading with one another.		Moves towards Common External Tariffs for Common Market Countries trade with other countries.	
		Per cent of national tariffs laid down in the original planned transitional period	Actual per cent of national tariffs applied under the accelerated timetable for the transitional period.	Per cent alignment of national tariffs towards the common external tariff — planned.	Per cent alignment of national tariffs —
	Treaty came into force 1 January 1958				
Stage 1	1959 1 January	90 %	90 %		
	1960 1 July	80 %	80 %		
	1961 1 January	—	70 %		
Stage 2	1962 1 January	70 %	60 %	30 %	30 %
	1 July	—	50 %		
	1963 1 July	60 %	40 %		
	1964 —	—	—		
	1965 1 January	50 %	30 %		
Stage 3†	1966 1 January	40 %	20 %	30 %	30 %
	1967 1 July	—	15 %	Common external tariff effective	
	1968 1 July	—	nil		
	1969				
	1970				

† In Stage 3 remaining duties were due to be removed at the latest by 1 January 1970.

* Where the difference between the national and the common tariff was 15 per cent or less the common tariff was adopted at the end of Stage 1.

The time-table for the three (Denmark, the Irish Republic and the United Kingdom) was:

	Tariffs between the Six and the four reduced by	Making a cumulative reduction of	Moves in adoption of Common External Tariff by the Four	Cumulative effect of moves towards Common External Tariff
	%	%	%	%
1 April 1973	20	20	—	—
1 January 1974	20	40	40	40
1 January 1975	20	60	20	60
1 January 1976	20	80	20	80
1 July 1977	20	100	20	100
		(i.e. tariffs abolished	(i.e. full use of E.T. by U.K.)	(i.e. full use of C.E.T. by U.K.)

customs union

A customs union is an agreement between two or more customs territories to abolish duties and other trade restrictions amongst themselves and to adopt a common policy, including a common external tariff, for trade with customs territories outside the Union. They are sometimes referred to as common markets or tariff unions. An early example in Europe was the *Zollverein* established by Prussia in 1833.

CXT

common external tariff but *see* C.C.T.

Cyprus

An association agreement, providing for the gradual introduction of a customs union in 1977, entered into force on 1 June 1973. Most industrial goods imported from Cyprus to the E.E.C. benefit from a 70% reduction in the common customs tariff. There are also reductions on a number of agricultural products. A wide range of E.E.C. exports to Cyprus benefited from reductions of 25% until 1 June 1977 and there is a planned increase to

35% from that date.

The E.E.C. Commission expressed concern at the Turkish invasion of Cyprus in 1974 and restated that the association agreement was based on the assumption that Cyprus remained independent and unified.

D

D.A.C.
Development Assistance Committee of the Organisation for Economic Co-operation and Development.

Dahomey
see Benin

dairy produce
The common price policy for milk came into operation in April 1968 and at the same time a common target price was established, this being the price which it was thought producers should receive for their milk delivered to dairies, subject to market outlets being available inside and outside the Community. Only about 25% of the milk produced in E.E.C. farms goes into liquid consumption and so the emphasis in price management is on dairy produce. The policy is to maintain the target price by providing intervention for butter and skim milk, and for cheese in Italy, where little butter is made.

On 1 April 1972 a regulation for trade in liquid milk came into force but without official Community pricing arrangements. All quantitative restrictions on trade between member countries were removed and quality standards were due to be aligned by then. Differing health regulations between member countries still prove some hindrance to intra-E.E.C. trade.

Production (in 1,000 mentric tons 1973)

	Milk	Butter	Cheese
Belgium	3,774	93	40
Denmark	4,778	136	131
France	29,491	546	879
German Federal Republic	21,482	497	549
Irish Republic	3,899	79	46
Italy	9,732	75	515
Luxembourg	231	8	1
Netherlands	8,988	163	320
United Kingdom	14,005	96	184
Total	96,380	1,687	2,665

E.E.C. producer prices are further protected from low import prices by threshold prices which are set out for twelve 'pilot' products. The importer pays a levy to cover the difference between the world c.i.f. price and threshold price. Threshold prices for other products are calculated from the pilot products.

Because production within the E.E.C. in the late 1960s and the 1970s was running well over self-sufficiency and stocks of butter and skim-milk powder was accumulating, various special subsidies were introduced to encourage the disposal of surpluses. Export restitutions were provided in the normal way to allow sales on world markets. In 1977 considerable quantities of surplus butter was sold to Eastern Europe. Grants have also been available to encourage the use of skim for animal feed and to provide general subsidies on butter. E.A.G.G.F. provides the finance for these measures and for the skim-milk powder exported to developing countries under Food Aid.

Danube Commission
The Danube Commission was constituted in 1949, based on the Convention relating to navigation control on the river Danube, which was signed in Belgrade on 18 Aug. 1948. This replaced the Paris Convention of 1921, on which the European Danube Commission was based (1856–1948). The Belgrade Convention reaffirmed that navigation on the

Danube from Ulm to the Black Sea, with access to the sea by the Sulina Canal, is equally free and unrestricted to the nationals, merchant shipping and merchandise of all states as to harbour and navigation fees, as well as conditions of merchant navigation.

The Danube Commission is composed of representatives from the countries on the Danube; one each for Austria, Bulgaria, Hungary, Romania, Czechoslovakia, U.S.S.R. and Yugoslavia. Since 1957 representatives of the Ministry of Transport from the Federal German Republic have attended the sittings and meetings of the Commission as guests of the secretariat.

The responsibilities of the Danube Commission are to check that the provisions of the Convention are carried out, to establish a uniform buoying system on all the Danube's navigable waterways and to see to the fundamental arrangements relating to navigation on the river. The Commission co-ordinates the regulations for river, customs and sanitation control, as well as the hydrometeorological service, and collects statistical data concerning navigation on the Danube.

The Danube Commission enjoys legal status. It has its own seal and flag and the members of the Commission and elected officers enjoy diplomatic immunity. The Commission's official buildings, archives and documents are inviolable. French and Russian are the official languages of the Commission. Since 1954 the headquarters have been in Budapest.

Davignon, Vicomte Etienne
Born Belgium, 1932. Political director of the Belgian Foreign Ministry. The 'Davignon' report was adopted in Oct. 1970, leading to greater political co-ordination between the member states of the Communities through regular meetings of Foreign Ministers outside the framework of the Council. Member of the E.E.C. Commission, 1977–.

Davignon Report
At the Hague summit in 1969 a decision was taken to examine the best means of achieving progress towards political unification, and a committee under the chairmanship of Vicomte Etienne Davignon subsequently prepared two reports. The final version of the second report was adopted by the E.E.C. Council of Foreign Ministers on 27 Oct. 1970.

death rate (1974)

Listing the objects of a united Europe the *Davignon Report* stated that it should be 'based on a common heritage of respect for the liberty and rights of man and bring together democratic states with freely elected Parliaments'.

Some of the proposals made in the report were that Foreign Ministers should meet at least once every six months, conferences of Heads of State or Government should be held when deemed desirable, and 'in the event of a serious crisis or special urgency' there should be extraordinary consultation between the member states' Governments.

death rate (1974)

country	*deaths per 1,000 inhabitants*
Belgium	11·9
Denmark	10·2
France	10·5
Federal German Republic	11·7
Irish Republic	11·2
Italy	9·5
Luxembourg	12·1
Netherlands	8·0
United Kingdom	11·9
E.E.C.	10·8

Decisions
Decisions are usually concerned with specific problems and may not necessarily be directed at the whole of the E.E.C. Many edicts of the Commission on the validity or otherwise of trading agreements go out as decisions and are binding on the parties to the agreements, even to the extent of the imposition of fines, which must be paid unless they are subsequently rescinded by the Court of Justice, to which appeal may be made.

deficiency payment
A United Kingdom Exchequer payment to producers or agricultural marketing boards in the United Kingdom which is based on the difference between the guaranteed price and market prices.

de Gaulle, Charles
Born Lille, France, 1890, died 1970. Head of French provisional Government, 1944. Head of temporary government with powers to draft a new constitution, 1958. First President of the Fifth Republic, 1958. He refused concessionary terms for United Kingdom entry to the E.E.C. in 1962–3 and again opposed United Kingdom entry in 1967–8. Consolidated Franco-German co-operation, 1963.

Dehousse, Fernand
Born Belgium, 1906. Senator, *Parti Socialiste Belge*, 1950. Belgian representative to the European Coal and Steel Community, 1952–60. Member of the Consultative Assembly of the Council of Europe, 1954–61, and of Western European Union Assembly, 1955. Member of the European Parliament, 1958. President of the European Commission for Saar Referendum, 1955, and Saar Commission of Western European Union, 1955–6. President of the Consultative Assembly of the Council of Europe, 1956–9. Belgian Minister for Community Relations, 1971.

dénaturation
see denaturing

denaturing
Denaturing is the act of making a commodity unfit for human consumption by, for example, contaminating wheat with fish oil. To encourage the use of wheat as animal feed, a denaturing premium can be granted to authorised users which makes wheat competitive with less expensive coarse grains. Sugar can also be denatured so that it must be used for animal feed.

Deniau, Jean François
Born 1928. Secretary-General of the Inter-Ministerial Committee on European Economic Co-operation, 1955–6, and delegate to the Organisation for European Economic Co-operation. Ambassador to Mauritania, 1963–6. Director of Commission on Countries seeking association with the E.E.C., 1959–61. Head of delegation to the Conference with States seeking membership of the E.E.C., 1961–3. Member of the combined Commission of E.E.C., E.C.S.C. and Euratom, 1967–73. Commissioner for Development Aid, European Communities, 1969–73. Secretary of State for Foreign Affairs, 1973. Ambassador to Spain, 1977.

Denmark
Denmark signed the Stockholm Convention (Efta) which came into force in 1960 but left Efta on signing the Treaty of Brussels (Treaty of Accession to the E.E.C.) in 1972.
Economic profile: Area 43,100 sq. km. Population (1973) 5,022,000 (male 2,485,000) density 117 per sq. km. Births (per 1,000 of pop. 1973) 14·3; marriages (1972), 6·2; deaths (1972), 10·2. Infant mortality (1972), 12·2.

Labour force (1972) 2,378,000; percentage in agriculture, 9·8; industry, 34·2; services, 56.

International trade (in millions of U.A.):

	1965	1970	1973	1976
Imports	2,811	4,385	6,161	9,808
Exports	2,273	3,290	4,951	7,199

	per 1,000 of population
Standard of living:	
Motor vehicles (1973)	240
Televisions (1972)	283
Telephones (1972)	356

Deutsche Grammophon case
The Deutsche Grammophon GmbH manufactured and sold records at controlled retail prices throughout the German Federal Republic. All

records sold under a particular mark were subject to resale price maintenance. Metro-SB Grossmärkte GmbH, the appellant company, refused to sign the undertaking to maintain the retail prices and obtained records indirectly from Deutsche Grammophon GmbH's French subsidiary, which they then sold in Germany at lower retail prices than those fixed by Deutsche Grammophon GmbH. Deutsche Grammophon GmbH obtained an injunction against Metro and the dispute came before the Court in Hamburg, by which it was referred to the Court of Justice under Article 177 of the Treaty. The questions asked were: (i) does an interpretation of Sections 97 and 85 of the statute concerning copyright, whereby the German manufacturer of sound recordings can prohibit the marketing in Germany of recordings which it has itself supplied to its French subsidiary, conflict with Article 85 of the Treaty? (ii) can the exercise of distribution rights by the manufacturer of recordings be regarded as abusive under Article 86 if the tied selling price is higher than the price of the same product re-imported from another member state, and at the same time the performers are tied by exclusive contracts to the manufacturer of the recordings?

The Court answered the first question in the affirmative thereby depriving Deutsche Grammophon GmbH of the protection it had claimed under German copyright law against imports of its own records sold at lower prices than those fixed for Germany. As to the suggestion of an abusive position under Article 86, the Court confirmed that a record manufacturer granted an exclusive right by national legislation did not have a dominant position under Article 86 merely because he exercised that right. The situation would be otherwise if the manufacturer was able to prevent effective competition in a considerable part of the market in question. The difference between the tied price and the price of the re-imported product did not justify a finding of an abuse of a dominant position, although it could be conclusive evidence if it was large and could not be explained on any objective grounds.

Deutsch Foundation European Prize
see awards

developing countries
see less developed countries

Development Assistance Committee of the Organisation for Economic Co-operation and Development (D.A.C.)
The Development Assistance Committee of the Organisation for Economic Co-operation and Development assumed the membership and functions of the former Development Assistance Group at the end of 1961. It provides a forum for consultations amongst donor countries on the subject of aid to the less developed countries. It is the principal instrument for international co-ordination of aid policies and programmes, and it holds an annual review of aid in which each country is examined by other member nations and its policies scrutinised. The Committee also undertakes studies of particular problems, *e.g.* it recently completed a preliminary study of the terms on which aid is given.

Development Funds, European
These funds were set up to provide aid to developing countries. The first three funds under the Yaoundé (Cameroon) Convention and the current fund under the Lomé (Togo) Convention signed 28 Feb. 1975 are all financed outside the general budget of the Communities, with the result that contributions by E.E.C. member states to the funds are in different proportion to that provided for in budgetary matters and do not need to follow the full budgetary process.

Under the Lomé Convention, E.E.C. member states contribute to the Fund in the following proportions:

	%
Belgium	6·25
Denmark	2·40
France	25·95
Federal German Republic	25·95
Irish Republic	0·60
Italy	12·00
Luxembourg	0·20
Netherlands	7·95
United Kingdom	18·70

The fund will distribute 3,000m. U.A.* over five years to A.C.P. countries as well as 150m. to overseas territories. In addition the European Investment Bank will make 400m. U.A. of loans over the period. The money will be provided over the five years as follows:

	A.C.P.	Overseas Territories	Total
	*millions of units of account**		
Subsidies and	2,100		
Special Loans	430	120	2,650
Risk Capital	95	5	100
Stabe	375	25	400
	3,000	150	3,150
E.I.B.	390	10	400
	3,390	160	3,550

* 'basket' unit of account (E.U.A.)

diplomas, mutual recognition of

The free movement of persons is one of the fundamental principles on which the European Treaties are based. Freedom of movement for employed people under Article 48 of the Treaties was agreed in 1964, but discrimination remains against a whole range of the liberal professions requiring national qualifications, practitioners of which are often self-employed. The problem of applying the principle to professional or semi-professional people remains because of the differing qualifications required by the member states in the practice of the professions. Thus the mutual recognition of diplomas is an essential element in the free movement of professional personnel. General practitioners and specialists may practice anywhere in the E.E.C. from Dec. 1976. Lawyers will similarly be free to practice, but not to establish themselves, by 1979. Apart from the doctors and lawyers very little practical headway has so far been made by the Council in the professions.

Directives

These are issued by the E.E.C. Council of Ministers and are binding as to the result to be achieved. It is left to each member state to decide how to achieve that result. This means that a member state may have to amend its own national laws or administrative practices to bring them into line with Community law.

discrimination

Discrimination consists of restrictive trade measures which favour one country at the expense of another.

disputes, industrial (1974)

country	working days lost per 1,000 employees
Belgium	183
Denmark	96
France	198
Federal German Republic	49
Irish Republic	741
Italy	. .
Luxembourg	0
Netherlands	2
United Kingdom	647

doctors

The Council of Health Ministers reached agreement in Feb. 1975 on the mutual recognition of diplomas for the medical profession and doctors are free to practise throughout the E.E.C. without restrictions from Dec. 1976. The directives apply to doctors trained in the member states and not to third-country diplomas.

72

D.P.C.
Defence Planning Committee of Nato.

dumping
Dumping is the export of a product at less than the domestic price of the product or, in the absence of sales on the home market, at less than the highest price for export to any third country, or at less than the cost of production plus a reasonable addition for selling cost and profit. Anti-dumping duties may be applied to cancel the effect of dumped imports where these cause or threaten material injury to domestic industry in the importing country. *See* anti-dumping policy of the E.E.C.

E

E.A.G.G.F.
European Agricultural Guidance and Guarantee Fund.

E.A.I.B.
European Association of International Booksellers.

E.A.T.
European Association of Teachers.

E.B.U.
European Broadcasting Union.

E.C.
European Communities/Community.

E.C.A.C.
European Civil Aviation Conference which was established in 1955 to promote the co-ordination and orderly development of European air transport.

E.C.E.
Economic Commission for Europe.

E.C.F.T.U.C.
European Confederation of Free Trade Unions in the Community.

E.C.G.D.
Export Credits Guarantee Department. A government body providing export credit insurance facilities to British exporters.

E.C.I.T.O.
European Central Inland Transport Organisation.

E.C.M.A.
European Computer Manufacturers' Association.

E.C.M.T.
European Conference of Ministers of Transport.

Economic and Social Committee of the E.E.C.
The Economic and Social Committee of the European Communities was established under Articles 194–195 Part III of the Treaty of Rome. There are 144 members (France, German Federal Republic, Italy and the United Kingdom have 24 each, Belgium and the Netherlands 12 each, Denmark and the Irish Republic 9 each, and Luxembourg 6). The Committee has been functioning since 1958. There are three groups consisting of

employers' organisations, trade unions and 'special interests' such as small craft industries, commerce, professional occupations, consumers and agriculturists. The Committee assists the Commission and the Council of Ministers of the E.E.C. in an advisory capacity and must be consulted on certain matters laid down in the Treaty.

President (1976–78): Basil de Ferranti (United Kingdom)

Vice-Presidents: Mathias Berns (Luxembourg) and Johannes M. W. van Greunsven (Netherlands).

Economic Commission for Europe

The Economic Commission for Europe is one of the five regional economic commissions established in 1947 by the United Nations Economic and Social Council.

The Committees of the Commission are: Agricultural Problems, Chemical Industry, Coal, Economic Advisers, Electric Power, Advisers on Environmental Problems, Gas, Housing Building and Planning, Advisers on Science and Technology, European Statisticians, Steel, Timber, Development of Trade, Inland Transport and Water Problems.

There is an annual plenary session and meetings of subsidiary bodies meet irregularly. The headquarters are in Geneva.

Economic Development Institute

see International Bank for Reconstruction and Development.

Economic Research, Association of European Institutes of

The Association was founded in 1957 and had a membership (1976) of twenty-two institutes in ten countries with headquarters in Bonn, Federal German Republic.

economic union

Work is progressing on common transport and external trade policies and the co-ordination of financial, commercial, economic and social policies. The Treaty forbids agreements or practices which restrict, prevent or distort free competition, and firms now have to submit such agreements to

75

the Commission, except in cases where Community regulations have exempted certain types of agreement.

At the Paris 'summit' of October 1972 the Nine affirmed the aim of 'Economic Union' by the end of 1980 and agreed to increase their collaboration in the fields of scientific research and advanced technology. The summit also laid the bases for environmental and social action programmes, and a regional policy and fund. The economic recession that followed the OPEC raising of oil prices in 1973, however, destroyed any hope of achieving economic union by the target date.

Ecrêtement

A proposal put forward for consideration by the E.E.C. at the Gatt Ministerial meeting in May 1963 on the basis of the French suggestion at a meeting of a Gatt Working Party. The plan would involve departing from the concept of a straight linear cut in tariffs by introducing the idea of target rates and reducing by 50% the difference between existing national rates and the target rates instead of the difference between existing tariff rates and nil. Thus it was suggested for discussion that, while the target rate for raw materials be taken as nil (so that the reduction on raw materials would be the same as under the linear tariff formula), that on semi-manufactured goods should be taken as 5% and on manufactured goods as 10%. This would have the effect of reducing the depth of a 50% linear cut on a semi-manufacture, on the figures suggested, by $2\frac{1}{2}$ percentage points, and on a manufactured article by 5 percentage points. The object would be to then ensure smaller reductions on lower rates of duty than on higher rates of duty. In fact it would also have meant that no tariff, except on a raw material, however high it was, would have been reduced by the full linear percentage. The Ecrêtement formula constitutes a move towards tariff harmonisation. It has not been proceeded with in the preparatory discussions in Geneva for the Kennedy Round, though there have been signs that the French at least may still be attached to it.

E.C.S.C.

see European Coal and Steel Community.

E.D.C.
European Defence Community.

E.E.C.
European Economic Community, *see also* history
Economic profile: Area 1,528,200 sq. km. Population (1973) 256,635,000
(male 124, 577, 000) density 168 per sq. km. Births (per 1,000 of pop. 1973)
14·1; marriages, 7·4; deaths, 11. Infant mortality, 19·8.

Labour force (1972) 103,370,000; percentage in agriculture, 9·6; industry, 43·4; services, 46·9.
International trade (in millions of U.A.):

	1965	1970	1973	1976
Imports	68,979	116,139	171,698	271,488
Exports	64,521	112,182	167,931	257,447

	per 1,000 of population
Standard of living:	
Motor vehicles (1973)	246
Televisions (1972)	247
Telephones (1972)	234

E.E.G.
Europese Economische Gemeenschap, European Economic Community.
(Dutch).

E.E.Z.
The exclusive economic zone refers to the coastal waters. At the United
Nations Conference on the Law of the Sea in 1976 there was discussion on
the introduction of a 200 mile E.E.Z. for coastal states for E.E.C. member
countries. Other major matters for consideration were the continental
shelf, the international sea-bed, protection of the marine environment,

marine scientific research, the transfer of technology and the settlement of disputes.

Efta
European Free Trade Association. An earlier proposal was for a European Free Trade Area.

E.G.K.S.
Europäische Gemeinschaft für Kohle und Stahl, European Coal and Steel Community (German).

Egypt
The Arab Republic of Egypt signed a preferential trade agreement with the E.E.C. under Article 113 of the Treaty of Rome which came into force on 1 Nov. 1973 for a period of five years. On 18 Jan. 1977 the E.E.C. signed a co-operation agreement with Egypt (and Jordan and Syria). There is no term set for the agreement but it will be reviewed in 1979 and 1984.

E.I.B.
European Investment Bank.

E.L.D.O.
European Launcher Development Organisation *now* E.S.A.

E.L.E.C.
European League for Economic Co-operation is an international non-party organisation which brings together experts in finance, economics and industry to study problemes and suggest solutions.

elections, direct, to European Parliament
At the session of the European Council held in Rome in Dec. 1976

agreement was reached that direct elections to the European Parliament should take place in May or June 1978.

E.M.
European Movement.

E.M.C.F.
European Monetary Co-operation Fund.

Employment, Standing Committee on
The Standing Committee on Employment, created in 1970 by decision of the Council of Ministers, advises the Council and Commission on all aspects of employment policy. It is composed of eighteen trade union and eighteen employer representatives, appointed by the European trade union and employers' organisations, plus the nine ministers of labour or social affairs and the member of the European Commission responsible for social affairs. It is serviced by the Council of Ministers' secretariat.

The European trade union movement campaigned strongly for the creation of the Standing Committee on Employment as part of its drive to orientate the E.E.C. more decisively towards social objectives. It was felt that more emphasis could be placed on employment questions by the establishment of this forum and that action could be attained more quickly through meetings where trade union representatives and ministers came face to face.

The Committee held several meetings but, after the enlargement of the Community on 1 Jan. 1973, for various reasons it was unable to meet for two years. One of the first actions of the European Social Conference in Dec. 1974 was to resuscitate the Standing Committee on Employment. Since then it has met frequently.

A new development within the Committee is the establishment of special committees to examine industrial sectors with high unemployment—automobile, chemicals, textile, construction and glass.

In its report on European Union published in July 1975, the European Commission mentions the need to strengthen the role of the Committee on employment, in the context of evolving a medium-term economic strategy.

employment, total civilian (1974)

Its view is as follows: 'Given the efforts and sacrifices entailed by this medium-term programme, it is essential that the two sides of industry should be more closely involved in the preparation of decisions on social and economic issues. There is a real need to set up a general framework for the purposes of ensuring permanent dialogue between Governments, institutions, and the two sides of industry. Without impinging on the role of the Economic and Social Committee, the role of the Committee on Employment should be strengthened'.

employment, total civilian (1974)

country	total	*foreign workers as %*
Belgium	3,801,000	6·9
Denmark	2,355,000	1·9
France	21,166,000	11·1
Federal German Republic	25,689,000	10·8
Irish Republic	1,047,000	0·2
Italy	18,715,000	0·4
Luxembourg	151,000	3·4
Netherlands	4,579,000	3·1
United Kingdom	24,767,000	5·6

E.M.U.A.
European Monetary Unit of Account, *see* unit of account

E.N.D.S.
Euratom Nuclear Documentation System.

energy policy
On 29 May 1974 the E.E.C. Commission approved a memorandum called *Towards a New Energy Policy Strategy for the European Community*.
  As objectives for 1985 on the demand side, the memorandum proposed

that (i) the rate of increase in the use of energy should be reduced by rationalisation and elimination of waste, so that the Community's internal consumption in 1985 was 10% below pre-crisis estimates for that year; and (ii) electricity consumption should be encouraged, without increasing dependence on oil, so as to ensure that 35% of total energy consumption was in this form (against 25% currently), thus creating a much larger market for nuclear energy.

On the supply side objectives for 1985 included: (i) the provision of 50% of electricity production by nuclear power; (ii) the maintenance of internal production of solid fuel at present levels, with increased requirements being met by imports; (iii) a 'great increase' in the internal production and importation of natural gas; and (iv) the restriction of oil consumption to specific uses (motor fuel and as a raw material).

The memorandum also stated that if these objectives were fulfilled, the Community's consumption of crude oil would reach a peak in 1980 and return to its 1973 level around 1985, thus reducing the share of imported energy, mostly oil, in the Community's total consumption from 63% to 42%. From 1985 onwards production from new oilfields within the Community, for instance the North Sea, could cut down still further the proportion of imports from non-member countries in the Community's oil supply.

It seemed certain in 1977 that the more optimistic target would not be reached and the E.E.C. Commission suggested that, even though the 1985 forecast energy requirement has been reduced by some 8%, the reduction to 50% is now in doubt. Even after allowing for North Sea production, an annual growth rate of 4–5%, the minimum to reduce unemployment, will probably mean that imported oil will represent about 45% of energy supplies as against the 37% aimed at in the (1974) strategy document.

environmental action

On 19–20 July 1973 the E.E.C. Council of Ministers adopted an initial two-year 'programme of environmental action' as a result of the Paris Summit of Oct. 1972.

Among the principles laid down in the programme as the basis for a Community environment policy were the following:
(i) 'The best protection of the environment consists in preventing at source the creation of pollution or nuisances, rather than subsequently trying to

counteract their effects.'

(ii) 'All exploitation of resources and the natural environment causing significant damage to the ecological balance must be banned.'

(iii) 'The cost of preventing and abolishing nuisances must be borne by the polluter.'

(iv) 'The Community and its member states must take into account in their environment policy the interests of the developing countries, and must in particular examine any repercussions of the measures contemplated under that policy on the economic development of such countries and on trade with them, with a view to reducing adverse consequences as far as possible.'

(v) 'For each different class of pollution, the level of action (local, regional, national, Community, international) best suited to the type of pollution and to the geographical zone to be protected should be sought.'

(vi) 'Environment policies should be harmonised in the Community, and national programmes on the environment should be co-ordinated among the member states and with the Community programmes on the basis of a common long-term plan.'

In its general definition of action to be taken in this field by the Community, the programme specified three types of project:

(i) 'Projects aimed at reducing and preventing pollution and nuisances. The main task is to set up a common framework for reference and methods, to limit the presence of pollutants in the environment and in products, to carry out research and to improve information and documentation.'

(ii) 'Projects intended to improve the environment and the quality of life. These projects involve protection of the natural environment, the problems posed by the depletion of certain natural resources, the optimum distribution of activities and people with a view to protecting or improving the environment, the improvement of the working environment, the establishment of an institution with the purpose of improving living and working conditions, and the information and education of the public.

Some of these projects will have to be worked out under an environmental policy and at the same time under more specific policies, e.g., social policy, agricultural policy and regional policy.'

(iii) 'Community action or, where appropriate, joint action on the part of the member states in the international organisations dealing with environmental questions.'

E.O.F.
Europaeiske okonomiske Faelleskab, European Economic Community
(Danish).

E.P.O.
European Patents Office.

E.P.U.
European Parliamentary Union.

E.P.U.
European Payments Union

equal pay
In 1964 the Council of Ministers recorded its agreement in principle to a
directive, published by the Commission, aimed at ensuring observance by
the end of 1975 of the principle of equal pay for men and women, in
accordance with Article 119 of the Treaty of Rome, covering the
elimination, for identical work or for work to which equal value had been
attributed, of all discrimination on grounds of sex with regard to all aspects
and conditions of remuneration.

The directive was also aimed at eliminating all discrimination which
might still exist in certain legal provisions, and at rendering null and void
any provisions in agreements or contracts which were contrary to this
principle. Member states would introduce into their national legislation
such measures as were necessary to enable all employees who considered
themselves aggrieved by the non-application of the principle of equal pay
to pursue their claims by legal processes after recourse to other competent
authorities. Protection for workers at shop-floor level was also ensured in
the event of arbitrary dismissal which could arise as a result of a request for
application of this principle.

Position in early 1975 on Equal Pay for Women:

Belgium   Royal decree of 24 Oct. 1967 allowed enforcement of
                   right to equal pay; decree replaced by law of 16 March

83

1971. Law of 5 Dec. 1968 gave trade unions right to take legal action on behalf of workers—even against workers' wishes.

Furthermore, collective agreements which are discriminatory can be replaced.

Denmark　No legal or statutory provisions requiring the implementation of equal pay.

France　Law of 13 July 1971 requires collective agreements to provide for 'equal wages for equal work'. If right to equal wage is not laid down by collective agreement, general legal principle on equality of sexes in preamble of 1946 Constitution provides basis for court proceedings. This is confirmed in the Law of 22 Dec. 1972. Infringements of rights to equal pay may warrant fines or other sanctions for the employer and the repeal of collective agreements, depending upon the source of infringements as determined by the inspector of labour. This stems from the Law of 27 March 1973.

Federal German Republic　Article 3 of 1949 Constitution of the Federal Republic stipulates equal rights. Legal standard determined by Federal Labour Tribunal. Laws on organisation of companies (11 Oct. 1952 and 19 Jan. 1972) and law on staff representation of 5 Aug. 1955 prohibit discrimination. Infringements may lead to invalidity of collective agreement. No official control.

Irish Republic　Anti-Discrimination (Pay) Bill 1974 requires as a general rule that pay rates must be related to job function rather than sex. Proposed implementation 1977.

Italy　Article 37 of 1948 Constitution stipulates equal rights and equal pay for equal work. There are specific provisions for certain professions and the civil service. Inspectors of labour have the function of supervising equal pay enforcement.

Luxembourg　Law of 23 June 1963 confirmed principle of non-discrimination for workers in public sector. Law of 12 June 1965 provides for equal pay in collective agreements. Law of 17 May 1967 confirms the equal pay

	provision of the I.L.O. convention.
Netherlands	No general legal or statutory provisions on implementation of equal pay principle. Rights to equal pay result solely from collective agreements on individual work contracts. Stipulation that collective agreements must be *erga omnes*.
United Kingdom	Equal Pay Act of 1970 assured general application of equal pay in the United Kingdom by 1975. Social Security Act 1973 required pensions benefits to be given to all; hence, including women in schemes by law.

Equatorial Guinea
Equatorial Guinea signed the Lomé Convention of 1975.

Erasmus Prize
see awards

E.R.P.
European Recovery Programme.

E.S.A.
European Space Agency.

E.S.C.
European Space Conference.

Eslab
European Space Laboratory.

E.S.R.O.
European Space Research Organisation *see* E.S.A.

establishment, right of
Restrictions on the freedom of establishment of nationals of a member country in the territory of another member country will be progressively abolished under Articles 52–58 of the Treaty of Rome. Such progressive abolition will also extend to restrictions on the setting up of agencies, branches and subsidiaries by nationals of any member country in another member country.

Freedom of establishment will include the right to engage in and carry on non-wage-earning activities, and also to set up and manage enterprises.

Progress in this area (by 1977) has been slow but it is closely linked to the problems of 'free movement of capital' and 'the alignment of qualifications'.

E.S.T.I.
European Space Technology Institute.

Ethiopia
Ethiopia signed the Lomé Convention of 1975.

E.T.U.C.
European Trade Union Confederation.

E.U.A.
see unit of account.

EUR
The EUR is the unit of account of the E.E.C. used by the Statistical office of the European Community.

EUR-6
The original six members of the E.E.C.

EUR-9
The nine members of the E.E.C. in 1977.

Euratom
The European Atomic Energy Community (Euratom) was set up in 1958 to help develop a civil nuclear industry in Europe and thereby help to raise living standards, which are closely linked to the level of energy consumption. In 1967 its executive was merged with E.E.C. and E.C.S.C. Between 1967 and the Hague Summit in 1973 there was very little progress in this Community. A four-year programme was then launched with a budget of £83.2m. to shift the emphasis from reactor technology towards public service research, including safety and the environment. In 1974 there were fifty-six nuclear reactors in the E.E.C. with a total capacity of 11.5m. kilowatts.

Euro-Arab dialogue
Negotiations on economic, financial and other co-operation between the European Communities and the Arab League, resulting from the Copenhagen summit of Dec. 1973, were still in progress in 1977.

Euro-Control
The European Organisation for the Safety of Air Navigation was established in 1963 to strengthen co-operation among member states (Belgium, France, the Federal German Republic, the Irish Republic, Luxembourg, the Netherlands and the United Kingdom) in matters of air navigation, and in particular to provide for the common organisation of air traffic services in the upper airspace.

Euroco-op
European Community of Consumers' Co-operatives.

Eurocrat
The colloquial term for a European Civil Servant. There are approx-

TABLE 1
The number of staff (permanent and temporary) authorised for 1976 was:

Category/grade		Parliament	Council	Economic and Social Committee	Audit Board	E.C.S.C. Auditor	Commission	Commission-research and investment	Court of Justice	Total
Non-Category		1	1	1	—					3
A	1	5	6	1	—	—	23	2	—	37
	2	21	16	3	1	1	125	12	2	181
	3	52	30	10	1	—	317	58	9	477
	4	40	32	5	4	—	554	168	7	810
	5	34	28	6	6	—	539	322	5	940
	6	34	29	6	2	—	315	106	6	498
	7	50	27	6	2	—	250	40	5	380
	8							1		1
	Total	236	168	37	16	1	2123	709	34	3324
LA	3	13	9	3	—	—	16	—	3	44
	4	58	45	12	—	—	198	—	15	328
	5	102	125	18	—	—	419	—	22	686
	6	60	71	11	—	—	248	—	14	404
	7	34	57	16	—	—	265	—	—	372
	8	—	—	—	—	—	1	—	—	1
	Total	267	307	60	—	—	1147	—	54	1835
B	1	34	18	5	4	1	391	109	5	567
	2	33	37	10	3	—	461	255	16	815
	3	49	44	10	4	2	447	235	15	806
	4	78	23	15	—	—	231	204	14	565
	5	—	11	4	—	—	134	60	11	220
	Total	194	133	44	11	3	1664	863	61	2973
C	1	130	119	16	1	1	349	82	12	710
	2	203	206	36	1	—	981	82	32	1541
	3	164	254	37	1	—	985	15	30	1486
	4	75	84	21	—	—	273	1	5	459
	5	—	36	21	—	—	83	—	—	140
	Total	572	699	131	3	1	2671	180	79	4336

TABLE 1
The number of staff (permanent and temporary) authorised for 1976 was:

Category/grade		Parliament	Council	Economic and Social Committee	Audit Board	E.C.S.C. Auditor	Commission	Commission-research and investment	Court of Justice	Total
Non-Category		1	1	1	–					3
D	1	44	37	6	–	–	172	–	19	278
	2	46	72	12	–	–	144	–	8	282
	3	44	84	11	–	–	62	–	9	210
	Total	134	193	29	–	–	378	–	36	770
Establishment staff								447		447
TOTAL		1404	1501	302	30	5	7983	2199	264	13,688

imately 14,000 Eurocrats spread over the various institutions and bodies of the Communities. In theory no posts are reserved for nationals of any specific member states and conversely all Eurocrats must be citizens of member states. The table above gives a detailed analysis of the numbers employed at each level in each institution.

Staff are divided into five categories, A, LA, B, C, and D. Category A is for the professional staff who perform administrative or advisory functions; a university or equivalent professional education is required. Category LA is similar to category A except that this category is occupied solely in translation, interpretation and similar duties. Category B requires an advanced level of secondary education. Category C covers clerical duties and requires secondary education. Category D covers manual or service duties and requires at least primary education. Brief job titles are given in table 2. Pay scales, net of tax, are given in table 2: in addition the Eurocrat receives an expatriation allowance equivalent to 16% and also certain other small allowances. Eurocrats can buy a small amount of duty-free

Table 2
Basic Pay and job titles
at 1 Jan 1977

		Lowest pay in category	Highest pay in category	Job titles.	The language service (LA category) and certain employees of Euratom have different job titles)
		BF	BF		
A and LA	1	184 674	230 684	Director General	
	2	165 175	209 075	Director	
	3	138 752	192 526	Head of Division	
	4	118 391	160 370	{ Principal	
	5	98 409	136 692	{ Administrator	
	6	83 791	117 314	{ Administrator	
	7	69 382	90 252		
	8	59 410	62 415	Assistant Administrator	
B	1	83 791	117 314	Principal Administrative Assistant	
	2	70 522	97 304	Senior { Administrative / Technical or / Secretarial } Assistant	
	3	56 134	79 675	{ Administrative	
	4	47 068	66 458	{ Technical or } Assistant	
	5	41 530	47 710	{ Secretarial	
C	1	48 205	65 341	Executive Secretary / Principal / Principal Clerical Officer	
	2	40 937	55 448	{ Secretary/Shorthand Typist	
	3	37 938	50 272	{ Clerical Officer	
	4	33 757	45 083	{ Typist	
	5	30 793	35 173	{ Clerical Assistant	
D	1	35 391	48 257	Head of Unit	
	2	31 826	43 033	Skilled employee	
	3	29 305	39 665	Unskilled employee	

alcohol twice a year and are exempted from national income taxes and
certain local taxes (*e.g.* on domestic servants, dogs and bicycles) although

they pay a Community income tax. Both Belgium and Luxembourg offer special car number plates to Eurocrats, which confer no privileges or exemptions. Staff above A4 level may be issued with a quasi-diplomatic *laissez passer*.

Euro-currency
see Euro-dollars

Euro-dollars
Euro-dollars are dollar balances held by private individuals or companies in European banks. They provide a stock of international currency not appearing in governmental returns. The traffic is not confined to dollars; it is also a fund of international short-term capital and generally flows to those countries offering highest interest rates. The system came into existence during the Suez crisis of 1957. Other currencies have also filled this role hence also the expression Euro-currency.

Euro-licence
Common Market citizens will be eligible for an optional European driving licence valid throughout the Community under plans approved by the European Parliament in 1976.

Euronet
It is planned that from June 1977 some 700 European research centres, high-technology industries and other bodies will be able to plug into a transmission system for data from more than twenty computer banks and get their answers within three minutes. This is the aim of an agreement concluded in 1975 between the telephone authorities of the nine Community countries. It provides for four communications centres, in London, Paris, Rome and Frankfurt, with four 'concentrators' in Dublin, Brussels, Copenhagen and Amsterdam, and local access in Luxembourg.

Europa
Europa the daughter of Agenor, King of Phoenicia, was abducted to Crete

by Zeus in the guise of a white bull. Also the name suggested for a parallel European currency proposed in a report by the Federal Trust.

Europabus
A network of road services, tours and excursions run under the control of the European railways both inside France and beyond its frontiers.

Europa Prize
see awards

European Agricultural Guidance and Guarantee Fund
The European Agricultural Guidance and Guarantee Fund (E.A.G.G.F.) finances the agricultural policy. The Guarantee section finances the public expenditure arising from the common organisation of agricultural markets and the Guidance section helps to finance the common policy of improving agricultural structure.

From 1964–74 nearly 4,800 projects were financed by the Fund involving a total of approximately 1,300m. U.A. Nearly 340m. U.A. were for land improvement and for irrigation and drainage. The chief beneficiary country was Italy for which 400m. U.A. were provided for some 1,800 projects, Germany received 330m. U.A. for 1,000 projects and France 264m. U.A. for 800 projects.

Since 1975 the financing of both the Guarantee and Guidance sections of the Fund has been charged to the budget of the European Communities. The receipts into this budget come from customs duties, agricultural levies and a charge on sugar. This produces 66% of the total and the balance consists of contributions assessed on the member states.

European Assembly
see Parliament, European

European Atomic Energy Community
see Euratom

European civil servants
see Eurocrat

European Coal and Steel Community
The European Coal and Steel Community (E.C.S.C.) was established in 1952 by the Paris Treaty and was the pioneer of European integration. It applied the Community method to the coal and steel industries as a first step towards the integration of the economy as a whole. A decision to merge the executives of the E.C.S.C. and Euratom with the E.E.C. came into effect on 1 July 1967.

European Communities Act
The European Communities Act, 1972, was the legislation enacted in the United Kingdom as a result of the signing of the Treaty of Accession.

The purposes were:

Part I. To give the force of law in the United Kingdom to present and future Community law in so far as that law would be directly applicable in the member states and would supersede national law.

Part II. To repeal and amend United Kingdom law:

(i) To enable the United Kingdom to implement its Community obligations and to exercise its rights as a member of the European Communities.

(ii) To share in the finances of the Communities as to both payments and receipts.

(iii) To conform to the Customs Duties of the Communities.

(iv) To set up an Intervention Board to operate the Common Agricultural Policy and to provide for the collection of levies on agricultural imports.

(v) To harmonise the work of the Restrictive Practices Act 1956 with the United Kingdom obligations under the Rules of Competition of the Treaty of Rome.

(vi) To amend the law to comply with the Regulations issued by the Commission on companies, food, seed, cine films, transport, animal and plant health, fertilisers, etc.

(vii) To fulfil all other obligations accepted by signing the Treaty of Accession.

Breaches against Community Regulations would be treated in the national Courts of the member states in the same way as breaches against national laws; for example against Community Regulations on Restrictive Trade Practices (Rules of Competition) by the Restrictive Practices Court; against Regulations of Companies under the Companies Acts; against making false statements before the European Court under the Perjury Acts; against disclosure of 'classified' information in Euratom under the Official Secrets Act.

European Convention of Human Rights
see Council of Europe.

European Council
At the Paris meeting of Heads of Government of the nine member countries 9–10 Dec. 1974 it was decided to meet, accompanied by the Ministers of Foreign Affairs, three times a year. These meetings have become known as the European Council which should not be confused with the Council of Ministers or the Council of Europe.

The European Council meets with representatives of the Commission present and is thus also the Council of the European Communities, a Community institution, and as such is empowered to adopt Community instruments in the form laid down by the Treaties. In spite of this it has to date confined itself to issuing general guidelines which have been acted upon by the Council proper, in its normal guise, and the Commission, in strict accordance with the Treaties.

The following European Councils have been held:

Dec.	1974	Paris	Heads of government of the Nine set up the European Council.
March	1975	Dublin	Major decisions taken enabling the United Kingdom government to recommend continued British membership of the Communities.
July	1975	Brussels	Concerned mainly with external affairs.
Dec.	1975	Rome	Decided that European Parliament should be elected by universal suffrage by 1978.

April   1976 LuxembourgAn inconclusive meeting.

July   1976 Brussels   Confirmed that Parliament should be elected by universal suffrage by 1978 and number of seats per member state decided. Roy Jenkins (U.K.) to be next president of the Commission.

Nov.   1976 The Hague   Routine matters, mainly economic, discussed.

March 1977 Rome   Twentieth anniversary of the Treaty of Rome.

European Development Fund
The European Development Fund is the main instrument for carrying out the Community's financial aid policy in the associated states and certain other countries. Although the Fund has taken different forms and developed greater flexibility through the years, the fundamental principles which underlay its creation have not been modified. Loans from the European Investment Bank have increased and reinforced the work of the European Development Fund.

The Fund's activities cover a very large field and can take many forms including:
(i) making immediately productive investments;
(ii) developing the rural economy;
(iii) investing in the economic and social infrastructure;
(iv) technical assistance before, during and after investment;
(v) training workers and managers;
(vi) providing experts and technicians;
(vii) undertaking feasibility studies;
(viii) helping to overcome serious difficulties resulting from drop in world prices for commodities;
(ix) helping to overcome problems arising from natural disasters;
(x) making advances to stabilisation funds to compensate for temporary fluctuations in world prices;
(xi) improving marketing and sales promotion.
There have, in fact, been four Funds: The first under the Treaty of Rome; the second and third under the two Yaoundé Conventions and the fourth under the Lomé Convention. Contributions to the first three Funds by the

Six were as follows (in millions of U.A.):

	Rome Treaty	Yaoundé I	Yaoundé II
Belgium	70·00	69·00	80·00
France	200·00	246·50	298·50
German Federal Republic	200·00	246·50	298·50
Italy	40·00	100·00	140·60
Luxembourg	1·25	2·00	2·40
Netherlands	70·00	66·00	80·00
total	581·25	730·00	900·00

For details of the fourth Fund *see* Lomé Convention page 146.

European Foundation for the Improvement of Living and Working Conditions

The European Foundation for the Improvement of Living and Working Conditions, established by the Council of Ministers in 1975, has a quadripartite management board of exactly the same composition as the European Centre for Vocational Training. Unlike the Centre the Foundation has, in addition, a committee of experts consisting of twelve members.

The Foundation aims to increase and disseminate knowledge contributing to the improvement of living and working conditions. More specifically its scope concerns the following areas: man at work; organisation of work and particularly job design; problems peculiar to certain categories of workers; long-term aspects of improvement of the environment; distribution of human activities in space and time. The Foundation is located in the Irish Republic.

European Free Trade Association (Efta)

Efta has six member countries: Austria, Iceland, Norway, Portugal, Sweden and Switzerland. A seventh country, Finland, is an associate member. The Stockholm Convention establishing the Association entered into force on 3 May 1960 and Finland became associated on 27 Mar. 1961. Iceland joined Efta on 1 Mar. 1970 and was immediately granted duty-free entry for industrial goods exported to Efta countries, while being given ten years to abolish her own existing protective duties. Two founder members of the European Free Trade Area, the United Kingdom and Denmark, left Efta on 31 Dec. 1972 to join the E.E.C.

When the Association was created it had three objectives: to achieve free trade in industrial products between member countries, to assist in the creation of a single market embracing the countries of Western Europe, and to contribute to the expansion of world trade in general.

The first objective was achieved on 31 Dec. 1966 when virtually all inter-Efta tariffs were removed. This was three years earlier than originally planned. Finland removed her remaining Efta tariffs a year later on 31 Dec. 1967. The achievement of free trade made Efta the world's first complete free trade area and intra-Efta trade more than doubled in the period 1959–68.

The fulfilment of the second aim was secured in 1972. On 22 Jan. 1972 the United Kingdom and Denmark signed the Treaty of Accession to the E.E.C. whereby they became members of the enlarged Community from 1 Jan. 1973. On 22 July five other Efta countries, Austria, Iceland, Portugal, Sweden and Switzerland signed Free Trade Agreements with the enlarged E.E.C. A similar agreement negotiated with Finland was signed on 5 Oct. 1973. Norway, whose intention of joining the E.E.C. was reversed following a referendum, signed a similar agreement on 14 May 1973. Through these agreements, virtually complete free trade in industrial goods will be achieved in sixteen Western European countries from 1 July 1977.

The third objective was to contribute to the expansion of world trade. In 1959 the trade between seven countries now in Efta amounted to $759m. and their exports to all markets totalled $6,852m. In 1975 the trade between them had risen to $9,849m. and their total exports to $52,758m.

Efta tariff treatment applies to those industrial products which are of Efta origin, and these are traded freely between member countries. Each Efta country remains free, however, to impose its own rates of duty on products entering from outside the Efta area.

Generally agricultural products do not come under the provisions for free trade, but bilateral agreements have been negotiated to increase trade in these products.

The operation of the Convention is the responsibility of a Council assisted by a small secretariat. Each Efta country holds the chairmanship of the Council for six months.

European Investment Bank

The European Investment Bank was created by the Treaty of Rome and came into force on 1 Jan. 1958. The Bank is an independent public institution within the E.E.C. and operates on a non-profit-making basis. Its basic function is to contribute to the balanced development of the Common Market.

The European Investment Bank grants long-term loans and gives its guarantee to enterprises, public authorities and financial institutions to finance investments which favour the development of less advanced regions and conversion areas, or which serve the interests of the Community as a whole.

The members of the European Investment Bank are the nine member countries of the Community, who have all subscribed to the Bank's capital which stands at 2,025m. units of account.

The Bank borrows the funds required to carry out its tasks on the capital markets of the Community and non-member countries, and on international markets.

The Bank's activities were initially confined to the territory of the member countries of the E.E.C. (special operations). Moreover, with the Association Agreements to other countries. Apart from its ordinary loans the Bank grants loans on special conditions to these countries through its Special Section, under mandate from and for the account of the member countries of the E.E.C. (special operations). Moreover, with special authorisation from its Board of Governors, the Bank may also grant financial aid to non-member countries, especially if the projects concerned are of direct interest to the member countries of the Community.

The Bank may grant loans from its own resources and give its guarantee (ordinary operations) to private or public enterprises, irrespective of their legal status, and to public authorities, to finance projects which conform with the conditions of Article 130 of the Treaty of Rome, or with the Association Agreements. The granting of financial aid does not depend on the nationality of the borrower.

The Bank's loans are intended to cover only part of the cost of a project, supplementing the borrower's own funds and credits from other sources. The Bank rarely lends more than 40 % of the cost of the fixed assets.

The Bank's loans generally range between 2m. and 16m. units of account and have so far never exceeded 30m. units of account. Some large projects have received more than one loan but the cumulative total has never exceeded 45m. units of account.

Loans to finance specific projects may be made directly to an enterprise or public authority or through a financial institution.In addition to these 'individual loans', the Bank also grants 'global loans' to financing institutions, which extend sub-loans for small and medium scale industrial investments after the Bank has given its approval for each individual project (appropriations from global loans).

The Bank disburses its loans in several currencies which it selects according to those actually held by it, after consulting the borrowers as to which currencies they would like to receive; repayments and the payment of interest are made in the currencies of the original loan.

The Board of Directors fixes the rate of interest on the loans. As the Bank operates on a non-profit-making basis, its interest rates are close to the average rates charged on the financial markets where it obtains its funds. The rate charged on each loan is generally that in force on the date when the contract is concluded and is not subject to revision. It is independent of the currency in which the loan is disbursed and the country in which the project is situated. The rate in force on 27 June 1974 was 9.875 % per annum irrespective of the term of the loan. The term of each loan (generally between eight and twelve years for industrial projects and up to twenty years for infrastructure projects) and the grace period depend upon the nature of the project concerned.

The Bank makes the granting of its loans conditional on the guarantee of a member country or other adequate security.

Finance arranged between 1958 and 1973 was for 480 loans, guarantees and equity participations and of these, 362 operations were in member countries, 44 in associated countries, 74 were for special operations. Of the 159 loans for infrastructure, 63 were for transport including 37 for roads and bridges. Agriculture, industry and services, such as tourism received 321. The total amount involved was 3,658.lm. U.A.

The European Investment Bank granted seventy-seven loans in 1975 amounting to 1,000m. U.A. to the following countries:

Belgium	10·8
Denmark	17·7
France	158·0
Irish Republic	37·7
Italy	358·8

United Kingdom	334·5
Greece	47·2
Mauritius	1·7
Turkey	35·0
Netherland Antilles	4·4
Guadeloupe	0·7

To finance this the Bank made twenty-six separate borrowing transactions in seven different currencies for a total of 814m. U.A. The head office is in Luxembourg.

European Monetary Co-operation Fund
The Fund was set up with the intention of becoming the embryo of a reserve system of the central banks, and to have operational responsibility in the field of a community currency exchange system.

The governors of the Fund are the governors of the member states' central banks. The Fund, which uses the Bank for International Settlements in Basle as its agent, intervenes on the foreign exchange markets at the request of member states. In addition the Fund also acts as a banker for the Communities in certain circumstances.

European Parliament
see Parliament, European

European Parliament, direct elections
see elections, direct, to European Parliament

Europan Parliament, strength of political groups
see Parliament, strength of political grouping in European

European People's Party
see Federation of Christian Democratic Parties

European Plan
A system of hotel management in which a guest pays for his room and services separately from his payment for meals, as against the American Plan in which the guest pays a fixed daily rate for room, meals and service.

European Recovery Programme
The European Recovery Programme, also known as the Marshall Plan, arose from the speech of Gen. George Marshall made at Harvard University on 5 June 1947 in which he outlined the serious shortage of United States dollars for the economic situation in Europe and suggested United States assistance in its economic recovery, on the understanding that the European countries reached some agreement about their requirements and the part that they would take in giving proper effect to the action of the United States.

Exploratory meetings were held during 1947 and on 16 April 1948 a Convention was signed by the European countries concerned to form the Organisation of European Economic Co-operation (O.E.E.C.)

European Science Foundation
Agreement was reached on 25 Sept. 1973 on the creation of a European Science Foundation to link the national research programmes of sixteen countries (Austria, Belgium, Denmark, France, Federal German Republic, Greece, the Irish Republic, Italy, the Netherlands, Norway, Portugal, Spain, Sweden, Switzerland, the United Kingdom and Yugoslavia). The initial objectives of the Foundation were announced as being to promote collaboration in research, to increase mobility among research workers, to assist exchanges of information and ideas among participating countries and to harmonise research activities and programmes. It was estimated that national research work costing about £500m. would be brought under the *aegis* of the new Foundation, which started functioning in 1975.

European Social Fund
see Social Fund Committee

European Space Agency
The Convention establishing the European Space Agency, which replaced the European Launcher Development Organisation and the European Space Research Organisation, was signed on 30 May 1975, in Paris, by representatives of the ten member countries (Belgium, Denmark, France, Federal German Republic, Italy, the Netherlands, Spain, Sweden, Switzerland and the United Kingdom).

It is expected that some $2,000m. will be spent on projects and activities controlled by the Agency by 1980 and members are committed to certain areas of co-operation such as studies on future projects, technological documentation and research, but each member country retains the right to decide whether to participate in specific major projects.

European Studies, Association of Institutes
The Association was founded in 1951 and had a membership (1976) of thirty-two institutes in nine countries, with headquarters in Geneva, Switzerland.

European Trade Union Confederation
In Feb. 1973 the European Trade Union Confederation was formed by trade unionists in fifteen Western European countries to deal with questions of interest to European working people arising inside and outside the E.E.C. All the founding organisations were I.C.F.T.U. affiliates but subsequently they accepted into membership European W.C.L. affiliates, the Irish Congress of Trade Unions and the Italian Communist trade union centre (C.G.I.L.). The membership now exceeds 36m. from thirty centres in seventeen countries.

Europêche
Association des organisations nationales d'entreprises de pêche de la C.E.E., Association of National Organisations of Fishing Enterprises of the E.E.C.

Europe Prize
see awards

Europoort
Construction of the Europoort in the Netherlands, covering nearly 4,000 acres, began in 1958 and is situated at the end of the *Nieuwe Waterweg* opposite the *Hoek van Holland*. Its main use is for the storage of ores and oil, transhipment, engineering, shipbuilding and chemicals. There are pipelines to the oil refineries of Pernis and Botlek and to parts of the German Federal Republic. Approximately 380,000 containers were loaded into and unloaded out of ships at the Europoort in 1974.

Eurostat
Statistical office of the European Communities.

Euro-sterling
Sterling deposits accepted and employed by banks outside the United Kingdom. The market in such sterling is centred in Paris, and is much smaller than that in Euro-dollars.

Eurosyndicat Index
An index number for European stock exchange securities.

Eurotox
European Standing Committee for the Protection of Populations against the Long-Term Risks of Intoxication.

E.V.G.
Europäische Verteidigungsgemeinschaft, European Defence Community (German).

E.W.G.
Europäische Wirtschaftliche Gemeinschaft, European Economic Community (German).

exclusive dealing agreements
These are agreements by which producers can grant absolute territorial protection to specified distributors, by guaranteeing to the holder of the concession the exclusive right to obtain supplies from the producer, and to be the only distributor to introduce the products into the territory allocated to him. This exclusive right is generally reinforced by prohibiting all resellers in other areas from exporting into the area allocated to the concession holder.

external relations
In 1961, the United Kingdom, the Irish Republic, Norway and Denmark opened negotiations for membership but these were broken off at the insistence of France in 1963. A fresh attempt in 1967 failed for the same reason.

After the retirement of President de Gaulle, and particularly after The Hague 'summit' meeting of the Six, it became clear that renewed efforts might succeed and on 30 June 1970 successful negotiations began. The basis of the agreement was that the principles of the 1957 treaty remain intact, and the great majority of the regulations made in it will continue to apply to the new Community of Nine.

Greece and Turkey are associated with the Community, with a view to eventual full membership when their economies have become strong enough to allow them to compete on the Community market. After the Greek *coup d'état* in April 1967 the Association Agreement was 'frozen' and no further steps towards a customs union were taken until democracy was restored. An Association Agreement with Malta was signed in Dec. 1970 and with Cyprus in Dec. 1972. By Jan. 1977, when Commercial Agreements with Egypt, Jordan and Syria were signed, the Community had negotiated economic links with all the Mediterranean Arab States except Lebanon

Association of eighteen African ex-colonies, now fully sovereign and independent, was renewed for a further five years by a convention signed at Yaoundé in 1963. This gave the eighteen free entry to the E.E.C. market and provides access to a special European Development Fund–additional to national aid–to which the Six allotted nearly $1,400m. for the years 1958–1969. The Convention, renewed in 1969, for the years 1970–1975, provided for another $1,000m. in aid grants and loans. Twenty-one developing Commonwealth countries have joined with the former associates and seven independent African states in the Lomé Convention, signed 28 Feb. 1975; under this the E.E.C. will expand by 3·7 times the amount of aid given, grant free access to imports and guarantee revenue levels for basic commodities. Trade agreements with India, Pakistan, Sri Lanka, Indonesia, Thailand, Brazil, Argentina, Uruguay, Israel, Lebanon, Egypt, Spain and Yugoslavia are in operation in addition to those with Efta countries, and negotiations are in progress with the remaining countries bordering on the Mediterranean, and Jordan. Regular contacts have been maintained between the Community and Latin-American countries with a view to future agreements. In the Paris 'summit' of Oct. 1972 the enlarged Community reaffirmed its determination to follow a common commercial policy towards Eastern Europe with effect from 1 Jan. 1973.

As a first step towards the creation of a political union, the Six agreed, in 1970, to hold twice-yearly consultation on foreign policy; since then 'political co-operation' meetings of foreign ministers have increased in frequency. In Dec. 1975, Leo Tindemans submitted a report on 'European Union' which had been requested at a meeting in Dec. 1974.

E.Z.U.
Europäische Zahlungs-union, European Payments Union (German).

F

F.A.O.
Food and Agriculture Organisation of the United Nations

Farm Fund
see European Agricultural Guidance and Guarantee Fund

F.A.T.I.S.

F.A.T.I.S.
Food and Agriculture Technical Information Service of O.E.E.C.

F.E.B.I.
Fédérations Européennes des Branches d'Industries.

Federal German Republic
see German Federal Republic

Federal Trust
Federal Trust for Education and Research is a British-based research organisation specialising in European affairs.

F.E.O.G.A.
Fond Européen d'Orientation et de Garantie Agricole, the European Agricultural Guidance and Guarantee Fund.

F.E.P.E.M.
Federation of European Petroleum Equipment Manufacturers.

F.I.D.E.
Fédération de l'industrie dentaire en Europe, Federation of the European Dental Industry.

F.I.G.E.D.
Fédération Internationale des Grande Entreprises de Distribution, Federation of large retail distributors.

Fiji
Fiji signed the Lomé Convention of 1975.

106

finances, Community
The main elements of Community finances are: (i) the general budget of the Communities; (ii) the European Coal and Steel Community operating budget and loans; (iii) the European Development Funds; (iv) Community Loans; (v) the European Monetary Co-operation Fund; (vi) the European Investment Bank

Finet Foundation, Paul, Prize
see awards

Finland
Finland became an associate member of Efta on 27 March 1961 and signed a Free Trade Agreement with the enlarged E.E.C. on 5 Oct. 1973.
Economic profile: Area 337,000 sq. km. Population (1973) 4,660,000 (male (1971) 2,220,000) density 14 per sq. km. Births (per 1,000 of pop. 1973) 12·7; marriages, 7·7; deaths, 9·6. Infant mortality, 11·3.
Labour force (1972) 2,162,000; percentage in agriculture, 18·9; industry, 35·6; services, 45·5.
International trade (in millions of U.A.):

	1965	1970	1973
Imports	1,646	2,637	3,472
Exports	1,427	2,306	3,072

	per 1,000 of population
Standard of living:	
Motor vehicles (1973)	175
Televisions (1972)	230
Telephones (1972)	270

fiscal federalism
Fiscal federalism is the economics of multi-level government finance.

fisheries
Five principles govern the common fisheries policy, which was completed
in Oct. 1970 and came into force in Feb. 1971. These principles are:
(i) Free access to Community waters and Community ports for fishermen
from member countries.
(ii) A free market for fish throughout the Community.
(iii) Reference price arrangements to control imports.
(iv) Market organisation and intervention to be the responsibility of
producer organisations.
(v) Help for modernisation from E.A.G.G.F.
   The main features of the E.E.C. fisheries policy agreed in 1976 are:
(i) The creation of a two hundred-mile E.E.C. fisheries zone from 1 Jan.
1977;
(ii) Negotiations can be initiated with third countries to agree rights of
access;
(iii) The establishment of a twelve-mile zone and around E.E.C. coasts to
protect the interests of inshore fishermen;
(iv) The maintenance of traditional rights within the twelve-mile zone;
(v) The introduction of E.E.C. catch quotas coupled with other conservation measures;
(vi) The adoption of a licencing system for E.E.C. fishing boats to allow
strict control of E.E.C. measures;
(vii) The allocation of 400m. U.A. over five years for rationalising and
modernising the fishing industry.

F.I.T.C.E.
*Fédération des ingénieurs des télécommunications de la communauté euro-
péenne*, Federation of Telecommunications Engineers in the European
Community.

flag discrimination
Flag discriminatory practices are designed to secure preferential treatment
for ships of a particular nationality, mainly in the assignment of cargo.

flags

Council of Europe	Dark blue with a ring of 12 gold stars in the centre.
NATO	Dark blue with a white compass rose of four points in the centre.
Belgium	Three vertical strips of black, yellow, red.
Denmark	Red with white Scandinavian cross (*Dannebrog*).
France	The Tricolour of three vertical stripes of blue, white, red.
German Federal Republic	Three horizontal stripes of black, red, gold.
Irish Republic	Three vertical strips of green, white, orange.
Italy	Three vertical strips of green, white, red.
Luxembourg	Three horizontal stripes of red, white, blue.
Netherlands	Three horizontal stripes of red, white, blue.
United Kingdom	A combination of the cross of St George with that of St Andrew (1606) to which the cross of St Patrick was added (1801).

flexible guarantee arrangement
An arrangement whereby a scale of bonuses or deductions is applied to the guaranteed price when United Kingdom production, or forecast production, falls below or rises above the level of the standard quantity.

Foratom
Forum atomique européen, European Atomic Forum.

Four
The Four were the countries which signed the Treaty of Accession (Denmark, Irish Republic, Norway and the United Kingdom) but because Norway did not ratify the Treaty the Four became the Three.

fourchette
The higher and lower price levels between which member states must operate their agricultural prices. The device was first introduced for cereals.

France

France signed the Treaty of Paris (E.C.S.C.) in 1951, the Treaties of Rome (E.E.C. and Euratom) in 1957 and the Treaty of Brussels (Treaty of Accession) in 1972

Economic profile: Area 547,000 sq. km. Population (1973) 52,133,000 (male 25,402,000) density 95 per sq. km. Births (per 1,000 of pop. 1973) 16·4; marriages, 7·7; deaths, 10·7. Infant mortality, 15·6.

Labour force (1972) 21,155,000; percentage in agriculture, 12·9; industry, 39·3; services, 47·7.

International trade (in millions of U.A.):

	1965	1970	1973	1976
Imports	10,336	18,922	29,574	50,844
Exports	10,048	17,739	28,453	44,024

	per 1,000 of population
Standard of living:	
Motor vehicles (1973)	268
Televisions (1972)	226
Telephones (1972)	185

freedom of movement for workers

Workers of member countries of the E.E.C. are entitled to look for and take up employment without a work permit, and automatically qualify for a residence permit, and they must be employed on exactly the same terms as workers of the host country, and there must be no discrimination either in granting jobs or in benefits.

A Council of Ministers Regulation of Oct. 1968, which lays down most of the conditions relating to the free movement of workers, and is now United Kingdom law, states:

'Any national of a member state, irrespective of his place of permanent residence, shall be entitled to take up and carry on a wage-paid occupation in the territory of another member state in accordance with the provisions governing the employment of nationals in that state imposed by law, regulation or administrative action.

110

He shall, in particular, receive the same priority with regard to availability of employment in the territory of another member state as nationals of that state.'

Employment in the public service is excluded from the provisions of the Regulation, but this is taken to mean positions at a policy making level, and would not exempt, for example, industrial, technical and clerical jobs in nationalised industries and public corporations.

The situation regarding professional jobs for which a qualification is necessary is complex. The Commission's aim is to harmonise professional qualifications, but this is a lengthy process and the positive results have so far been small. At present one has to check whether a certain diploma is recognised in another country on a case-by-case basis.

The regulation also prohibits all national laws and practices if they restrict the right of non-nationals in any way to engage in employment. This however, does not apply to conditions regarding knowledge of languages required by the nature of the job.

A worker who is a national of a member state may not on grounds of his nationality be treated differently, in the territory of other memeber states, from national workers in respect of all the conditions of his employment and work, in particular as regards remuneration, dismissal and vocational reinstatement or re-employment if he has become unemployed.

He enjoys the same social and tax advantages as national workers.

He also has the same right to benefit under the same conditions as national workers from the instruction in vocational schools and centres of rehabilitation or retraining.

Any clause in a collective or individual agreement or in any other collective regulations on eligibility for employment, employment itself, remuneration and the other conditions of work and dismissal will be automatically null and void in so far as it makes provision for or authorises discriminatory conditions as regards workers who are nationals of other member states.

A national of a member state who is working in the territory of another member state will receive equality of treatment as regards affiliation to trade unions and the exercise of union rights, including the right to vote; he may be excluded from participation in the administration of bodies under public law (*droit public*) and from the exercise of any functions under public law. He also has the right to be eligible for bodies representing workers in the undertaking.

A national of a member state who is working in the territory of another member state has all the rights and benefits granted to national workers as regards accommodation, including the possibility of ownership of the accommodation he needs.

Any such worker has the same right as a national to put his name on the housing list in the district in which he is employed, if there is one, and he shall receive the benefits and priorities arising therefrom.

A worker can take his wife and their children (under 21 or dependent on him) whatever their nationality and any other dependants living under his roof in the United Kingdom.

A worker is allowed to live in a country without a permit in the following circumstances:

(i) if he is in a job which is not expected to last more than three months;
(ii) if he has a permanent home in one country but goes every day, or at least once a week to another country to work;
(iii) if he does seasonal work for which he has a proper contract.

A worker has the right to live permanently in another member state if:

(a) at the time of his retirement he is entitled, by the national law, to an old age pension and has been working in the country for at least the last year and has lived there for more than three years;
(b) he has been living in the country for the last two years but can no longer as a result of permanent incapacity.

Freedom of Movement for Workers, Advisory Committee on

The Advisory Committee on Freedom of Movement for Workers, a Commission advisory committee on social policy, was created by the E.E.C. Council of Ministers in 1961. The Committee has fifty-four members, and twenty-seven substitutes, divided equally between unions, employers and governments. It is chaired by a member of the Commission. The members are appointed by governments. The Committee is serviced by the Commission.

free trade area

A group of two or more customs territories in which duties and other restrictions on trade are eliminated on most of the trade between the members. Unlike the Customs Union, however, free trade area territories do not pursue a common external trade policy and do not therefore have any common external tariff.

G

Gabon
Gabon signed the Yaoundé Conventions of 1963 and 1969 and the Lomé Convention of 1975.

Gambia, The
The Gambia signed the Lomé Convention of 1975.

Gasperi, Alcide de
Born Italy, 1881, died 1954. Member of the Italian Parliament from 1911. Imprisoned under Mussolini. Italian Prime Minister, 1946–54. Supported French initiative in creating a European Assembly, 1948. Addressed the Congress of Europe, 1948 and took Italy into the Council of Europe as a founder-member, 1949.

Gatt
see General Agreement on Tariffs and Trade, The

g.d.p.
see gross domestic product.

General Agreement on Tariffs and Trade, The
The General Agreement on Tariffs and Trade, generally known as Gatt, was negotiated in 1947 and entered into force on 1 Jan. 1948. Its twenty-

three original signatories were members of a Preparatory Committee appointed by the United Nations Economic and Social Council to draft the charter for a proposed International Trade Organisation. Since this charter was never ratified, the General Agreement, intended as an interim agreement, has instead remained as the only international instrument laying down trade rules accepted by countries responsible for most of the world's trade. In Sept. 1976 there were eighty-three full contracting parties, three countries had acceded provisionally with a further twenty-four countries participating under special arrangements.

Gatt functions both as a multilateral treaty that lays down a common code of conduct in international trade and trade relations and as a forum for negotiation and consultation to overcome trade problems and reduce trade barriers. Key provisions of the Agreement guarantee most-favoured-nation treatment (exceptions being granted to customs unions and free trade areas, and for certain preferences in favour of developing countries); require that protection be given to domestic industry only through tariffs; provide for negotiations to reduce tariffs (which are then 'bound' against subsequent increase) and other trade distortions; and lay down principles (particularly in Part IV of the Agreement, added in 1965) to assist the trade of developing countries. The Agreement also provides for consultation on, and settlement of, disputes, for 'waivers' (the grant of authorisation, when warranted, to derogate from specific Gatt obligations) and for emergency action in defined circumstances.

Six major trade negotiations, most recently the highly successful Kennedy Round of 1964–7, took place in Gatt up to 1973. In Sept. 1973 a Ministerial conference in Tokyo launched new negotiations of unprecedented scope, in which some ninety countries are engaged. The negotiations are guided by the Tokyo Declaration, which provides that the negotiations shall cover tariffs, non-tariff barriers and other measures which impede or distort international trade in industrial and agricultural products, including tropical products and raw materials and, in particular, products of export interest to developing countries and measures affecting their exports. The negotiations are based on the principles of mutual advantage, mutual commitment and overall reciprocity (*i.e.* that the totality of concessions made by each developed country should balance those received) with the joint aim of achieving an overall balance of advantage at the highest possible level. In addition, special terms have been agreed upon for the participation of developing countries as well as specific aims for the negotiations as regards their trade. A firm technical basis for the negotiations is provided by a comprehensive work programme undertaken in Gatt since 1967.

To assist the trade of developing countries Gatt established in 1964 the International Trade Centre (since 1968 operated jointly with the United Nations Conference on Trade and Development) to provide information and training on export markets and marketing techniques. Other Gatt action in favour of developing countries includes training courses on trade policy questions.

generalised system of tariff preferences
A system of preferences granted by the E.E.C. to less developed countries in 1971 following the U.N.C.T.A.D. New Delhi meeting in 1968. The system is renewable annually, for ten-year periods.

The system introduced a tariff-free quota for a variety of industrial manufactured goods but not for industrial raw materials.

German Federal Republic
The German Federal Republic signed the Treaty of Paris (E.C.S.C.) in 1951, the Treaties of Rome (E.E.C. and Euratom) in 1957 and the Treaty of Brussels (Treaty of Accession) in 1972.

Economic profile: Area 248,600 sq. km. Population (1973) 61,973,000 (male 29,533,000) density 249 per sq. km. Births (per 1,000 of pop. 1973) 10·3; marriages, 6·4; deaths, 11·8. Infant mortality, 22·7.

Labour force (1972) 26,372,000; percentage in agriculture, 7·8; industry, 49·1; services, 43·1.

International trade (in millions of U.A.):

	1965	*1970*	*1973*	*1976*
Imports	17,472	29,814	43,421	69,281
Exports	17,892	34,189	53,552	80,029

	per 1,000 of *population*
Standard of living:	
Motor vehicles (1973)	264
Televisions (1972)	270
Telephones (1972)	249

Ghana

Ghana signed the Lomé Convention of 1975.

Gibraltar

The Treaty of Accession provisions apply to Gibraltar as a European Territory for whose external relations a member state is responsible, but Gibraltar is not included in the customs area of the enlarged Community as she is not part of the United Kingdom's customs territory.

G.I.E.

Groupement d'Intérêt Economique is a form of business enterprise for inter-company co-operation, created by legislation in France in 1967.

G.I.I.P.

Groupement international de l'industrie pharmaceutique des pays de la C.E.E., International Pharmaceutical Industry Group for the E.E.C. countries.

G.m.b.H.

Gesellschaft mit beschränkter Haftung, company with limited liability in the Federal German Republic.

g.n.p.

see gross national product.

golden triangle
The area of the E.E.C. bounded by Paris, the Ruhr and Milan, containing
the areas of economic growth.

Greece
Greece signed an agreement under Article 238 of the Treaty of Rome on 9
July 1961 and as a result Greece became associated with the E.E.C. on the
basis of a customs union with the prospect of full membership of the
Community at a later date. In 1976 Greece formally applied for full
membership of the E.E.C.
Economic profile: Area 132,000 sq. km. Population (1972) 8,950,000 (male
(1971) 4,280,000) density 68 per sq. km. Births (per 1,000 of pop. 1973)
15·7; marriages, 6·7; deaths, 8·6. Infant mortality, 27·3.
    Labour force (1972) 3,378,000; percentage in agriculture, 35·7; industry,
25·2; services, 39·2.
    International trade (in millions of U.A.):

	1965	*1970*	*1973*
Imports	1,134	1,958	2,744
Exports	328	643	1,162

	per 1,000 of population
Standard of living:	
Motor vehicles (1973)	25
Televisions (1972)	11
Telephones (1972)	137

'green pound'
The 'green pound' represents the rate at which the prices fixed under the
Common Agricultural Policy are translated into sterling. These prices are
fixed in units of account (U.A.) originally based on the United States
dollar. The 'green pound' rate was 1.7559 units of account (Oct. 1976).

Grenada
Grenada signed the Lomé Convention of 1975.

---

gross domestic product (g.d.p.)
The total of goods and services produced in a country over a given period of time, usually a year.

gross domestic product at current market prices

(millions of dollars, current exchange rates)

Country	1973	1974	1975[1]
Belgium	45,000	52,600	61,400
Denmark	27,300	30,600	35,700
France	249,500	266,200	309,800
Federal German Republic	344,100	381,200	420,300
Irish Republic	6,400	6,700	8,600
Italy	138,600	149,800	174,000
Luxembourg	1,800	2,100	2,100
Netherlands	59,500	69,300	80,000
United Kingdom	174,100	189,200	248,600
Community	1,046,300	1,147,700	1,340,500

[1] Provisional estimates

The importance of the E.E.C. in terms of gross domestic products is much greater than its importance in terms of area and population. The total gross domestic product of the nine countries of the Community amounted in 1975 to US$1,341,000m., which is nearly as high as the g.d.p. of the United States of America. In the last ten years the average growth rate in the Community as a whole has been around 4% per annum.

gross domestic product at current market prices (in % of total) origin

		Agricultural, forestry and fishery products	Fuel and power products	Manu- facturing products	Building and Con- struction	Services and Adjustments
Belgium	1970	3·5	5·1	29·3	7·5	54·6
	1974	2·7	4·6	28·2	7·5	57·0
Denmark[1]	1970	8·8	2·1	32·1	11·0	46·0
	1974	8·9	1·7	31·0	10·0	48·4
France	1970	6·3	5·8	30·3	9·9	47·7
	1974	5·3	5·2	30·7	9·6	49·2
Federal German Republic	1970	3·2	5·5	38·8	9·4	43·1
	1974	2·8	5·3	36·1	8·6	47·2
Irish Republic[1]	1970	16·8	2·8	25·7	8·6	46·1
	1974	—	—	—	—	—
Italy	1970	8·8	6·0	27·7	8·5	49·0
	1974	8·4	5·0	28·5	8·2	49·9
Luxembourg	1970	4·1	2·9	45·6	6·8	40·6
	1974	3·3	2·7	44·2	7·7	42·1
Netherlands	1970	5·9	5·6	27·2	7·7	53·6
	1974	—	—	—	—	—
United Kingdom	1970	2·1	6·8	33·1	6·1	51·9
	1974	2·2	5·4	28·9	7·2	56·3

[1] gross value added at factor prices

gross national product (g.n.p.)
This is equal to gross domestic product *plus* income from abroad *less* income paid abroad. g.n.p. is equal to *gross national income*—the total of incomes of the residents of a country from *all* sources.

groupes de travail
working groups *see* committees

Group of Ten
Under the general arrangements to borrow, ten of the main industrial countries in the International Monetary Fund stand ready to lend their currencies to the I.M.F. up to specified amounts when supplementary

119

resources are needed by the I.M.F. The resources of the general arrangements to borrow can be called upon if the I.M.F. needs supplementary resources to provide assistance to a member which is a participant of the arrangements. The general arrangements to borrow were used on a number of occasions between 1964 and 1970 to help finance exchange transactions with the United Kingdom and France. The total of the credit arrangements amounts approximately to 5,500m. special drawing rights.

Grundig-Consten

In 1964 the E.E.C. Commission issued a specific prohibition of an agreement between the Grundig Sales Company in the Federal German Republic and the Consten Company in France. The purpose of the agreement was to make Consten the sole distributor of Grundig products in France, for which purpose Grundig had imposed a ban on all their dealers in other countries so that French purchasers could buy Grundig products only from Consten. In addition Grundig and Consten had signed a supplementary agreement on the use of a special trade mark (Gint), the purpose of which was to hinder the importation by firms other than Consten of Grundig products into France.

Consten sought to uphold its claim to exclusive dealership by taking action against a rival importer, Unef, of Paris, which was importing Grundig products from German wholesalers. Consten contended that Unef had not respected the established sales organisation and was introducing unfair competition. The case came before the Paris Courts and was adjourned pending a decision by the Commission on the compatibility of the exclusive distribution agreement between Grundig and Consten with the Rules of Competition of the Treaty.

The Commission decided that the agreement offended against the ban in Article 85 (1) of the Treaty and that it could not be approved under the provisions of Article 85 (3). In addition the Commission forbade Grundig to obstruct rival imports of their products into France. The Commission held that the agreement constituted a restraint of competition, because freedom of business activity of the parties to the agreement was restricted and that of firms outside the agreement was impaired. Customers for Grundig products were denied the possibility of making their purchases from other suppliers.

The agreement had been signed between two firms established in

120

different member states and regulated trade between those member states in such a way that such trade was wholly in the hands of Grundig and Consten. It was considered by the Commission that the protection which the agreement gave Consten went beyond any restraint of competition which might conceivably be necessary for the improvement of production and distribution.

The two companies involved in this case exercised their right to challenge the legality of the decision by the Commission and they appealed to the Court of Justice in Luxembourg. Except for a technicality, that the inclusion of certain provisions in the agreement were irrelevant in the case submitted to the Court, the Court upheld the Commission's interpretation of the Regulations and the exclusive dealing agreement between the two firms remains 'incompatible with the E.E.C.' and illegal in terms of the Treaty.

G.S.P.
Generalised System of Tariff Preferences, more properly G.S.T.P.

G.S.T.P.
Generalised System of Tariff Preferences.

guaranteed price
Prices determined at the United Kingdom's Annual Price Review, held in accordance with the Agricultural Acts of 1947 and 1957, as being the prices which farmers, as a whole, should receive for specified agricultural commodities.

G.U.D.
Gestion de l'Union Douanière is part of the E.E.C. Commission, with responsibility for administration of the customs union.

guide price
The price level which the system proposed for beef and veal is designed to

achieve. It is not necessarily connected with the intervention price. (*see also* recommended price.)

Guinea
Guinea signed the Lomé Convention of 1975.

Guinea-Bissau
Guinea-Bissau signed the Lomé Convention of 1975.

Guyana
Guyana signed the Lomé Convention of 1975.

H

Hague summit
see summits

Hallstein, Walter
Born Mainz, Germany, 1901. Chairman of the German Commission Unesco, 1949–50; led German delegation to Schuman Plan Conference, 1950. Secretary of State for Foreign Affairs, 1951–8. President of the Commission of the E.E.C., 1958–67. President of the European Movement, 1968– . Member of *Bundestag*, 1969–72. Awarded the Robert Schuman Prize, 1969.

Heath, Edward
Born Broadstairs, England, 1916. Member of the United Kingdom Parliament from 1950. Lord Privy Seal, 1960–3. Leader of the United Kingdom delegation to Brussels Conference for countries seeking entry to

the E.E.C., 1961–3. Secretary of State for Industry, Trade and Regional Development and President of the Board of Trade, 1963–4. Prime Minister, 1970–4. Awarded the Charlemagne Prize, 1963, and the Stresemann Medal, 1971. As Prime Minister he successfully proposed United Kingdom membership of the E.E.C.

Hillery, Patrick
Born Miltown Malbay, Irish Republic, 1923. Member of the Irish Parliament from 1951. Minister for Education, 1959–65. Minister for Industry and Commerce, 1965–6. Minister for Labour, 1966–9. Minister of Foreign Affairs, 1969–73. Vice-President, Commission of European Communities, and Commissioner for Social Affairs, 1973–6. President of the Irish Republic, 1976–

history
On 25 March 1957 in Rome, six European countries, Belgium, France, the German Federal Republic, Italy, Luxembourg and the Netherlands signed the Treaties, concluded for an unlimited period, setting up the European Economic Community (Common Market) and the European Atomic Energy Community (Euratom). The Treaties, which came into force on 1 Jan. 1958, also provided for the creation of the European Investment Bank (E.I.B.), the basic task of which is to finance regional development projects, industrial and agricultural innovation in the Community and associated countries, and projects of common interest to member states.

The E.E.C. was established for the purpose of promoting harmonious development of economic activities, continuous and balanced expansion, increased stability and raising of the standard of living within, and closer relations between, the member states.

The activities of the E.E.C. include:
(i) the elimination, as between member states, of customs duties and of quantitative restrictions on the import and export of goods, and of all other measures having equivalent effect;
(ii) the establishment of a common customs tariff and of a common commercial policy towards third countries;
(iii) the abolition, as between member states, of obstacles to freedom of movement for persons, services and capital;

(iv) the adoption of a common agricultural policy;

(v) the adoption of a common transport policy;

(vi) the institution of a system to ensure that competition in the E.E.C. is not distorted;

(vii) the application of procedures by which the economic policies of the member states can be co-ordinated and disequilibria in their balances of payments remedied;

(viii) the approximation of the laws of member states to the extent required for the proper functioning of the Common Market;

(ix) the creation of a European Social Fund in order to improve employment opportunities for workers and to contribute to the raising of their standard of living;

(x) the establishment of a European Investment Bank to facilitate the economic expansion of the E.E.C. by opening up new sources of financing;

(xi) the association of overseas countries and territories in order to increase trade and to promote economic and social development.

Under the Treaty, the E.E.C. enjoys in each of the member states the most extensive legal capacity granted to legal entities in that country and in particular may acquire and transfer property and may sue and be sued in its own name.

There are at present three European Communities, the European Coal and Steel Community (E.C.S.C.) established 1951, the European Economic Community (Common Market) and the European Atomic Energy Community (Euratom) sharing one Commission since 1965 but each having separate legal personality.

The year 1968 was marked by the completion of the Customs Union and the freedom of movement of workers in the Community. In 1969 work began on the economic and monetary union, the bases for which were fixed by the resolution taken by the Council of Ministers on 22 March 1971. By a treaty signed on 22 Jan. 1972, which entered into force on 1 Jan. 1973, the Kingdom of Denmark, the Irish Republic and the United Kingdom of Great Britain and Northern Ireland acceded to the Community.

Hitler

If Napoleon administered Europe for France, Adolf Hitler (1889–1945) tried to conquer it for Germany. There was no mistake about the ultimate aim, a docile, hardworking European proletariat governed by a German master-race. When in 1941 Hitler embarked on his attempted conquest of Russia, he hoped to attract the reluctant partners of his European Empire by proclaiming a European crusade against Russian Communism. The presence of 'volunteers' from Spain, France, Italy, Hungary, Romania, the Netherlands and Belgium in Hitler's armies may have given a spurious European aspect to his rule. In one sense, of course, Hitler was the father of European unity: it was the experiences of the war which he unleashed that determined Robert Schuman to begin to press for some institutional framework that would make sure it could never happen again.

holidays

	Minimum annual paid holiday —excluding public holidays days	Public holidays days
Belgium	18	10
Denmark	24	9–10
France	24	9
Federal German Republic	15–24	10–13
Irish Republic	10–12	7–8
Italy	12–30	17
Netherlands	18–23	6– 7
Luxembourg	18–24	10
United Kingdom	15	6

Holland
see Netherlands, The

Hong Kong
Hong Kong was included in the E.E.C. scheme of generalised preferences as part of the terms of the United Kingdom's entry into the Community and can be offered association with the E.E.C. under Part IV of the Treaty of Rome.

hot money

This term is nearly impossible to define. It is often used about capital movements, usually of a short-term character, which take place either for speculative reasons (*e.g.* to reap the advantage of, or avoid the loss arising from, an impending change in exchange rates) or in response to interest rate differentials. Hot money cannot be identified statistically because it depends on the motive of the owner. Generally it means overseas funds placed in a country at short-term which are liable to rapid withdrawal if confidence in a currency is shaken or if interest differentials swing against the country where the money is deposited.

I

I.A.E.A.
International Atomic Energy Agency.

I.B.R.D.
see International Bank for Reconstruction and Development of the United Nations. The 'World Bank'.

I.C.A.O.
International Civil Aviation Organisation

I.C.C.
International Chamber of Commerce.

Iceland
Iceland signed the Stockholm Convention (Efta) and joined on 1 March

1970. Iceland was immediately granted duty-free entry for industrial goods and was given ten years to abolish her own existing productive duties.

I.C.F.C.
Industrial and Commercial Finance Corporation established under the auspices of the Bank of England and other institutions to provide finance for industrial development which are in the national economic interest. It also administered a bloc loan from the European Investment Bank.

I.C.F.T.U.
see International Confederation of Free Trade Unions.

I.D.A.
International Development Association of the United Nations, *see* International Bank for Reconstruction and Development.

I.F.C.
see International Finance Corporation of the United Nations.

I.F.C.T.U.
International Federation of Christian Trade Unions.

I.F.T.U.
International Federation of Trade Unions.

I.L.O.
see International Labour Organisation and International Labour Office.

I.M.C.O

I.M.C.O.
Intergovernmental Maritime Consultative Organisation is a specialised agency of the United Nations established in 1959 to facilitate co-operation between governments on technical matters affecting international shipping, such as navigation, safety and pollution control.

I.M.F.
see International Monetary Fund.

immigrants
Nationals of member states are able to reside and work in other member states under the free movement of workers rules. The Governments of member states may define their nationals.

The definition of United Kingdom nationals in the United Kingdom Declaration (included in the Final Act of the Treaty of Accession) was: '(i) persons who are citizens of the United Kingdom and Colonies or British subjects not possessing that citizenship or the citizenship of any other Commonwealth country or territory, who in either case, have the right of abode in the United Kingdom, and are therefore exempt from United Kingdom immigration control;
(ii) persons who are citizens of the United Kingdom and Colonies by birth or by registration or naturalisation in Gibraltar, or whose father was so born, registered or naturalised.'

Incoterms
International rules for the interpretation of terms used in foreign trade contracts.

India
India signed a five-year (renewable) trade co-operation agreement in Dec. 1974 under Articles 113–4 of the Treaty of Rome, and under Article 113 she signed a trade agreement covering certain handicrafts for an unlimited period which came into force on 1 Sept. 1969.

indicator price system
An arrangement whereby the deficiency payment to United Kingdom producers is based on the difference between the guaranteed price and an indicator price. This represents a price which producers might reasonably be expected to secure if the market is not overloaded.

industrial property
Industrial property is a generic classification for patents, trade marks, copyright, 'know-how' and agreements relating to these.

Information offices of the E.E.C.
Belgium   Rue de la Loi 244, 1049 Brussels
Chile   Avenida Ricardo Lyon 1177, Santiago 9
Denmark   Gammel Torv 4, 1004 Copenhagen K
France   61 rue des Belles-Feuilles, 75782 Paris Cedex 16
German Federal Republic   Zitelmannstrasse 22, D-5300 Bonn (sub office attached to Bonn) Kurfüstendamm 102, 1000 Berlin 31
Irish Republic   29 Merrion Square, Dublin 2
Italy   Via Poli 29, 1–00187, Rome
Japan   Kowa 25 Building, 8–7 Sanbancho, Chiyoda-Ku, Tokyo 102
Luxembourg   Centre europeen, Luxembourg-Kirchberg
The Netherlands   Lange Voorhout 29, The Hague
Switzerland   37–39 rue de Vermont, Ch–1202, Geneva
Turkey   13 Bogaz Sokak, Kavaklidere, Ankara
United Kingdom   20 Kensington Palace Gardens, London W8 4QQ
United States of America   2100 M Street, N.W. Washington D.C. 20037 (sub office attached to Washington) 277 Park Avenue, New York, N.Y. 10017
Uruguay   Calle Bartolome Mitré 1337, Montevideo

INSEAD
Institut Européen d'Administration des Affaires, European Institute of Business Administration.

Institutions of the Community

The Institutions of the Community are the Council of Ministers, the Commission, the European Parliament and the Court of Justice.

Interlaine

Comité des industries lainières de la C.E.E., Committee for the Wool Industries of the E.E.C.

International Bank for Reconstruction and Development

The International Bank for Reconstruction and Development began operations in June 1946. Its purpose is to provide funds and technical assistance to facilitate economic development in its poorer member countries. Also known as the World Bank.

The Bank obtains its funds from the following sources: Capital subscribed by member countries; sales of its own securities; sales of parts of its loans; repayments; and net earnings. The subscribed capital of the Bank amounted to \$25,578m. at 30 June 1975. 10% of this amount is paid-in while the remainder is subject to call if needed to meet the Bank's obligations. Borrowing in the market had reached \$20,882m. by 30 June 1975, of which \$12,287m. was outstanding, and sales of portions of Bank loans from portfolio had totalled \$2,511m. The Bank is self-supporting. Its net earnings for the year ending 30 June 1975 amounted to \$275m.; in addition the Bank had reserves of \$1,902m.

By 30 June 1975 the Bank had made 1,161 loans totalling \$27,874m. in ninety-four of its 125 member countries. Excluding loans of \$460m. to its affiliate, the International Finance Corporation (I.F.C.), its lending had been for the following purposes: agriculture, \$3,933m.; education, \$769m.; industry, \$5,016m.; non-project, \$1,653m.; population, \$52m.; electric power, \$6,980m.; telecommunications, \$735m.; tourism, \$127m.; transportation, \$7,598.; urbanisation, \$160m.; water supply and sewerage, \$835m.; and technical assistance, \$16m.

In order to eliminate wasteful overlapping of development assistance and to ensure that the funds available are used to the best possible effect, the Bank has organised consortia or consultative groups of aid-giving nations for the following countries: Colombia, Ethiopia, Ghana, India, Korea, Malaysia, Morocco, Nigeria, Pakistan, Peru, the Philippines, Sri

Lanka, the Sudan, Thailand, Tunisia, Zaïre and East Africa (Kenya, Uganda, Tanzania). The Bank furnishes a wide variety of technical assistance. It acts as executing agency for a number of pre-investment surveys financed by the United Nations Development Programme. Permanent missions have been established in East and West Africa, India, Indonesia, Thailand and elsewhere primarily to assist in the preparation of projects. The Bank helps member countries to identify and prepare projects for the development of agriculture, education and water supply by drawing on the expertise of the F.A.O., W.H.O., U.N.I.D.O. and Unesco through its co-operative agreements with these organisations. The Bank maintains a staff college, the Economic Development Institute in Washington, D.C., for senior officials of the member countries.

To help nations whose borrowing capacity is limited by foreign-exchange stringency, member countries of the Bank established the International Development Association (I.D.A.) in 1960. I.D.A. grants development credits on a long-term, interest-free basis. By 30 June 1975 I.D.A. had extended 595 credits to sixty-eight countries, totalling $6,938m., for the same general purpose as bank loans. I.D.A.'s primary lending resources have been the subscriptions and supplementary contributions of member countries, chiefly the twenty-one wealthiest. In addition it has negotiated interest-free loans from Switzerland and New Zealand. The World Bank has made grants to I.D.A. out of its net income; the Association also has a small flow of net income of its own. The headquarters are at Washington, D.C., U.S.A.

International Carriage of Dangerous Goods by road
see A.D.R.

International Confederation of Free Trade Unions
The first congress of I.C.F.T.U. was held in London in Dec. 1949. The constitution as amended provides for co-operation with the United Nations and the International Labour Organisation and for regional organisations to promote free trade unionism, especially in under-developed countries.

The congress meets every three years. It elects the Executive Board of twenty-nine members nominated on an area basis for a three-year period; the Board meets at least twice a year. Various committees cover policy *vis-à-vis* such problems as those connected with Atomic Energy and also the administration of the International Solidarity Fund. There are joint I.C.F.T.U.-I.T.S. Committees for co-ordinating activities and also for women workers' problems. Headquarters: 37–41, rue Montagne aux Herbes Potagères, Brussels 1, Belgium.

Regional organisations exist in America, office in Mexico City; Asia, office in New Delhi; Africa, office in Addis Ababa.

The total membership in 1973 was about 51m. The biggest groups were the British Trades Union Congress (10m.), the West-German Deutscher Gewerkschaftsbund (7.2m.), the Federation of Indonesian Islamic Trade Unions (2.8m.), the Confederazione Italiana Sindacati Lavoratori (2m.), the Confederación de Trabajadores de Mexico (2m.), the Indian National Trade Union Congress (2m.), the Swedish Landsorganisationen (1.7m.), the Canadian Labour Congress (1.6m.), the Österreichischer Gewerkschaftsbund (1.5m.), the French Confédération Générale du Travail Force Ouvrière (1.1m.), and the Belgian General Federation of Labour (950,000).

The American Federation of Labor and Congress of Industrial Organisations disaffiliated in Feb. 1969. (*see also* trade unions)

International Development Association of the United Nations

The International Development Association was established in 1960. It has the status of a United Nations Specialised Agency and is an affiliate of the I.B.R.D., having the same management and staff, but is a separate legal entity with separate funds.

It was established to meet the problem of a growing number of less developed countries whose need for outside capital is greater than their ability to service conventional loans. It accordingly grants credits for projects of high development priority, whether or not they yield a direct financial return, on terms easier than those on which the International Bank can lend.

Membership of the Association is open to all countries which belong to the International Bank and their subscriptions provide the Association's capital.

International Finance Corporation of the United Nations
The International Finance Corporation, an affiliate of the World Bank, was established in July 1956. Paid-in capital at 30 June 1975 was $107.3m., subscribed by 100 member countries. In addition it has a general reserve of $70.7m. I.F.C. supplements the activities of the World Bank by encouraging the growth of productive private enterprises in less developed member countries. Chiefly I.F.C. makes investments in the form of subscriptions to the share capital of privately-owned companies, or long-term loans, or both. The Corporation will help finance new ventures and will also assist established enterprises to expand, improve or diversify their operations.

At 30 June 1975 I.F.C. had made commitments, amounting to $1,262m., in fifty-seven countries. The total amount of loans and equity which I.F.C. had sold, or agreed to sell, to other investors as of that date was $391.6m. Standby and underwriting commitments totalled $33.7m.

International Labour Organisation
The International Labour Organisation (I.L.O.) was established under the Treaty of Versailles in 1919 and became affiliated to the United Nations in 1946. The aims are the improvement of the conditions of work throughout the world, the spread of social security and the maintenance of standards of social justice. In addition the Organisation gives technical assistance, especially for training, to developing countries.

International Monetary Fund
The International Monetary Fund was established on 27 Dec. 1945 as an independent international organisation; its relationship with the United Nations is defined in an agreement of mutual co-operation which came into force on 15 Nov. 1947. The quotas of the 126 members was SDR29, 189·4m. at 31 Dec. 1974. At the same date the Fund's assets included SDR, 5,369·5m. in gold, SDR457m. in SDRs, SDR49·9m. in subscriptions receivable and SDR25,752·6m. in various national currencies, and SDR43·1m. in other assets. (One special drawing right (SDR) is equal in value to 0.888671 gramme of fine gold.)

The Fund is authorised under its Articles of Agreement to supplement its resources by borrowing. In Jan. 1962, a four-year agreement was concluded with ten industrial members (Belgium, Canada, France, Federal

German Republic, Italy, Japan, Netherlands, Sweden, the United Kingdom, the United States of America) who undertook to lend the Fund up to $6,000m. in their own currencies, if this should be needed to forestall or cope with an impairment of the international monetary system. These agreements, extended in 1965 until 1970 and for a further five years in 1970, were again renewed in 1974 for a five-year period from 24 Oct. 1975 and were used to finance drawings made by the United Kingdom in 1964, 1965, 1968 and 1969, and by France in 1969 and 1970. By Aug. 1971 all such borrowings had been repaid in full to the Fund.

Purposes: To promote international monetary co-operation, the expansion of international trade and exchange stability; to assist in the removal of exchange restrictions and the establishment of a multilateral system of payments; and to alleviate any serious disequilibrium in members' international balance of payments by making the resources of the Fund available to them under adequate safeguards.

Activities: Each member of the Fund undertakes to establish and maintain an agreed par value for its currency, and to consult the Fund on any change in excess of 10% of the initial parity. Countries retaining exchange controls are required to hold annual consultations with the Fund regarding the restrictions in use, the balance of payments justification for them, and the possibilities for their removal. The Fund makes its foreign exchange resources available, under proper safeguards, to its members to meet short-term or medium-term payments difficulties. The Fund also supplements, as and when needed, the existing reserve assets of participants in the Special Drawing Account. The first allocation of special drawing rights was made on 1 Jan. 1970, in a total amount equivalent to $3,500m. The second allocation, on 1 Jan. 1971, was equivalent to $2,900m. and the third, on 1 Jan. 1972, was equivalent to $2,900m.

Following serious monetary disturbances in 1971, a Report on Reform of the International Monetary System was submitted to the Board of Governors at the 1972 annual meeting. During the meeting the Committee on Reform of the International Monetary System and Related Issues, generally known as the Committee of Twenty, held its first session, with the mandate to advise and report to the Board on all aspects of the international monetary system, including proposals for any amendments of the Articles of Agreement. The Committee of Twenty ceased to exist after submitting its final report in 1974. An interim Committee of the Board of Governors on the International Monetary System, and a Joint

134

Ministerial Committee of the Boards of Governors of the World Bank and the Fund on the Transfer of Real Resources to Developing Countries (Development Committee) were established and held their meetings in Jan. 1975.

Organisation: The highest authority in the Fund is exercised by the Board of Governors on which each member Government is represented. Normally the Governors meet once a year, although they may take votes by mail or other means between annual meetings. The Board of Governors has delegated many of its powers to the executive directors in Washington, of whom there are twenty, five appointed by the five members with the largest quotas and the other fifteen elected by groups of countries. Each appointed director has voting power proportionate to the quota of the government he represents, while each elected director casts all the votes of the countries which elected him. The five appointed executive directors represent the United States, United Kingdom, Federal German Republic, France and Japan.

The managing director is selected by the executive directors; he presides as chairman at their meetings but may not vote except in the case of a tie. His term is for five years but may be extended or terminated at the discretion of the executive directors. He is responsible for the ordinary business of the Fund, under general control of the executive directors, and supervises a staff of 1,400. The headquarters is at Washington, D.C., U.S.A.

International Standard Industrial Classification
A categorisation of economic activity used in compiling and presenting official statistics issued by the United Nations.

International Trade Federations
see trade unions

International Trade Organisation
The Charter for the I.T.O., usually known as the Havana Charter, was drawn up in March 1948 in order to tackle postwar trade problems, but in Dec. 1950 it became clear that the Charter would not be submitted again to

the United States Congress and the attempt to establish the I.T.O. had to be abandoned. As a result, Gatt has remained the only international instrument which lays down rules of conduct for trade and which has been accepted by many leading trading nations.

International Trade Secretariats
see trade unions

intervention price
The price at which support buying inside E.E.C. markets can take place. In the case of cereals the intervention prices are 5 % to 10 % below the target prices.

Investment Bank, European
see European Investment Bank

Irish Republic
The Irish Republic signed the Treaty of Brussels (Treaty of Accession) in 1972.
Economic profile: Area 70,300 sq. km. Population (1973) 3,051,000 (male 1,531,000) density 43 per sq. km. Births (per 1,000 of pop. 1973) 22·3; marriages, 7·4; deaths, 10·9. Infant mortality, 17·8.

Labour force (1972) 1,108,000; percentage in agriculture, 25·7; industry, 30·3; services, 44.

International trade (in millions of U.A.):

	1965	1970	1973	1976
Imports	1,041	1,569	2,225	3,311
Exports	611	1,035	1,697	2,632

	per 1,000 of population
Standard of living:	
Motor vehicles (1973)	146
Televisions (1972)	166
Telephones (1972)	109

I.S.I.C.
International Standard Industrial Classification

I.S.O.
International Standards Organisation.

Israel
Israel signed a preferential trade agreement with the E.E.C. on 1 July 1975 for an unlimited period, and under Article 113 of the Treaty of Rome she agreed to establish a free trade area by 1989. The financial aid protocol to this agreement was not signed until Feb. 1977.

Italy
Italy signed the Treaty of Paris (E.C.S.C.) in 1951, the Treaties of Rome (E.E.C. and Euratom) in 1957 and the Treaty of Brussels (Treaty of Accession) in 1972.

Economic profile: Area 301,300 sq. km. Population (1973) 54,901,000 (male 26,747,000) density 182 per sq. km. Births (per 1,000 of pop. 1973) 16·0; marriages, 7·6; deaths, 9·9. Infant mortality, 27.

Labour force (1972) 18,837,000; percentage in agriculture, 18·2; industry, 44·3; services, 37·5.

International trade (in millions of U.A.):

	1965	*1970*	*1973*	*1976*
Imports	7,378	14,970	22,259	34,454
Exports	7,200	13,206	17,794	29,328

	per 1,000 of population
Standard of living:	
Motor vehicles (1973)	228
Televisions (1972)	191
Telephones (1972)	188

I.T.O.
International Trade Organisation.

I.T.S.
International Trade Secretariats.

I.T.U.
International Telecommunication Union

Ivory Coast
The Ivory Coast signed the Yaoundé Conventions of 1963 and 1969 and the Lomé Convention of 1975.

J

Jamaica
Jamaica signed the Lomé Convention of 1975.

Japan
At the European Council's meeting in Nov. 1976 held at The Hague discussions took place about the growing inbalance in commercial exchanges between the E.E.C. and Japan. The E.E.C. officials urged Japan

to place voluntary restrictions on certain categories of its exports to E.E.C. Certain concessions were made and in its reply the Japanese Government stated 'Regarding the Japan-E.E.C. trade imbalance, we are of the view that trade among developed countries should not aim at a balance on a bilateral basis but at a balance in a global context.'

Economic profile: Area 369,000 sq. km. Population (1973) 108,350,000 (male (1972) 52,639,000) density 293 per sq. km. Births (per 1,000 of pop. 1971) 19·2; marriages, 10·5; deaths, 6·6. Infant mortality, 12·4.

Labour force (1972) 51,820,000; percentage in agriculture, 14·8; industry, 36·3; services, 49.

International trade (in millions of U.A.):

	1965	*1970*	*1973*
Imports	8,184	18,881	30,657
Exports	8,456	19,318	29,549

	per 1,000 of population
Standard of living:	
Motor vehicles (1973)	117
Televisions (1972)	222
Telephones (1972)	282

J.D.I.

The joint declaration of intent is annexed to the Treaty of Accession and states that the Nine will examine with Bangladesh, India, Malaysia, Singapore and Sri Lanka any trade problems that may arise from the implementation of the Treaty, and will aim at seeking appropriate solutions.

Jenkins, Roy Harris

Born Wales, 1920. Member of the British Parliament since 1948. Minister of Aviation, 1964–5. Home Secretary, 1965–7. Chancellor of the Exchequer, 1967–70. Deputy Leader of the Labour Party, 1970–2. Awarded the Charlemagne Prize and Robert Schuman Prize, 1972. Member of the council of Britain in Europe. Deputy Chairman of the Common Market

Jet

Campaign. President of the Commission of European Communities, 1977–

Jet
see Joint European Torus.

J.O.C.E.
Journal Officiel des Communautés Européennes, Official Journal of the European Communities.

Joint European Torus
Jet is a machine for undertaking research into fusion, the combination process occuring in the interior of the sun. Because of the great costs involved, the Council of the European Communities acting under the Euratom Treaty decided in 1973 to undertake a research programme using a Community financed Joint European Torus. Plans on how the Jet should be built, including a timetable and budget, was presented to the Council in 1975 by the team of scientists specially formed for this purpose.

Since 1975, however, there has been no agreement among the member states as to where the Jet should be built. Five nations, Belgium, German Federal Republic, France, Italy and the United Kingdom, have each proposed sites in their own territory. This inability to decide on a site, has in its turn delayed the start of construction of the plant and hence the research.

Jordan
Jordan signed a co-operation agreement with the E.E.C. on 18 Jan. 1977.

J.R.C.
Joint Research Centre of Euratom.

K

Kennedy Round

The Kennedy Round covered three elements in the trade negotiations which the ministerial meeting in the Gatt in May 1963 agreed to launch on 4 May 1964, and were completed 30 June 1967. These were:

(i) a substantial reduction in tariffs and other barriers to trade;

(ii) measures to improve access to world markets for agricultural products; and

(iii) expansion of outlets for the exports of less developed countries.

The trade negotiations have been named after the late President Kennedy because they were made possible by the exceptional powers obtained by President Kennedy in the Trade Expansion Act, 1962, which among other things allows the United States Administration to negotiate on a basis of reciprocity a substantial reduction in tariffs, generally up to 50% with larger concessions on agricultural and tropical products in certain circumstances and on duties not exceeding 5% *ad valorem*. The term 'Kennedy Round' is sometimes used to cover only the tariff element in these negotiations.

Kenya

Kenya signed the Arusha Convention in 1968 and because this agreement was not ratified by the expiry date she signed a subsequent Arusha Convention on 24 Sept. 1969. She also signed the Lomé Convention of 1975.

Konzern

A Konzern is the aggregate of enterprises which are bound together by one enterprise exercising control of the others by holding shares in them or in other similar ways.

L

L.A.F.T.A.

The Latin American Free Trade Association was formed in 1961 by Argentina, Brazil, Chile, Mexico, Paraguay, Peru and Uruguay. Colombia, Ecuador and Venezuela joined later. The aim is an eventual Latin American Common Market. The permanent secretariat is at Montevideo.

'lake'

A dispute between France and Italy over trade in wine assumed the proportions of a major Community crisis in March 1975, when the French authorities banned all wine imports for at least a month following widespread demonstrations by French wine producers. They were protesting against continuing imports of cheap, mainly Italian, wine when French wine prices had fallen to the levels guaranteed under the common agricultural policy and consequent intervention buying had built up a surplus Community wine 'lake' of some 2,400m. litres of mainly French wine. On 1 April the Italian Government requested an emergency session of the E.E.C. Council of Ministers to discuss the French ban, and on 8 April the European Commission decided to open proceedings against France for alleged contravention of the common agricultural policy rules. However, the Commission rescinded this decision when, on 15 April, the Agriculture Ministers of the Nine reached a compromise solution in which, in return for the French Government agreeing to end its import ban and to consider ways of reducing French wine production, the Council agreed to an additional 460m. litres of stored wine being distilled into industrial alcohol.

languages

For most practical purposes the main working language of the European Communities is French, though the six official languages (Danish, Dutch, English, French, German, Italian) all have equal status. Most official acts such as directives, decisions and regulations and the *Official Journal* must

142

be published in all six languages.

For legal purposes no language takes precedence over another and where there is a conflict in meaning between a document in one language and a version of the same document in another language, the true meaning is only decided by looking at all the remaining four versions. There is no concept of an 'original' version for language purposes.

The Commission employed 1147 interpreters (simultaneous speech) and translators (written documents) in 1976 and it has been estimated that when back-up personnel are taken into account as much as 38% of the Commission's staff are employed on language work.

lawyers
Lawyers will be free to practise, but not to establish themselves, by 1979.

l.d.c.'s
see less developed countries.

Lebanon
Lebanon signed a trade and technical co-operation agreement under Article 113 of the Treaty of Rome which came into force on 1 July 1965 and is renewable annually. On 18 Dec. 1972 she signed a five-year preferential trade agreement and on 16 Feb. 1977 she initialled an agreement for trade and co-operation as part of the E.E.C. Mediterranean Policy but Lebanon expressed concern at the low level of financial aid.

L.E.C.E.
Ligue européenne de coopération économique, European League for Economic Co-operation.

legal status
The European Economic Community has a personality of its own. Accordingly the Community as such can be a party to a contract, whether

143

governed by public or private law, and can defend its interest at law, without any intervention on the part of the member states.

The Community also has the capacity to conclude agreements with third states, unions of states and international organisations. By the end of 1975 the number of states with missions accredited to the Community was 103. In addition the Community has entered into association agreements with a large number of countries, and into commercial agreements with certain other countries.

Lesotho
Lesotho was a signatory of the Lomé Convention of 1975.

less developed countries
The United Nations definition implies poor countries with low income per head of population, little industrial development and limited economic and social infrastructure. The following examples are of various interpretations of the term in United Nations documents: (i) all countries in Africa except the Republic of South Africa, in North and South America except Canada and the United States, and in Asia except Japan; (ii) countries in Africa excluding South Africa, in South and South-East Asia excluding Japan, in Latin America, in the Middle East and Greece, Iceland, Irish Republic, Portugal and Spain; (iii) Africa excluding South Africa, Asia and the Far East excluding Japan, the Middle East and Latin America which covers all countries and territories in Central America, the Caribbean and South America; (iv) countries other than the United States, Canada, those in Western Europe, Australia, New Zealand, Republic of South Africa, Japan, those in Eastern Europe, mainland China, North Korea, North Vietnam and Mongolia.

levy
In essence a levy is merely a form of duty, whether it takes the form of a charge on imports or of a charge applying both to imports and to the domestic product. The precise meaning of the word must be judged in the context in which it is used; in practice today 'levy' often signifies a charge applied to imports in addition to any tariff or import duty. In the

agricultural sphere the term often denotes an import duty that is subject to variation, in contrast to a tariff which normally remains unchanged for considerable periods.

levy subsidy
A subsidy to producers or suppliers of a commodity financed by a levy on sales of that commodity. The subsidy might be payable to domestic producers or to certain overseas suppliers; and the levy might be raised on all sales or simply on imports.

Liberal and Democratic Parties within the E.E.C.
At a meeting held in March 1976 in Stuttgart, Federal German Republic, fourteen Liberal parties from eight E.E.C. countries agreed to form a 'Federation of Liberal and Democratic Parties within the E.E.C.', the purpose initially being to prepare for the direct elections to the European Parliament.

Liberia
Liberia was a signatory of the Lomé Convention of 1975.

linear tariff cuts
As with across-the-board tariff reductions, this term means a uniform reduction in tariffs; uniform, that is, in relation to the different sectors of a national tariff and, at least in the context of the Kennedy Round, in tariffs of different countries participating.

loans, Community
After the balance of payments crises caused by the increased oil prices imposed by Opec in 1973 and 1974, the Community decided in 1975 to borrow up to $3,000m. capital and interest and re-lend it to those countries worst affected. So far Italy and the Irish Republic have received loans of $1,000m. and $300m. respectively, the product of a money-raising operation in the spring of 1976.

Lomé, Togo
Capital of Togo and port situated on the Bight of Benin. Exports coffee, cocoa and palm kernels. E.E.C. Convention establishing an overall trading and economic co-operation relationship with forty-six developing A.C.P. countries was signed in Lomé in 1975. Population in 1971 was estimated at 200,100.

Lomé Convention
The E.E.C. invited twenty Commonwealth countries in Africa, the Caribbean, and the Pacific to negotiate links with it. In April 1973 it extended this offer to other countries with economies similar to those of the African associates. These offers were intended to coincide with the expiry in 1975 of the second Yaoundé Convention, enabling its signatories to negotiate with the Community at the same time as the British Commonwealth and other countries concerned. All countries were offered the same terms.

Negotiations began on 21 Nov. 1973 between the E.E.C. and forty-three countries, which became forty-six when Equatorial Guinea, Guinea-Bissau and Grenada joined them on attaining independence.

The forty-six countries are: Bahamas, Barbados, Benin, Botswana, Burundi, Cameroon, Central African Republic, Chad, Congo, Equatorial Guinea, Ethiopia, Fiji, Gabon, Gambia, Ghana, Grenada, Guinea, Guinea-Bissau, Guyana, Ivory Coast, Jamaica, Kenya, Lesotho, Liberia, Madagascar, Malawi, Mali, Mauritania, Mauritius, Niger, Nigeria, Rwanda, Senegal, Sierra Leone, Somalia, Sudan, Swaziland, Tanzania, Togo, Tonga, Trinidad and Tobago, Uganda, Upper Volta, Western Samoa, Zaïre and Zambia.

Agreement was reached in 1977 that the Cape Verde Islands, São Tomé and Principe, Papua New Guinea, Comoro Islands, Surinam and the Seychelles should also adhere to the Lomé Convention. This brought the membership to fifty-two.

The Convention's main provisions covered the granting by the E.E.C. of duty-free access on a non-reciprocal basis to all industrial and 96% of agricultural imports from A.C.P. countries; the creation of an export stabilisation scheme, Stabex, guaranteeing the A.C.P. countries a certain level of income on exports of their primary products; increased development aid for the A.C.P. countries from Community sources; increased industrial co-operation between the Nine and the A.C.P. countries; and the creation of three new bodies to provide the institutional framework for the operation of the agreement.

Under its special arrangements the Convention also provided for continued imports into the Community of up to 1.4m. tonnes of cane sugar a year from A.C.P. countries, the bulk of it to come from Commonwealth producers for the United Kingdom market.

In addition the agreement provided for the accession of any other state of comparable economic structure and production, subject to the agreement of the Nine and the A.C.P. countries themselves—the Community having already made known its willingness to consider applications from the former Portuguese territories in Africa currently in the process of attaining independence (*i.e.* Mozambique, Angola, the Cape Verde Islands, and São Tomé and Principe).

The Convention was to be of five years' duration from the date of signature, *i.e.* until 28 Feb. 1980, except in the case of the special arrangements for sugar, which were to last for an unspecified period.

The trading provisions of the new Convention came into force by 1 Aug. 1975. On this basis the Community's trading arrangements under the Yaoundé and Arusha Conventions, as well as Britain's Commonwealth arrangements, all of which had been due to expire on 31 Jan. 1975, were extended to 31 July 1975.

The Lomé Convention contained several features which did not form part of the previous relationship between the original E.E.C. member countries and the former associated states, or between Britain and the developing Commonwealth countries; notably the provision that the A.C.P. countries were required to grant only most-favoured-nation treatment to E.E.C. exports rather than reverse preferences as under the former arrangements. In addition the old term 'association' was dropped in the wording of the new agreement.

The detailed provisions of the Convention are:

TRADE Subject to the necessary origin requirements, all industrial goods and most agricultural products from the A.C.P. countries would enter the Community completely free of protective duties, levies or quotas. The excepted agricultural items, which amounted to 4% of the A.C.P. countries' agricultural exports to the E.E.C., mainly comprised produce covered by the E.E.C. common agricultural policy, as well as a few items of fresh temperate horticultural produce and fresh oranges, but they were generally given preferential treatment as compared with similar products from third countries. Special arrangements were made in respect of beef, rum, bananas and sugar.

The A.C.P. countries undertook to grant to all E.E.C. trade equal treatment no less favourable than that given to other developed countries, although other developing countries could be given preferential treatment. The formula would enable A.C.P. countries to continue their participation in regional economic and trade groupings with other developing countries (for example, Caricom) without damaging their trading relationship with the E.E.C. It would also enable A.C.P. countries to give preference to E.E.C. imports if they wished to do so, provided such preferences applied to all E.E.C. member countries.

Beef; the A.C.P. countries would be able to export to the Community a duty-free annual quota of beef and veal based on exports in the best of the years 1969–74 (with an annual growth factor of 7%) even when beef imports from third countries were banned by the E.E.C. It was anticipated that this provision would greatly assist Botswana, which depended on beef exports to the United Kingdom for a substantial part of its export earnings.

Rum; a tariff-free quota would be fixed each year (with an annual growth factor of 40% for imports into the United Kingdom, and 13% for imports into the rest of the Community) based on the largest annual quantities exported to the Community in the previous three years. The object of these provisions was to enable Commonwealth Caribbean supplies to increase their sales in both the United Kingdom and the other member states without damaging the interest of the French overseas departments of Martinique and Guadeloupe in their own traditional Community markets.

Bananas; A.C.P. bananas were to enjoy duty-free access and were also to be included in the Stabex scheme (*see below*). In addition the Community undertook that no A.C.P. state would be less favourably placed than before as regards access to the E.E.C., and also that a joint effort would be made to increase the Community's consumption of bananas.

Sugar; the Community undertook to buy, and the A.C.P. states to supply, a maximum of 1·4m. tonnes of sugar a year, expressed as quotas for each producing country, namely, Barbados, Congo, Fiji, Guyana, Jamaica, Kenya, Madagascar, Malawi, Mauritius, Swaziland, Tanzania, Trinidad and Tobago, and Uganda. A number of non-independent Caribbean territories (Belize, St Kitts, Nevis, Anguilla and Surinam) and India were also to be covered by these arrangements.

148

RULES OF ORIGIN   The rules of origin to be applied under the Convention were broadly similar to those applied under the free trade agreements between the E.E.C. and Efta countries, but also provided for a system of 'full cumulation' under which products originating in any A.C.P. or E.E.C. country would be regarded as originating in any other A.C.P. country where they were further worked or processed. In addition the Community undertook to consider, within six months, requests from A.C.P. states for derogations from these rules, in particular where this would assist industrial development in the A.C.P. countries.

SAFEGUARD PROVISIONS   A safeguard clause was included to enable the Community or individual member countries to take action to remedy (i) serious economic disturbances either within the Community or in respect of its external financial stability, or (ii) difficulties which might damage particular regions of the Community. The A.C.P. countries would be immediately notified of such action, which would be as limited as possible.

STABILISATION OF EXPORT EARNINGS   In the first agreement of its kind between industrialised and developing countries, the Convention established an export stabilisation scheme (Stabex) under which reductions in A.C.P. earnings from twelve basic export products—bananas, cocoa, coconut products, coffee, cotton, groundnut products, palm products, hides and skins, sisal, tea, timber and iron ore (together with their main processed derivatives, making a total of twenty-nine items in all)—would be cushioned by payments from Community sources.

AID   The Convention provided for total Community aid for the A.C.P. countries in the five-year period of U.A. 3,390m. (about $4,270m. compared with $918m. under the second Yaoundé Convention) of which U.A. 3,000m. was to be made through a new European Development Fund (E.D.F.) made up of U.A. 2,100m. in grants, U.A. 430m. in low-interest loans, U.A. 95m. in risk capital and U.A. 375m. for the Stabex scheme. The remaining U.A. 390m. was to come from the European Investment Bank (E.I.B.) in the form of ordinary loans. In addition a further U.A. 160m. would be provided for the overseas territories, departments and dependencies of E.E.C. member countries (compared with $82m. U.A. under the second Yaoundé Convention), of which U.A. 150m. would come from the E.D.F. and U.A. 10m. from the E.I.B.

INDUSTRIAL CO-OPERATION   Under a wide-ranging chapter on industrial co-operation, which was considered by the A.C.P. countries as an essential element of the new agreement, the Community undertook to assist the A.C.P. countries in specific industrialisation schemes, training programmes, research, the transfer of technology, advisory services and assistance to small and medium-sized firms.

INSTITUTIONS Three new institutions were created under the Convention: a Council of Ministers, a committee of ambassadors and a Consultative Assembly.

Lomé scholarships

The European Development Fund allotted U.A. 8m. for scholarships and training grants for nations of all A.C.P. countries in the 1977 academic year. Until the multi-annual scholarship programme and the training programme for each state have been established, this will enable the most urgent requests to be met.

Ltd

Limited, denoting a company limited in its liability and applying to companies in the Irish Republic and the United Kingdom.

Luns, Joseph

Born Rotterdam, the Netherlands, 1911. Second Secretary of the Netherlands Ministry for Foreign Affairs, 1943–4. Second, then First Secretary of the Dutch Embassy in London, 1944–9: Permanent delegate to the United Nations, 1949–52. Co-Minister for Foreign Affairs, 1952–6. Minister of Foreign Affairs, 1956–71. Signatory to the Treaty of Rome, 1957. President of the Nato Council, 1958–9. Chairman of the Council of Organisation for Economic Co-operation and Development, 1964. Secretary-General of Nato, 1971– . Awarded the Charlemagne Prize, 1967.

Luxembourg

Luxembourg signed the Treaty of Paris (E.C.S.C.) in 1951, the Treaties of Rome (E.E.C. and Euratom) in 1957 and the Treaty of Brussels (Treaty of Accession) in 1972.

Economic profile: Area 2,600 sq. km. Population (1973) 353,000 (male 172,000) density 135 per sq. km. Births (per 1,000 of pop. 1973) 10·9; marriages, 6·0; deaths, 12. Infant mortality, 15·3.

Labour force (1972) 151,000; percentage in agriculture, 9·3; industry, 48·3; services, 42·4.

International trade: (*see* Belgium).

	per 1,000 of population
Standard of living:	
Motor vehicles (1973)	319
Televisions (1972)	227
Telephones (1972)	346

Luxembourg Agreement

The Luxembourg Agreement arose from a considered opinion of the Commission that the new budget procedure would be a step towards full budgetary powers for the European Parliament, which it would exercise when elected by direct universal suffrage.

The President of the Commission (Walter Hallstein) had informed the European Parliament, at its session of 22–6 March 1965, that the Commission intended to submit to the Council proposals on financing the Common Agricultural Policy and the provision of independent revenue for the E.E.C. The Parliament adopted a resolution approving the principle that the proceeds of agricultural levies and duties on imports from non-member countries should accrue to the Community, but urged that the burdens should be fairly shared; it also expressed the view that the creation of independent revenue for the Community should be conditional upon transfer to the Parliament of power to fix revenue and expenditure.

The E.E.C. Commission's scheme was considered by the Council of Ministers at a meeting in Brussels which opened on 28 June 1965 under the chairmanship of M. Couve de Murville, the French Foreign Minister.

M. Couve de Murville immediately rejected the Commission's proposals, maintaining that political conditions had been imposed by the Commission which were totally unacceptable to France, and that the sole question to be settled was the renewal of levies after the expiry of the existing agricultural finance regulations on 30 June.

The Constitutional Crisis: Dr Luns, the Netherlands Foreign Minister, on the other hand, strongly urged the adoption of the Commission's proposals, being supported by Dr Schröder and Signor Fanfani, the Federal German and Italian Foreign Ministers. M. Spaak, however, expressed the view that the renewal of the agricultural finance regulations must be decided by 30 June as demanded by France, while the other points raised by the Commission could be dealt with at a later date.

Professor Hallstein, on behalf of the Commission, defended its proposals by reason of its authority to pursue economic integration under the Treaty and under subsequent Council regulations on agriculture. He nevertheless indicated the Commission's willingness to reconsider its proposals, but M. Couve de Murville refused to agree, although the other Foreign Ministers were in favour of continuing the debate.

On 1 July M. Couve de Murville declared that agreement was impossible and proposed that the Council should adjourn. In spite of suggestions that the clock be 'stopped' and that the Commission be asked to work out immediately a compromise proposal for further consideration, the discussion ended without result in the early hours of 2 July.

Following the temporary breakdown of the talks, the French Government announced on 5 July 1965 the withdrawal of its representatives from the Commission's working committees on agriculture, foreign relations, and the association agreement with Nigeria then under negotiation; the chief French Representative to the European Communities (M. Jean-Marc Boegner) was recalled to Paris on 6 July, and France boycotted a meeting of the Common Market representatives in Geneva on 6 July called to co-ordinate the tactics of the Six in the 'Kennedy Round' trade negotiations. M. Giscard d'Estaing failed to attend a meeting of the Finance Ministers in Stresa in July, and at the next meeting of the Council of Ministers on 26–7 July France was not represented, officials at the Quai d'Orsay defining the French boycott as the 'policy of the empty chair'.

Prior to this Council meeting, and in an effort to help solve the crisis, the Commission had published a memorandum on 22 July 1965 dealing with the problems which had caused the crisis. The Commission proposed in this memorandum that:

(i) Independent revenue for the E.E.C. should be postponed until 1970, as 1967 was not acceptable to all member countries;

(ii) Between 1967 and 1970 a compensation fund should be created to redistribute, among member countries, the duties collected at points of entry. The common external tariff would become effective from 1967 and redistribution of duties would be essential because the points of entry would not always be in the country of use or consumption;

(iii) The existing system of financing farm policy would remain in effect until such time as the Agriculture Fund progressively took over the financing from member countries;

(iv) A decision on these proposals should be made by 1 Nov. 1965;

(v) The new finance regulations should be linked to enforcement of common policies for sugar, fats and oils, fruit and vegetables, on which no agreement had so far been reached;

(vi) A ceiling should be placed on the financial cost to Italy;

(vii) When agreeing the final stages of the agricultural policy as from 1 July 1967, the complete elimination of Customs duties between member countries and the introduction of the common external tariff on all goods entering the E.E.C. should be introduced on the same date.

The memorandum was discussed by the Council after M. Spaak had raised the question whether in France's absence the meeting was legally constituted. The Council decided that it would discuss the memorandum but left open the question whether it was to take material decisions.

During the autumn of 1965 much diplomatic activity took place in an effort to encourage France to return and take a full part in the Community's proceedings. On 30 Nov. a further request by the 'Five' led to discussions between Signor Colombo, President of the Council, and M. Couve de Murville in Rome. Two days following the second ballot in the French presidential election the French Government accepted an invitation to meet the Council of Ministers in Luxembourg in Jan. 1966 to try to reach a settlement.

The Council's Luxembourg meetings were devoted almost entirely to the discussion of the French requests concerning the non-application of majority decisions and the role of the Commission, a satisfactory solution of which the French Government had made a condition for resuming its active participation in the E.E.C.

It will be seen that 'procedures' and aspects of politics play a greater part in the Luxembourg Agreement than the subject of Agriculture, but it was on the question of Agriculture that France took her political stand and therefore the subject must be included here.

Explaining the French objections to the principle of majority decisions, M. Couve de Murville said that in questions of vital interest only unanimous agreement was politically conceivable. Without pressing for an amendment of the Treaty the French Government therefore suggested a political agreement among the member countries, whereby the Council would abstain from deciding by majority vote if any member should so request because of the vital importance of the question for his country.

The other members refused any formal settlement which would involve giving a member country a permanent right to veto; they felt, however, that this was in practice largely a false problem, since unanimity would always be sought on major issues.

The solution eventually agreed upon was announced in a communiqué at the end of the second session on 29 Jan. 1966, as follows:

(i) 'When issues very important to one or more member countries are at stake, the members of the Council will try, within a reasonable time, to reach solutions which can be adopted by all members of the Council while respecting their mutual interests, and those of the Community, in accordance with Article 2 of the Treaty.' (This article aims at approximating the economic policies of E.E.C. members to create a common market.)

(ii) 'The French delegation considers that, when very important issues are at stake, discussion must be continued until unanimous agreement is reached.'

(iii) 'The six delegations note that there is a divergence of views on what should be done in the event of a failure to reach complete agreement.'

(iv) 'They consider that this divergence does not prevent the Community's work being resumed in accordance with normal procedure.'

Dealing with the role of the Commission and its relations with the Council, M. Couve de Murville put forward a list of ten points as a suggestion to assist subsequent discussion:

(i) The Commission should consult the member Governments at the appropriate level before submitting proposals for Community action of particular importance to the Council.

(ii) Commission proposals should not be made known to the European Parliament or the public before their submission to the Council.

(iii) The executive powers granted to the Commission in any policy field should be precisely formulated, leaving no room for its discretion.

(iv) Commission directives for Community policy should not specify the detailed manner of their application by the member states.

(v) The Council should reassert its prerogatives in diplomatic relations, particularly as regards accepting letters of credence.

(vi) Approaches to the Commission by non-member countries should be brought to the early attention of the Council.

(vii) The Council should decide the nature and extent of the Community's relations with international organisations.

(viii) Commission members should observe political neutrality in public statements.

(ix) Community information policy should be a joint Council-Commission responsibility.

(x) The Council should exercise a closer control over the Commission's budget.

Following discussion of the French aide-memoire it was found that there were possibilities of agreement and, according to the communiqué, the Council adopted seven points for improving its relationship with the Commission. These were:

(i) It was desirable that the Commission, before adopting a proposal of particular importance, should, through the Permanent Representatives, make appropriate contacts with the Governments of the member states, without this procedure affecting the right of initiative which the Commission derived from the Treaty.

(ii) Proposals and all other official acts which the Commission addressed to the Council and the member states should only be made public after the latter had formally taken cognisance of them and had the texts in their possession.

The *Official Gazette* should be arranged so that legislative acts having a binding force were distinguished as such.

(iii) The credentials of Heads of Mission of non-member states accredited to the Community should be presented to the President of the Council and the President of the Commission, meeting together for this purpose.

(iv) The Council and the Commission would inform each other rapidly and fully of any approaches relating to fundamental questions made to either institution by non-member states.

(v) Within the scope of the application of Article 162, the Council and the Commission would consult together on the advisability of, the procedure for, and the nature of any links which the Commission might establish, under Art. 229 of the Treaty, with international organisations.

(vi) Co-operation between the Council and the Commission on the Community's information policy, which had been examined by the Council on 24 Sept. 1963, would be strengthened so that the programme of the Press and Information Service could be drawn up and carried out jointly, in accordance with procedures to be defined later and which might include an *ad hoc* body.

(vii) Within the framework of the financial regulations for drawing up and putting into effect the Communities' budgets, the Council and the Commission would define methods of increasing the efficiency of control over the acceptance, authorisation, and execution of the Communities' expenditures.

It was provided that these points would be discussed between the Council of Ministers and the Commission under Article 162 of the Treaty.

At the last sitting on 29 Jan. 1966 M. Couve de Murville put forward a tentative programme of work comprising, on the one hand, certain outstanding problems such as the budget, agricultural finance regulation, and the second alignment towards a common Customs tariff, and on the other hand the entry into force of the Treaty on the merger of the Executives and decisions on the composition of the new single Commission. During the discussion reservations were expressed by other members on the principle of such a timetable, no decision being taken.

At a press conference after the end of the Council meeting on 29 Jan., Signor Colombo and M. Spaak made statements which indicated that the most drastic effects of the crisis within the Community had been overcome and that the way had been opened for a resumption of French co-operation.

Signor Colombo said: 'We can say that the European Community is starting work again, and that is what is most important from the political point of view. We have reached some agreement, come to some understanding, and have defined certain practices, but the Treaty, with its rules and institutions remains intact. And it is according to these rules and through these institutions that the life of the Community will start again. We can only express the hope that crises like that which we have lived through in the second half of 1965 and the opening weeks of 1966 will not recur. . . .'

M. Spaak declared: 'One cannot say that all the difficulties have been overcome by any means, but we have succeeded in what we had to do. . . . As for majority voting, we are obliged to recognise that we are not entirely in agreement. But what is essential is that we recognise that the disagreement which continues does not hinder France from coming back to Brussels, nor, therefore, the Community from resuming its activities.'

The E.E.C. Commission itself issued the following communiqué on 2 Feb. 1966:

'The Commission is pleased that, after the Council meeting in Luxembourg, the Community can now resume its normal activities, both internal and external. There is a great deal of work to be done in the coming months, and many decisions must be taken, to make real progress towards economic union. The Commission is ready to hold consultations with the Council, in due course, in a spirit of co-operation and in accordance with Article 162 of the Treaty in order to make even closer the collaboration between itself and the Council.'

Luxembourg declaration
see Luxembourg Agreement

M

Macmillan, Harold
Born London, England, 1894. Member of the British Parliament, 1924–9, 1931–64. Minister-Resident of North-West Africa and Central Mediterranean, 1942–5. Diplomatic Representative with French National Committee, 1943–4. Chairman of the Advisory Council for Italy, 1944–5. Secretary of State for Air, 1945; Minister of Housing and Local Government, 1951–4; Minister of Defence, 1954–5; Secretary of State for Foreign Affairs, 1955; Chancellor of the Exchequer, 1955–7 and Prime Minister, 1957–63. British delegate to the first consultative assembly of the Council of Europe, 1949.

Madagascar
Madagascar was a signatory of the Yaoundé Conventions of 1963 and 1969 and the Lomé Convention of 1975.

Maghreb Agreement

Trade agreements were signed with Algeria, Morocco and Tunisia (the Maghreb countries) in April 1976. For each country it meant that from 1 July 1976 there was duty free entry of industrial goods into the Nine except for certain petroleum products and cork. In addition there were some tariff concessions on agricultural goods.

E.E.C. aid to the Maghreb (in millions of U.A.) for a five-year period.

	Algeria	*Morocco*	*Tunisia*	*Total*
E.I.B. loans	70	56	41	167
Loans on special terms	19	58	39	116
Grants	25	16	15	56
Total	*114*	*130*	*95*	*339*

Maghreb citizens employed in the E.E.C.

	Algerians	*Moroccans*	*Tunisians*	*Total*
Total	444,400	187,900	84,800	717,100
of which:				
in France	440,000	130,000	70,000	640,000
in Belgium	3,000	30,000	2,000	35,000
in German Federal Republic	1,400	16,400	12,000	29,800
in the Netherlands	–	9,500	800	10,300
in the United Kingdom	–	2,000	–	2,000

majorities

The Council exercises the powers conferred on it by the three Treaties (European Coal and Steel Community, Euratom, E.E.C.) by unanimous vote, absolute majority or qualified majority. Although the definitions of each type of majority are basically the same in each Treaty the few variations which do exist are given below.

Unanimous vote. Each member state has one vote and abstentions do not prevent a vote being unanimous, except in certain cases specified by Article 28 of the E.C.S.C. Treaty.

Absolute majority. Each member state has one vote. In the E.C.S.C. Treaty (only) the majority must also include at least two states each producing at least one eighth of the coal and steel output of the Community.

Qualified majority. Member states have the following number of votes each: Belgium 5, Denmark 3, France 10, Federal German Republic 10, Irish Republic 3, Italy 10, Luxembourg 2, the Netherlands 5, United Kingdom 10. Forty-one votes cast by not less than six members constitute a majority. In the Euratom and E.E.C. Treaties the qualified majority, so long as it has the forty-one votes necessary, does not need to be cast by the minimum of six member states where the vote is on a proposal by the Commission.

Since the Accords of Luxembourg, however, almost all Council votes have been unanimous. This unanimity flows from the realisation that, on the one hand, it would be dangerous to rely on a legalistic interpretation of the Treaties to bind the Communities together when genuine national interests are in conflict and, on the other hand, it is politically short-sighted to humiliate a fellow politician by outvoting him. This has meant that, even without any legal veto existing, the Council has become the scene of much political bargaining among its members so that each package of proposals is acceptable to all member states.

Malawi
Malawi was a signatory of the Lomé Convention of 1975.

Mali
Mali was a signatory of the Yaoundé Conventions of 1963 and 1969 and the Lomé Convention of 1975.

Malta
Malta signed an Association agreement with the E.E.C. which came into force on 1 April 1971. It provided for a customs union to be established within ten years. There were to be two phases of five years each. In the first phase Malta would reduce customs duties on most goods by 55%. In the return, the E.E.C. would reduce its duties on imports from Malta by 70%. In April 1976 the provisions of the 1971 agreement were extended until 30 June 1977 or until the entry of the second stage of the agreement. The 1971

agreement was also extended to include the three new members of the E.E.C. with effect from 1 June 1976.

Man, Isle of

Free trade in agriculture and industrial goods between the Isle of Man and members of the E.E.C. was agreed under the Treaty of Accession but the island is exempt from other E.E.C. rules and regulations, including V.A.T., free movement of labour, freedom of establishment and competition policy.

Mansholt Plan

The E.E.C. Commission presented to the Council of Ministers a ten-year plan for agricultural reform in Dec. 1968. It had been drawn up by Dr Sicco Mansholt, then a vice-president of the Commission and spokesman on agriculture. The plan was also known as *Agriculture 1980.*

The Mansholt Plan proposed a restructuring of agriculture in the E.E.C. with the aim of raising the living standards of farmers and workers and also of halting the persistent increase in the common agricultural policy's costs. It was proposed that:

(i) There should be a reduction in the emphasis on market and price policies, and priority should be given to the removal of economic and legal barriers that made it difficult to increase the size of agricultural holdings and to improve the mobility of labour;

(ii) There should be a reduction in the acreage of farmland within the E.E.C.;

(iii) The drift from the land should be encouraged so that the estimated labour force of 10m. in 1968 be reduced to 5m. by 1980.

The plan envisaged the establishment of large agricultural units and that this would come about by voluntary methods. It also saw a large education and re-training programme for workers leaving the land and payments made to farmers for leasing their land to the larger agricultural concerns. The cost of implementing the plan was estimated in 1968 at 2,500m. U.A. per annum.

Mansholt, Sicco
Born Groningen, Netherlands, 1908. Minister of Agriculture, Fisheries and Food, 1945–8; 1951–2 and 1956–8. Led the Netherlands delegation on agriculture to the United Nations. Took part in negotiations creating Benelux Union, 1946. Prepared the 'Mansholt Plan' for the E.E.C., 1953; Vice-President of the E.E.C. Commission, 1958–67. Vice-President of the combined executives of E.E.C., E.C.S.C. and Euratom, 1967–72, and President, 1972–3. Awarded the Robert Schuman Prize in 1968.

margin, price, preference, tariff
The difference between two rates, of price or duty. A preference margin in Gatt terms is the absolute difference between a most-favoured-nation rate of duty and a preferential rate of duty for the like produce (preference); it is not the proportionate relation between those rates.

Marshall, George
Born Pennsylvania, U.S.A., 1880, died 1959. Chief of Staff, United States Army, 1939–45. Special representative of the President in China, 1945–7. Secretary of State, 1947–9, and originator of Marshall Plan for the financial and economic rehabilitation of war-shattered Europe. On 5 June 1947, speaking at Harvard University as U.S. Secretary of State, he said: 'It would be neither fitting nor efficacious for this Government to undertake to draw up unilaterally a programme designed to place Europe on its feet economically. This is the business of Europeans. The initiative must come from Europe. The role of this country should consist of friendly aid in drafting a European programme; and of later support of such a programme so far as it may be practical to do so. The programme should be a joint one, agreed to by a number of, if not all, European nations. . . . Our policy is directed not against any country or doctrine but against hunger, poverty, desperation and chaos. United States assistance should not be doled out as crises develop. Any assistance this Government may render in future should provide a cure rather than a palliative. Any Government

which manoeuvres to block the recovery of other countries cannot expect help from us. Furthermore, Governments, political parties, or groups which seek to perpetuate human misery in order to profit therefrom politically or otherwise will encounter the opposition of the United States'.

Marshall Plan
see European Recovery Programme

Mashrag countries
The Mashrag countries (Egypt, Jordan, Lebanon and Syria) signed trade and co-operative agreements in Jan. and Feb. 1977 and thus completed the E.E.C. Mediterranean Policy.

Maudling, Reginald
Born England, 1917. Member of the British Parliament since 1950. Minister of Supply, 1955–7. Paymaster-General, 1957–9. President of the Board of Trade, 1959–61. Secretary of State for the Colonies, 1961–2. Chancellor of the Exchequer, 1962–4. Home Secretary, 1970–2. Chairman of a committee to set up an industrial free trade area among O.E.E.C. members, 1957–8.

Mauritania
Mauritania was a signatory of the Yaoundé Conventions of 1963 and 1969 and the Lomé Convention of 1975.

Mauritius
Mauritius was a signatory of the Lomé Convention of 1975.

M.C.A.
see monetary compensatory amounts.

M.E.
Mouvement européen, European Movement.

M.E.C.
Mercato Comune Europeo, European Common Market (Italian).

medical help for travellers in the E.E.C.
Medical help for travellers is available provided they make the proper arrangements in advance. Most people visiting Community countries for a short time, *e.g.* on holiday or business, are entitled, if they are taken ill or have an accident, to receive medical treatment on the same terms as the people of those countries.

This treatment may not be entirely free but, and provided proper procedures are followed, only a small percentage of the costs should be borne by the visitor.

In general, only those people and their dependants covered by Class I national employment insurance or in receipt of benefit, *e.g.* retirement or disablement pension, are eligible to participate in the arrangements. Self-employed or non-employed people are not eligible unless they fall in the above category. If not covered by private insurance, they are liable to pay the full cost of treatment.

Before travelling, unless visiting Denmark or the Irish Republic, British nationals entitled to participate should obtain an Entitlement Certificate (E. 111) from the local Social Security office. This should be done some weeks in advance, and the form will be valid from the date of issue to one month after the expected date of return. Slightly different forms are needed if dependants are going abroad alone, or make frequent trips abroad, or are going to the Federal German Republic.

Normally a visitor is only entitled to treatment for an ailment requiring immediate attention, though pensioners or someone in receipt of Industrial Injuries benefit may be able to obtain a wider range of care. In some cases, also, sickness benefit can be claimed if application is made within three days to the local sickness institution.

Mediterranean Policy

The E.E.C. Mediterranean Policy is to establish a global relationship with the countries of the Mediterranean basin. The discussions on the trade and co-operation agreements between individual countries have been protracted but once agreed they will be for an unlimited period with a review of the workings of the agreements in 1979 and 1984.

Medium-Term Economic Policy Committee of the E.E.C.

The committee was established in 1964 and it studies the probable development of the Communities' economies over the medium-term.

merger of the Communities

A Treaty for the merger of the separate executives of the three Communities, the Commission of the European Economic Community, the High Authority of the European Coal and Steel Community, and the Commission of the European Atomic Energy Community, was signed by the member countries on 8 April 1965 and the merger took place on 1 July 1967. This agreement was contained in the subsidiary conventions and protocols signed at Rome on 25 March 1957 that:

(i) there should be one Assembly common to the three European Communities; (ii) there should be a Common Court of Justice and (iii) the E.E.C. and Euratom should share a single Economic and Social Committee.

Messina Conference

The Foreign Ministers of the six member countries of the E.C.S.C., Paul-Henri Spaak (Belgium), Antoine Pinay (France), Walter Hallstein (Germany), Gaetano Martino (Italy), Joseph Bech (Luxembourg) and Johan Willem Beyen (Netherlands), met at Messina on 2–4 June 1955, to discuss proposals for further European economic integration which had been made by the three Benelux countries on 20 May 1955, to the Governments of the member countries. The Benelux proposals called for:

(i) the establishment of a 'common organisation' to study development plans for a European network of roads, canals and railways, and for the co-ordination of civil aviation policies;

(ii) the study of methods of co-ordinating power policy in Europe:

(iii) the creation of a 'common authority' for the development of atomic energy for peaceful purposes, with the pooling of investment funds, technical knowledge and research facilities; and

(iv) the progressive integration of the national economies of the six member countries and the harmonisation of economic, financial and social policies. To implement this programme the Benelux Governments proposed that a conference should be called to work out:

(i) a Treaty on the pooling of transport, power and atomic energy;

(ii) a Treaty on general economic integration; and

(iii) a Treaty defining the European institutions necessary to carry out the programme.

After discussing these proposals the Ministers finally agreed on a resolution known as the Messina Resolution, which adopted the objectives of the Benelux programme but set out different procedures for, and a more gradual approach to, their implementation.

Messina Resolution

The Messina Resolution stated 'The Governments of Belgium, France, German Federal Republic, Italy, Luxembourg and the Netherlands consider that the moment has arrived to initiate a new phase on the path of constructing Europe. They believe that this has to be done principally in the economic sphere, and regard it as necessary to continue the creation of a United Europe through an expansion of joint institutions, the gradual fusion of national economies, the creation of a common market, and the gradual co-ordination of social policies. Such a policy seems to them indispensable to preserve for Europe its place in the world, to restore its influence, and to improve steadily the living standards of its population'. The following aims were agreed:

(i) The joint development of large-scale communications facilities, including the construction of a European network of canals, *autobahnen*, and electrified railway-lines, as well as the standardisation of equipment and the improved co-ordination of aerial traffic.

(ii) The development of exchanges of gas and electric power, and a reduction of their cost, through co-ordination of the production and consumption of power and the formulation of a joint policy.

(iii) The creation of a joint organisation having 'the responsibility and the facilities' for ensuring the development of atomic energy for peaceful purposes, 'taking into account any special agreements of individual Governments with third countries'.

These facilities would be:
(i) the creation of a common fund, financed by member countries, for the construction of atomic energy plants and atomic research;
(ii) free and sufficient access to raw materials, and free exchange of information, technicians, by-products and special equipment;
(iii) the sharing of the results of such research without discrimination, and the provision of financial aid for their practical implementation; and
(iv) co-operation with non-member countries.

'The six Governments agreed that the aim of this course in the field of economic policy is the creation of a common European market free from all Customs barriers and quantitative restrictions. They believe that this market has to be realised by stages.' This would require an examination of the following questions:
(i) The 'procedure and rhythm' of the gradual abolition of trade barriers between the participating countries and of suitable measures for the gradual unification of their Customs system *vis-à-vis* third countries.
(ii) Measures for the co-ordination of their general policy in the financial, economic and social spheres.
(iii) Measures for the co-ordination of their monetary policy with a view to the creation of a common market.
(iv) A system of protective clauses.
(v) The creation and functioning of a 're-adaptation fund'.
(vi) The gradual realisation of a common labour market.
(vii) The drafting of rules that would guarantee free competition within the common market in such a way as to exclude any national discrimination.
(viii) The 'appropriate institutional means' for the realisation and oper-ation of a common market.

The question of the creation of a European investment fund was under examination; the purpose of such a fund would be 'the joint development of Europe's economic potential, and especially of the under-developed areas of member countries'.

The six Governments also regarded it as 'indispensable to examine the progressive harmonisation of national social policies', especially those relating to working hours, payment for overtime and paid holidays.

Instead of calling an immediate treaty-drafting conference, as had been proposed by the Benelux countries, the Foreign Ministers decided to appoint in the first instance a committee of Government representatives and experts, working under the direction of an 'eminent political personality', to study the problems raised, prepare drafts of treaties or agreements, and report back on 1 Oct. 1955 at the latest. Meanwhile the Foreign Ministers would meet again before that date to study any interim reports of the committee and issue further directives. The United Kingdom Government was invited to attend the committee's meetings because of Britain's membership in the West European Union and her associate membership of the Coal and Steel Community. The Foreign Ministers would decide at a later date whether other countries should also be invited to participate in the treaty-drafting conferences.

metric system
The metric system of weights and measures was introduced in France in 1799 and is now widely accepted by many countries of the world, including all members of the E.E.C., although it was only adopted by the United Kingdom and Ireland in 1971.

Mexico
Mexico has a five-year non-preferential trade agreement with the E.E.C. dating from 1 Nov. 1975.

Mezzogiorno,
The traditional name of that part of the Italian mainland which lies approximately to the south of Rome and includes the two large offshore islands, Sicily and Sardinia. It has an area of order 130,000 sq. km. and a population of about 20m. For the purpose of development planning it also includes the provinces of Frosinone and Latina, in lower Lazio, a number of communes in the provinces of Rome, in Rieti in upper Lazio and in the province of Ascoli Piceno in the Marche, as well as the islands of Elba, Giglio and Capraia off the Tuscan coast.

m.f.n.

m.f.n.
see most-favoured-nation.

Migrant Workers, Advisory Committee on Social Security for
The Advisory Committee on Social Security for Migrant Workers, a
Commission advisory committee on social policy, was created by the
E.E.C. Council of Ministers in 1971. The composition and servicing are the
same as for the Advisory Committee on Freedom of Movement for
Workers.

military service
The Nine

Belgium	eleven months, nine months if service in Federal German Republic.
Denmark	nine months.
France	twelve months.
German Federal Republic	fifteen months.
Irish Republic	voluntary.
Italy	army and air force twelve months, navy eighteen months.
Luxembourg	voluntary.
Netherlands	army fourteen months, navy and air force eighteen to twenty-one months.
United Kingdom	voluntary.

Other European countries

Albania	army two years, air force, navy and special units three years.
Austria	six months, followed by sixty days' reservist training, for twelve years.
Bulgaria	army and air force two years, navy three years.
Czechoslovakia	two years.
Finland	eight to eleven months.
German Democratic Republic	eighteen months.
Greece	twenty-eight to thirty-two months.
Hungary	two years.

168

Norway	army twelve months, navy and air force fifteen months.
Poland	army, internal security forces and air force two years; navy and special services three years.
Portugal	army fifteen months.
Romania	army and air force sixteen months, navy two years.
Spain	eighteen months.
Sweden	army and navy seven and a half to fifteen months, air force nine to fourteen months.
Switzerland	four months' initial training, refresher training of three weeks a year for eight years, two weeks for three years and one week for two years.
Turkey	twenty months.
U.S.S.R.	army and air force two years, navy and border guards two to three years.
Yugoslavia	army and air force fifteen months, navy eighteen months.

Mines Safety and Health Commission

The Mines Safety and Health Commission was created in 1957 by decision of the Council, following the pit disaster at Marcinelle, Belgium. In 1974 the Council extended its competence to cover extractive industries, mining or non-mining. It has thirty-six members, two government and one trade union representative and one employer per country. It is serviced by the Commission, which also provides the chairman. There are twelve working parties and four committees of experts on different aspects of health and safety.

Monetary Committee

A consultative body set up under Article 105 of the Treaty of Rome in order to promote co-ordination of the policies of the member states in the monetary field to the full extent needed for the functioning of the Common Market.

The Committee is composed of two members from each member state (normally from the Treasury and Central Bank) and two members from the

169

Commission. The secretariat is provided by the Commission.

The Committee must be consulted before the Commission takes action when member states take 'protective measures' restricting the freedom of movement of capital or goods between states so as to protect their balance of payments.

monetary compensatory amounts
These are applied in inter-Community agricultural trade and are altered weekly as currencies fluctuate.

Monnet, Jean
Born at Cognac, France, 1888. First Deputy Secretary-General of the League of Nations. Chairman Franco-British Economic Co-ordination Committee, 1939. Commissioner on French Committee of National Liberation, 1943–4. Originator of the French Modernisation Plan 1946. Initiator of the Schuman Plan which launched the European Communities and of the 'relaunching of Europe' in 1955 which led to the Common Market and Euratom. First President E.C.S.C. High Authority, 1952–5. Chairman Action Committee for a United State of Europe, 1956. Awarded the Charlemagne Prize, 1953 and the Schuman Prize, 1966. At a meeting of Heads of State in Luxembourg in April 1976, it was decided to confer the title 'Honorary Citizen of Europe' on Jean Monnet for his work as a founder of the European Community.

montant de soutien
One of the main features of the Mansholt proposals for dealing with agriculture in the Kennedy Round was the binding of the amount of support, *montant de soutien*. All agricultural produce, with only the most limited exceptions, were dealt with under the 'support approach'. This involves, for any given commodity: (i) agreeing a world price or reference price which is taken as the 'norm' for international commercial transactions; (ii) each country concerned with that commodity would then submit for international confrontation the total remuneration received by its producers for that item; (iii) the world or reference price would then be subtracted from the total remuneration and this difference would con-

stitute the amount of support (*montant de soutien*) which would be bound for three years.

montant forfaitaire
The sum by which the levy on imports from one member state to another is reduced so as to give E.E.C. suppliers a preference over outside suppliers. This sum is to be increased by stages so that at the end of the transitional period the levies on trade between member states will be eliminated. Also known as '*abattement forfaitaire*'.

Morocco
Morocco signed a preferential trade agreement with the E.E.C. which came into force on 1 July 1976 and is of an unlimited duration. This agreement was part of the E.E.C. Mediterranean Policy.

most-favoured-nation
The concept, embodied in the Gatt, of granting to other countries any advantage, favour, privilege or immunity which is granted to the trade of a country receiving the most favourable treatment. An exception to this is made in the Gatt for preferential tariff margins existing at the inception of the Gatt.

'mountain'
From time to time the prices of certain agricultural products, especially beef and milk products, have been set at prices high enough to encourage over-production. This has necessitated heavy Community intervention to support prices, with the result that stocks or 'mountains' in the intervention stores have risen. The skimmed-milk mountain rose from 166,000 tonnes in early 1974 to 1.11m. tonnes two years later. Costs of keeping food in intervention, i.e. warehousing, were very heavy and in 1976 were budgetted at 1,110m. U.A., equivalent to 14% of the total budget of the European Communities. Attempts to reduce the mountains run into difficulties because they either reduce agricultural incomes or are obviously illogical—such as using milk-powder as cattle food or selling butter at low prices to non-E.E.C. buyers.

171

MTN's

Multinational trade negotiations.

---

multinationals

Because of the influence of multinational companies on the economies of the member states of the E.E.C., the Commission proposed a seventh Directive under Article 54 (3) (g) of the Treaty of Rome to ensure that companies situated within the Community publish comparable information drawn up on uniform lines in order to provide a minimum degree of protection for shareholders, employees and third parties.

In seeking to categorise the companies involved the E.E.C. Commission has based its definitions on a fairly wide concept of the undertaking. There would be no justification, it argues, for limiting the scope of the directive to certain legal forms, since investments which allow a significant degree of influence to be exerted may be held in all forms of undertaking. Thus the directive defines companies as follows:

(i) Associated company—one over which another company exercises directly or indirectly a significant influence. Thus a company is presumed to be associated with another company where the latter holds directly or indirectly 20 % or more of the capital, or of the votes attaching to shares issued by the former. An example is a joint venture.

(ii) Dependent company or subsidiary, one over which another company, the dominant undertaking, directly or indirectly exercises a dominant influence because it either holds the major part of the subscribed capital, controls the majority of votes attaching to shares, or can appoint more than half of the members of the dependent company's administrative, managerial or supervisory body.

A Group of Companies is defined as one where the dominant undertaking and undertakings dependent on it are managed on a central and unified basis by the dominant company, vertical structure, or, irrespective of dependency, the companies are managed centrally, as in a consortium, horizontal structure.

The advantage of this definition is that it covers cases where an undertaking is controlled through a minority holding. At the same time short-term investments, however large, are excluded.

Where the head company has its registered office within the E.E.C., it will have to draw up group accounts once the company itself, or another

172

member of the group, is a company incorporated with limited liability. This consolidation will be world-wide in that the annual accounts of all the undertakings belonging to the group, irrespective of where their head office is situated, must be consolidated. A group undertaking may not be excluded from the consolidated accounts unless it is of only minor importance; the Commission would like to see banks and insurance companies covered by the directive.

Consolidated accounts must also be drawn up where dependent companies, with a head office outside the Community, are limited companies established within the Community, each of which heads a sub-group within the Community. This provision is particularly important as regards multinational groups which, while being controlled from outside the Community, have multiple interests and activities inside it.

If the directive is adopted the principle of a 'true and fair view' of company activity will not be a formality but have full legal effect. Group accounts, therefore, cannot be presented merely as a collection of statistics derived from the annual accounts, or in the form of the individual accounts of a company otherwise excluded from consolidation.

As proposed in the directive, group accounts must comprise the group consolidated balance sheet, the group consolidated profit and loss account and notes to the accounts. They must give a true and fair view of the group's assets, liabilities, financial position and results, and the methods of consolidation must not be changed from one year to the next.

The proposal lays down a number of principles governing consolidation in order to ensure that it is carried out uniformly through the Community. Thus debts and claims and transactions between group undertakings must be eliminated to prevent group accounts giving a false impression of the group's assets, liabilities and results. The annual accounts of undertakings to be included in the consolidation must also be drawn up as at the same date, so that the consolidated accounts refer to the same period and cover comparable accounting items.

The group's annual report must also give particulars of important events that have occurred during the year, as well as the activities of the group regarding research and development and the projected cost.

To ensure proper comparisons it is proposed that items incorporated in group accounts must be valued using identical methods, although a degree of flexibility will be allowed in applying these principles as there may be practical difficulties in exceptional cases.

Thus the directive prescribes a special valuation method for group accounts in respect of holdings of group undertakings in the capital of other companies not belonging to the group, but where, by virtue of the holdings, a substantial influence is exerted on the running of the companies, as in a joint venture. The purpose of the valuation method laid down in the directive is to put a more realistic value on such holdings. Compulsory use of this valuation method is justified by the Commission on the grounds that the information given on this matter must be comparable throughout the Community.

Finally the directive requires certain information to be given in the notes to group accounts, mainly to disclose the structure of the group, the identity of the group undertakings and the relationship between them.

N

N.A.C.E.
The Nomenclature Générale des Activités Economiques des Communautés, used by the Six for the classification of economic activities, is an alternative to the International Standard Industrial Classification.

Napoleon I
The reputation of Napolean (1769–1821) as a great European is seemingly based on the survival of parts of the *Code Napoleon* and the habit of driving on the right throughout Europe. His conquests, as represented by neo-classical artists, smacked of ancient Rome, as did his creation of Republics and other new political entities throughout Europe. He in fact abolished the venerable Holy Roman Empire in 1806. But whilst he administered 'throughout' Europe, creating the Continental System to keep out British trade and recruiting men for his armies, he did not administer 'for' Europe. It is even doubtful whether he administered for France. Indeed, the nationalism he unleashed against the Europe of the *ancien régime* was quickly imitated elsewhere. The propaganda paintings of Goya in Spain,

the rising of Andreas Hofer in the Tyrol, the patriotism of Baron Stein of Prussia, the spontaneous hostility of the Prussian people were part of the backlash of nationalism that he created. By 1815 the nations of Europe were far more aware of their differences than before his appearance. Napoleon may be truly said to have created European nationalism and not a united Europe.

National Referendum Campaign

The National Referendum Campaign was the anti-Common Market 'umbrella' organisation active in the United Kingdom during the run-up to the referendum. Affiliated organisations were: Anti-Common Market League, Anti-Dear Food Campaign, British Business for World Markets, British League of Rights, Common Market Safeguards Committee, Get Britain Out, National Council of Anti-Common Market Associations, Plaid Cymru, Scottish National Party, United Ulster Unionists, Conservatives Against the Treaty of Rome and Liberals 'No' to the Common Market.

Nato

see North Atlantic Treaty Organisation.

Netherlands, The

The Netherlands signed the Treaty of Paris (E.C.S.C.) in 1951, the Treaties of Rome (E.E.C. and Euratom) in 1957 and the Treaty of Brussels (Treaty of Accession) in 1972.

Economic profile: Area 40,800 sq. km. Population (1973) 13,439,000 (male 6,676,000) density 329 per sq. km. Births (per 1,000 of pop. 1973) 14·5; marriages, 8·0; deaths, 8·2. Infant mortality, 11·5.

Labour force (1972) 4,678,000; percentage in agriculture, 6·9; industry, 36·6; services, 56·5.

International trade (in millions of U.A.):

	1965	*1970*	*1973*	*1976*
Imports	7,464	13,393	19,539	31,557
Exports	6,393	11,767	19,255	31,727

	per 1,000 of *population*
Standard of living:	
Motor vehicles (1973)	232
Televisions (1972)	244
Telephones (1972)	280

newspapers

Belgium: La Cité, La Dernière Heure, Echo de la Bourse, La Libre Belgique, Le Peuple, Le Soir, De Financieel Ekonomische Tijd, Gazet van Antwerpen, Het Laaste Nieuws, De Nieuwe Gids, De Standard. *Denmark*: Aktuelt, Berlinske Tidende, Børsen, Ekstra-Bladet, Information, Jyllands-Posten, Politiken. *France*: L'Aurore, La Croix, Les Echos, Le Figaro, France-Soir, L'Humanité, Le Monde, Le Nouveau Journal, Le Quotidien de Paris. *Germany*: Blick durch die Wirtschaft, Frankfurter Allgemeine Zeitung, Frankfurter Rundschau, Generalanzeiger, Handelsblatt, Stuttgarter Zeitung. Süddeutsche Zeitung, Vereinigte Wirtschaftsdienste, Die Welt. *Irish Republic*: Cork Examiner, Irish Independent, Irish Press, Irish Times, Sunday Independent. *Italy*: Avanti, Corriere della Sera, Gazzetta del Mezzogiorno Il Giornale, Il Giorno, Il Messaggero, La Nazione, Paese Sera, Il Popolo, La Republica, Il Sole/24 ore, La Stampa, L'Unità, La Voce Repubblicana. *Luxembourg*: Journal, Luxemborger Wort, Tageblatt. *Netherlands*: Het Financieele Dagblad, N.R.C. Handelsblad, De Telegraaf. *United Kingdom*: Daily Express, Daily Mail, Daily Telegraph, Financial Times, Guardian, Times.

Niger

Niger was a signatory of the Yaoundé Conventions of 1963 and 1969 and of the Lomé Convention of 1975.

Nigeria

When the Association Convention with the French-speaking African states was concluded at Yaoundé on 20 July 1963, the member states of the E.E.C. declared their readiness to negotiate in a sympathetic spirit with any other country who so requested and whose economic structure and production was comparable with those of the Associated States. An agreement, which would have made Nigeria an associated member of the European Economic Community, was signed in Lagos in 1966. This agreement was never ratified, partly because of the Nigerian civil war, but Nigeria signed the Lomé Convention of 1975.

Nimexe
The nomenclature for the Foreign Trade Statistics of the E.E.C.

Nine
The Nine consist of the original Six E.E.C. members (Belgium, France, Federal German Republic, Italy, Luxembourg, the Netherlands) and the Three (Denmark, the Irish Republic and the United Kingdom).

non-tariff barriers
A substantial reduction in tariffs tends to bring into greater prominence other obstacles to trade, which can include Government purchasing policy, flag discrimination, arbitrary use of standards regulations, discriminatory use of anti-dumping regulations, irregular valuation rules for assessing customs duties.

Nordic Council
A Treaty was signed in Helsinki in 1953 between the Nordic countries, and came into force in 1962. According to the treaty the Nordic countries should further develop co-operation in the fields of legislation, of cultural, social, and economic policies and of transport and communications. Through the revised agreement of 1971, the Nordic Council of Ministers was established, and at the same time the procedures and rules of co-operation were changed.

The Nordic Council provides a means for joint discussions between the parliaments and governments of the Nordic countries on questions of co-operation between them. The Council is an advisory as well as controlling body and can make recommendations to the governments. The Council consists of seventy-eight elected members and of governmental representatives. The Danish Parliament elects sixteen members, the Finnish seventeen members, the Icelandic six members, the Norwegian and Swedish Parliaments each eighteen members. The Legislature of the Faeroe Islands elects two members and the County Council of Åland one member. In addition the governments appoint Ministers as their representatives, who take part as members but without the right to vote. The Executive of the Faeroe Islands and the County Board of Åland each appoints one representative among members. Normally, about forty-five Ministers participate in the annual plenary sessions of the Council, so that the total number of delegates is about 125.

The Nordic Council has at least one session annually. The Council's Presidium has a permanent secretariat in Stockholm which, assisted by the Council's national secretariats, attends to the current matters of the Council. The Council's five permanent committees, among which the elected members are distributed, meet several times between the sessions and prepare motions that have been proposed by members of the Council and by the governments. The Council's recommendations are to a large extent implemented by the governments and the parliaments.

Since 1975 the Nordic Council has had a special budget and control committee which takes part in yearly budget discussions with the Council of Ministers about joint Nordic allowances, and which at the same time has been given controlling functions on behalf of the Nordic Council *vis-à-vis* the governments.

The Council of Ministers is assisted in its work by a number of standing committees of civil servants, each of them responsible for a specific field. The Council of Ministers has two secretariats, one in Oslo and one in Copenhagen. The secretariat of the Council of Ministers situated in Oslo is divided into four sections. The co-ordinating section is in charge of , *inter alia*, legislation matters, planning, budgets and administration. The section for economic co-operation also deals with manufacturing industries and regional policies as well as with the building industry. A third section covers labour market policies, environmental questions and social policies. Finally there is a section for transport and communications, including consumer policies.

The secretariat of Nordic Cultural Co-operation in Copenhagen was set up in accordance with the Nordic Cultural Agreement which was signed in 1971 and enforced in 1972. The Cultural secretariat is the secretariat of the Council of Ministers as regards the co-operation fields of the cultural agreement, education, research, and other cultural activities. In principle, the secretariat has the same field of competence as the standing committee dealing with cultural matters in the Nordic Council.

The twenty-third session of the Nordic Council in Feb. 1975 in Reykjavik passed recommendations on co-ordinated efforts to establish and protect equal rights for men and women in the legislation of the Nordic countries, on a Nordic action programme for increased food production and on special cheap 'Nord-turist' tickets for youth to promote travelling within and between the Nordic countries.

In Nov. 1975 the first extraordinary session of the Nordic Council was held in Stockholm. Proposals were on the agenda from the Council of Ministers concerning a joint Nordic Investment Bank, a programme for co-ordinated Nordic labour market policy and the question of the right for Nordic citizens living in another Nordic country to participate in local elections in the country of residence.

Nordiska Radet
see Nordic Council

North Atlantic Treaty Organisation (Nato)
On 28 April 1948 the Canadian Secretary of State for External Affairs broached the idea of a 'security league' of the free nations, in extension of the Brussels Treaty of 17 March 1948. The United States Senate, on 11 June, recommended 'the association of the United States with such regional and other collective arrangements as are based on continuous self-help and mutual aid, and as affect its national security'. Detailed proposals were subsequently worked out between the Brussels Treaty powers, the United States of America and Canada.

On 4 April 1949 the Foreign Ministers of Belgium, Canada, Denmark, France, Iceland, Italy, Luxembourg, the Netherlands, Norway, Portugal, the United Kingdom and the United States of America met in Washington and signed a Treaty which came into force on 24 Aug. 1949. Greece and Turkey were admitted as parties to the Treaty in 1951 (effective Feb. 1952), the Federal German Republic in Oct. 1954 (effective 5 May 1955).

As reorganised by the Council at its session in Lisbon in Feb. 1952, the structure of Nato is as follows:

The Council, the principal body of the organisation, 'charged with the responsibility of considering all matters concerning the implementation of the provisions of the Treaty', incorporates the Council and the Defence Committee originally envisaged. The Council is a council of governments, on which Nato nations are normally represented by their Minister for Foreign Affairs and/or the Minister of Defence, or by other competent Ministers, especially those responsible for financial and economic affairs.

The Council normally meets at ministerial level two or three times a year.

Each member government appoints a Permanent Representative to represent it on the Council when its ministerial representatives are not present. Each Permanent Representative also heads a national delegation of advisers and experts. The Permanent Representatives meet once or twice a week and can be called together at short notice at any time.

In carrying out its role the Council is assisted by a number of committees, some of a permanent nature, some temporary. Like the Council, the membership of each committee is made up of national representatives. They study questions submitted to them by the Council for recommendation. The work of the committees has a direct bearing on the activities of the International Secretariat.

The Political Committee, charged with preparing the political agenda for the Council, dates from 1957, as does the Economic Committee which studies and reports to the Council on economic issues of special interest to the Alliance. In 1963 a Defence Planning Committee was established as the civilian co-ordinating body for the defence plans of member countries. Since France's withdrawal in 1966 from Nato military organisations, this Committee is composed of the Permanent Representatives of the eighteen countries which take part in Nato's integrated common defence. Like the Council, it also meets at ministerial level. At the Ministerial meeting in Dec. 1966 two bodies for nuclear planning were established: the Nuclear Defence Affairs Committee and a Nuclear Planning Group of seven to eight members.

Among other important Committees are: the Science Committee and the Infrastructure Committee, whose varied tasks are directly linked to fundamental and applied research; the Senior Civil Emergency Planning Committee; the Committee for European Airspace Co-ordination; the Committee for Pipelines; the Committee for Information and Cultural Relations; and the Civil and Military Budget Committees, who carefully supervise the expenditures of Nato funds for the maintenance of the International Secretariat and military headquarters. In Nov. 1969 the Council established a Committee on the Challenges of Modern Society to consider problems of the human environment. This new Committee examines methods of improving the exchange of views and experience among the Allied countries in the task of creating a better environment for their societies.

More recently the Armaments Committee has been replaced by the

Conference of National Armaments Directors.

Norway

Norway signed the Stockholm Convention (Efta) which came into force in 1960. A decision to join the E.E.C. was taken and the Treaty of Accession was signed but, as a result of a referendum, it was not ratified. Norway therefore continued her membership of Efta.

Economic profile: Area 323,900 sq. km. Population (1973) 3,960,000 (male (1972) 1,948,000) density 12 per sq. km. Births (per 1,000 of pop. 1973) 16·3; marriages, 7·3; deaths, 10. Infant mortality, 12·8.

Labour force (1972) 1,677,000; percentage in agriculture, 12·2; industry, 34·1; services, 53·6.

International trade (in millions of U.A.):

	1965	*1970*	*1973*
Imports	2,206	3,697	4,975
Exports	1,443	2,455	3,744

	per 1,000 of population
Standard of living:	
Motor vehicles (1973)	216
Televisions (1972)	229
Telephones (1972)	307

N.R.C.

see National Referendum Campaign.

nurses

Two draft Directives were submitted to the E.E.C. Council of Ministers for consideration, concerned with (i) 'the mutual recognition of diplomas, certificates and other evidence of the formal qualifications of nurses responsible for general care' and (ii) 'the co-ordination of provisions laid down by law, regulation or administrative action in respect of the activities of nurses responsible for general care'.

181

The draft Decisions propose the setting up of an Advisory Committee on Training in Nursing, and an amendment to the responsibilities of a Committee of Senior Officials on Public Health to cover the nursing profession as well as doctors.

Nurses to be covered by the Directives are those who, whether employed or self-employed, hold the qualifications necessary to practise in their own country. In the United Kingdom this means State Registered Nurses, or Registered General Nurses in Scotland, but exceptions can be made in certain cases where, though the certificates and other evidence of formal training do not satisfy all the minimum qualifying requirements before the implementation of the Directive, evidence is provided that the nurse has been responsible for general care for at least three years during the five years prior to the date of the issue of a certificate to this effect.

The proposals put great emphasis on proof of 'good character and good repute'. Where this is automatically included in national registration qualifications no further proof may be required; but if not, the host country will be entitled to ask for a 'judicial record', or equivalent document, as evidence to this effect.

Further, the country of origin may be obliged, in confidence, to provide the host state with information regarding disciplinary measures or criminal penalties imposed on the nurse in connection with professional duties and, where this is a condition of national qualifications in the host country, a certificate of physical or mental health.

It would be necessary, however, for a nurse from one country to register with the professional organisation of the host country if he/she were going to provide only a temporary service in that country, although he/she may be required to notify the professional organisation. A nurse taking up permanent residence would, of course, be expected to register with the professional organisation. Whether temporary or resident the nurse would be subject to the same rights and obligations as nurses in the host country.

Nurses wishing to work in another country would be expected to acquire the linguistic knowledge necessary for the exercise of their profession.

Provided all these conditions are met and the Council approves, nurses will be able to practise anywhere in the Community.

N.V.
Naamloze vennootscap, company with limited liability in the Netherlands.

O

objectives, E.E.C.
(i) To establish the basis for a closer union among the European nations.
(ii) To further the economic and social progress of the member countries by jointly eliminating the barriers dividing them.
(iii) To further the improvement of working and living conditions within the Community.
(iv) To act together to promote steady expansion, balanced trade and fair competition.
(v) To strengthen the unity of member countries' economics, by bringing the various regions into line with each other, and assisting developing areas.
(vi) To abolish restrictions on international trade by means of a common commercial policy.
(vii) To strengthen the bonds between Europe and countries overseas.
(viii) To combine resources to promote peace and freedom.
 A wide series of measures to achieve these objectives were drawn up, the major areas being:
(i) The elimination of customs duties and trade restrictions between member countries.
(ii) The establishment of a uniform external customs tariff and a common commercial policy towards non-member countries.
(iii) The removal of restrictions on the freedom of movement of labour, capital and services.
(iv) The establishment of a common transport policy.
(v) The establishment of a common agricultural policy.
(vi) The setting up of a system to prevent distortion of competition within the Community.
(vii) The co-ordination of member countries' economic policies.
(viii) The modification of national laws to bring them into line with each other, in cases where such laws have an effect on the establishment or functioning of the Common Market.
(ix) The establishment of a European Social Fund to improve employment possibilities for workers and to help raise the standard of living.
(x) The creation of a European Investment Bank to further economic

expansion within the Community.

(xi) The association of non-member countries with the Community in order to expand trade and assist economic and social development, both within the Community and abroad.

O.C.D.E.

Organisation de coopération et de développement économiques, Organisation for Economic Co-operation and Development.

Ockrent Report

The Ockrent Report was the E.E.C.'s statement on the establishment of a Free Trade Area running parallel with the E.E.C. The plan for a Free Trade Area of the Six and the Seven non-member countries was worked out in London during 1956, and a decision to open discussion was taken in 1957. In Oct. 1957 O.E.E.C., including France, approved the principle of a Free Trade Area. On 17 Oct. 1957 the Council of O.E.E.C. passed a resolution in which it declared its determination to secure the establishment of a European Free Trade Area which, taking into consideration the objectives of the European Economic Community, would take effect parallel with the Treaty of Rome. To this resolution France subscribed.

The Federal German Republic wanted a Free Trade Area, as did the Netherlands and, to a lesser extent, Belgium. The German Foreign Ministry had certain reservations because it did not want to upset its new relationships with France. Italy was somewhere half way between the two. France paid lip service to the O.E.E.C. Plan.

The French pinned their faith on the problem of 'origin' as the most plausible grounds on which to oppose a Free Trade Area, on the pretext that the privileges enjoyed within the Commonwealth would distort conditions of competition for the Common Market and make it difficult to prevent many Commonwealth products which enjoy duty free entry into the United Kingdom from getting into Europe by the back door. For over a year the French delegation raised one technical objection after another to the system which was emerging from the negotiations and which is now successfully used in Efta.

Challenged on this, the Community produced the Ockrent Report which, while reaffirming that the E.E.C. was determined to arrive at an agreement for a Free Trade Area associated with the Community on a multilateral basis, nevertheless reiterated many of the supposed difficulties. France then fell back upon her second line of defence by raising every conceivable obstruction on the step-by-step examination of the difficulties as they emerged.

At the end of 1958 the French Government abruptly denounced the whole plan and the negotiations were immediately broken off.

O.C.T.

Overseas Countries and Territories of member states of the E.E.C. associated under Part IV of the Treaty of Rome.

O.D.A.

The Overseas Development Administration is a department of the United Kingdom's Foreign and Commonwealth Office.

O.E.C.D.

see Organisation for Economic Co-operation and Development, *formerly* O.E.E.C.

O.E.C.E.

Organisation européenne de coopération économique, Organisation for European Economic Co-operation.

O.E.C.Q.

Organisation européenne pour le contrôle de la qualité, European Organisation for Quality Control.

O.E.E.C.
see Organisation for European Economic Co-operation, *now* O.E.C.D.

O.E.R.S.
Organisation européenne de recherches spatiales, European Space Research Organisation.

oil
see energy policy

O.J.E.C.
Official Journal of the European Communities.

O.R.E.
Organisation régionale européenne de la Conféderation internationale des syndicats libres, European Regional Organisation of the International Confederation of Free Trade Unions.

Orgalime
Organisme de liaison des industries métaliques européenes, Liaison body for the European engineering and metal industries.

Organisation for Economic Co-operation and Development (O.E.C.D.)
On 30 Sept. 1961 the Organisation for European Economic Co-operation (O.E.E.C.), after a history of 14 years, was replaced by the Organisation for Economic Co-operation and Development. The change of title marks the Organisation's altered status and functions: with the accession of Canada and U.S.A. as full members it ceased to be purely a European body; while at the same time it added development aid to the list of its other activities. The member countries are now Australia, Austria, Belgium, Canada, Denmark, Finland, France, Federal German Republic, Greece, Iceland, Irish Republic, Italy, Japan, Luxembourg, the Netherlands, New Zealand,

Norway, Portugal, Spain, Sweden, Switzerland, Turkey, the United Kingdom and the United States of America. Yugoslavia participates in certain of the Organisation's activities with a special status.

The aims of the reconstituted Organisation, as defined in the convention signed on 14 Dec. 1960, are as follows: (*a*) to achieve the highest sustainable economic growth and employment and a rising standard of living in member countries, while maintaining financial stability, and thus to contribute to the development of the world economy; (*b*) to contribute to sound economic expansion in member as well as non-member countries in the process of economic development; and (*c*) to contribute to the expansion of world trade on a multilateral, non-discriminatory basis in accordance with international obligations. Responsibility for the achievement of these aims has been vested in the numerous committees, notably the Economic Policy Committee, the Development Aid Committee and the Trade Committee. The second of these is made up of representatives of all the seventeen principal capital-exporting member countries, together with the Commission of the European Communities. Other committees and working parties deal with economic and development review; the environment; technical co-operation; balance of payments problems; monetary and foreign exchange matters; payments; invisible transactions; insurance; fiscal matters; agriculture; fisheries; education; science policy; manpower and social affairs; energy, consumer policy, industry, oil, tourism, maritime transport, etc.

The European Nuclear Energy Agency (E.N.E.A.) founded in 1957 became the O.E.C.D. Nuclear Energy (N.E.A.) in 1972.

An O.E.C.D. Development Centre began work in 1963. In 1968 a Centre for Educational Research and Innovation was established.

Organisation for European Economic Co-operation (O.E.E.C.)
On 5 June 1947, the U.S. Secretary of State, George Marshall, made a speech at Harvard University in which he outlined the seriousness of the shortage of dollars for the economic situation of Europe. He suggested American assistance in its economic recovery, on the understanding that the European countries reached some agreement about their requirements and the part they themselves would take in giving proper effect to the action of the United States.

An exploratory conference of the foreign ministers of the United

Kingdom, France and the U.S.S.R. was held in Paris from 27 June to 3 July 1947, when it broke down as M. Molotov maintained that an overall economic programme for Europe would infringe on national sovereignty and interfere with existing economic arrangements. Thereupon the United Kingdom and France invited all the European countries (with the exception of Spain) which desired to participate in a programme on the lines suggested in Mr. Marshall's speech. The invitation, issued on 4 July, was accepted by Austria, Belgium, Denmark, Greece, Iceland, the Irish Republic, Italy, Luxembourg, the Netherlands, Norway, Portugal, Sweden, Switzerland and Turkey; it was declined by Bulgaria, Czechoslovakia, Finland, Hungary, Poland, Romania and Yugoslavia.

The conference of the sixteen nations willing to work the Marshall plan began in Paris on 12 July and set up the Committee of European Economic Co-operation (C.E.E.C.). On 22 Sept. the sixteen countries signed a report formulating an economic recovery programme which aimed at restoring European economy by the end of 1951.

A second report of the Secretary-General of the Committee of European Economic Co-operation, issued on 15 March 1948, demonstrated the need for a permanent co-ordinating body. For this purpose the sixteen nations and the Anglo-American and French occupation zones of Germany signed a convention for European economic co-operation in Paris on 16 April 1948. From 31 Oct 1949 Germany was represented in O.E.E.C. by the government of the Federal Republic. On 2 June 1950, Canada and the United States accepted the invitation to associate themselves with the work of the Organisation relating to the study of economic problems of common interest to, and affecting the immediate future of, the countries of Western Europe and North America.

Part I of the Convention dealt with the general obligations which the sixteen countries and the Anglo-American and French occupation zones of Germany had undertaken towards each other in the field of economic co-operation.

Part II contained the constitution of the permanent Organisation.

The Organisation made decisions for implementation by its members; it entered into agreements with its members, non-member countries, the United States Government and international organisations; and it made recommendations to the United States Government and other governments.

Decisions of the Organisation were taken by mutual agreement of all

188

members (unless otherwise decided) and the abstention of any one of them declaring himself not to be interested in any subject under discussion did not invalidate decisions.

The machinery of the Organisation consisted of:

(i) a Council, on which all the members were represented and which was responsible for all policy decisions;

(ii) an Executive Committee of seven members designated annually by the Council, to which the Committee was responsible. Any member state not represented on the Council took part in its work on any subject of particular interest to it;

(iii) the Secretariat, which was selected by the secretary-general who, in turn, was appointed by the Council. The secretariat personnel had international status, owing allegiance to the Organisation and not to individual governments;

(iv) a number of *ad hoc* committees.

The Organisation established relations with the United Nations, its principal organs and specialised agencies, and it also maintained relations with other international bodies.

The functions of the O.E.E.C. when it was set up in 1947 were essentially twofold: on the one hand to develop economic co-operation between member countries, and on the other to assist the United States government in carrying out its programme of aid to Europe. The first of these functions came to an end in June 1952, with the completion of the 'Marshall Plan'. In 1948 the main emphasis was on the increase of production, in 1949 on internal financial stability, in 1950 on European co-operation in the liberalisation of trade and payments, in 1951 on dealing with the raw material shortages, and in 1952 on the serious balance-of-payments positions of France and the United Kingdom and the continuing deficits of most European countries with the dollar area. The dollar position of most member countries improved considerably in 1953, and the Organisation was thus able to study further measures towards the re-establishment of currency convertibility and trade liberalisation.

The main activities of O.E.E.C. could be summarised as follows:

As from 1 July 1950 the European Payments Union (E.P.U.) superseded the previous Intra-European Payments Agreements. It provided an automatic multilateral system for offsetting monthly surpluses and deficits of each member country with all other members and the determination of a resulting single balance owed to or by the Union; the automatic granting of credits, coupled with gold and dollar payments which increased when the country's indebtedness rose, facilitated the overbridging of short-run fluctuations in the balance of payments; the position of each country included that of its monetary area, *e.g.* in the case of the United Kingdom, the net position determined each month was that of the whole of the sterling area *vis-à-vis* all other member countries.

In addition to this mechanism the Union provided, through its Managing Board, for guidance and consultation between member countries concerning their commercial, monetary and fiscal policies.

The Organisation of European Economic Co-operation was replaced by the Organisation for Economic Co-operation and Development (O.E.C.D.) in 1961.

Ortoli, François-Xavier
Born Ajaccio, Corsica, 1925. Inspector of Finances, 1948—51; Government adviser, 1951—4. Secretary-General of the Franco-Italian Committee of the E.E.C., 1955. Director-General of Internal Market Division of the E.E.C., 1958. Secretary-General, Inter-Ministerial Committee for Questions of European Economic Co-operation from 1961. President of the Commission of European Communities, 1972—6. Vice-President of the Commission of the European Commmittee 1977— .

O.T.C.
Organisation for Trade Co-operation of Gatt.

P

Pakistan
Pakistan signed a five-year commercial co-operation agreement which came into force on 1 July 1976.

Papua New Guinea
Papua New Guinea became a member of the Lomé Convention in 1977.

Paris Club
An informal group of representatives of European countries which meets *ad hoc* in Paris to discuss common problems of financial relations with Latin American countries, including the co-ordination, where appropriate, of balance of payments assistance to them. The press also sometimes describe the I.M.F. Borrowing Scheme as the Paris Club.

Paris, Treaty of
The draft Treaty creating the European Coal and Steel Community was initialled in Paris on 19 March 1951. A summary is as follows:
Preamble
'The President of the German Federal Republic, H.R.H. the Prince Royal of Belgium, the President of the French Republic, the President of the Italian Republic, H.R.H. the Grand Duchess of Luxembourg, and H.M. the Queen of the Netherlands;

'Considering that world peace may be safeguarded only by creative efforts equal to the dangers which menace it;

'Convinced that the contribution which an organised and vital Europe can bring to civilisation is indispensable to the maintenance of peaceful relations;

'Conscious of the fact that Europe can be built only by concrete actions which create a real solidarity and by the establishment of common bases for economic development;

'Desirous of assisting through the expansion of their basic production in raising the standard of living and in furthering the works of peace;

'Resolved to substitute for historic rivalries a fusion of their essential interests; to establish, by creating an economic community, the foundation of a broad and independent community among peoples long divided by bloody conflicts; and to lay the bases of institutions capable of giving direction to their future common destiny;

'Have decided to create a European Coal and Steel Community and . . . have designated . . . plenipotentiaries . . . and have agreed to the following provisions';

Paris, Treaty of

The European Coal and Steel Community
Article 1 'By the present Treaty the High Contracting Parties institute among themselves a European Coal and Steel Community, based on a common market, common objectives, and common institutions.
Article 2 'The mission of the European Coal and Steel Community is to contribute to economic expansion, the development of employment and the improvement of the standard of living in the participating countries through the institution, in harmony with the general economy of the member states, of a common market as defined in Article 4.

'The Community must progressively establish conditions which will in themselves assure the most rational distribution of production at the highest possible level of productivity, while safeguarding the continuity of employment and avoiding the creating of fundamental and persistent disturbances in the economies of the member states.'
Article 3 Within the framework of their respective powers and responsibilities, the institutions of the Community should: '(i) see that the common market is regularly supplied, taking account of the needs of third countries; (ii) assure to all consumers in comparable positions within the common market equal access to the sources of production; (iii) seek the establishment of the lowest prices which are possible without requiring any corresponding rise either in the prices charged by the same enterprises in other transactions or in the price-level as a whole in another period, while at the same time permitting necessary amortisation and providing normal possibilities of remuneration for capital invested; (iv) see that conditions are maintained which will encourage enterprises to expand and improve their ability to produce and to promote a policy of rational development of natural resources, avoiding inconsiderate exhaustion of such resources; (v) promote the improvement of the living and working conditions of the labour force in each of the industries under its jurisdiction so as to make possible the equalisation of such conditions in an upward direction; (vi) further the development of international trade and see that equitable limits are observed in prices charged on external markets; (vii) promote the regular expansion and the modernisation of production, as well as the improvement of its quality, under conditions which preclude any protection against competing industries, except where justified by illegitimate action on the part of such industries or in their favour.'
Article 4 The following were recognised to be incompatible with the common market for coal and steel, and were therefore 'abolished and

192

prohibited' within the Community: (i) import and export duties, or charges with an equivalent effect, and quantitative restrictions on the movement of coal and steel; (ii) measures or practices discriminating among producers, buyers, or consumers, specifically as concerned prices, delivery terms and transportation rates, as well as measures or practices which hampered the buyer in the free choice of his supplier; (iii) subsidies or state assitance, or special charges imposed by the state, in any form whatsoever; (iv) restrictive practices tending towards the division of markets or the exploitation of the consumer.

Article 5 The Community would accomplish its mission with 'limited direct intervention', and to this end it would: 'enlighten and facilitate the action of the interested parties' by collecting information, organising consultations, and defining general objectives; place financial means at the disposal of enterprises for their investments and participate in the expenses of re-adaptation; assure the establishment, maintenance, and observance of normal conditions of competition, and take direct action with respect to production and the operation of the market only when circumstances made it absolutely necessary, publish the justifications for its action and take the necessary measures to ensure observance of the rules set forth in the Treaty. The institutions of the Community should carry out these activities with 'as little administrative machinery as possible' and in close co-operation with the interested parties.

Article 6 Provided that the Community should have 'juridical personality' and that it should enjoy, in its international relationships, 'the juridical capacity necessary to the exercise of its functions and the attainment of its ends'.

Economic and Social Provisions

General Provisions (Articles 46–8) The High Authority might at any time consult the governments, the various interested parties (enterprises, workers, consumers and dealers) and their associations, as well as any experts, and should by these means

(i) carry on a permanent study of markets and price tendencies;

(ii) periodically draw up non-compulsory programme forecasts dealing with production, consumption, exports, and imports;

(iii) periodically work out general programmes with respect to modernisation, the long-term orientation of manufacturing and the expansion of productive capacity;

(iv) at the request of the interested Governments, participate in the study of the possibilities of re-employment, either in existing industries or through the creation of new activities, of workers set free by the evolution of the market or by technical transformations;

(v) gather all information necessary to the appraisal of the possibilities of improving the living and working conditions of the labour force in the industries under its jurisdiction, and of the risks which menaced such living conditions.

The High Authority would not divulge information which by its nature was considered a professional secret, and in particular information pertaining to the commercial relations or the breakdown of the costs of production of enterprises. With this reservation, it should publish such data as might be useful to governments or to any other interested parties. The High Authority might impose fines and daily penalty payments upon those enterprises which evaded their obligations resulting from decisions made in application of these provisions, or which knowingly furnished false information.

The right of enterprises to form associations was not affected by the Treaty, but membership of such associations must be voluntary; these associations could engage in any activity which was not contrary to the provisions of the Treaty or to the decisions or recommendations of the High Authority.

Financial Provisions (Articles 49–53) The High Authority was empowered to procure the funds necessary to the accomplishment of its mission (i) by placing levies on the production of coal and steel and (ii) by borrowing, whilst it might also receive grants. The levies were intended to cover administrative expenses, the non-reimbursable assistance provided for re-adaptation, and expenditures to encourage technical and economic research, but the funds obtained by borrowing might be used by the High Authority only to grant loans. The levies would be assessed annually on the various products according to their average value, but the rate of levy might not exceed 1 % unless previously authorised by a two-thirds majority of the Council.

Investment and Financial Assistance (Articles 54–6) The High Authority might facilitate the carrying out of investment programmes by granting loans to enterprises, or by giving its guarantee to loans which they might obtain elsewhere. With the concurrence of the Council acting by unanimous vote, the High Authority might assist by the same means in financing works and installations which contributed directly and principally to increase production, lower production costs, or facilitate marketing of products subject to its jurisdiction. In order to encourage co-ordinated development of investments, however, the High Authority might require enterprises to submit individual programmes in advance.

If the High Authority found that the financing of a programme or the operation of the installations which it entailed would require subsidies, assistance, protection, or discrimination contrary to the Treaty, it could prohibit the enterprise concerned from applying to resources other than its own funds to put such programme into effect.

The High Authority would encourage technical and economic research concerning the production and the development of consumption of coal and steel, as well as labour safety in these industries, and to this end would establish appropriate contacts among existing research organisations. After consultation with the Consultative Committee, the High Authority might initiate and facilitate the development of such research work either by encouraging joint financing by the interested enterprises, or by earmarking for that purpose any grants it might receive.

If the introduction of technical processes or new equipment within the framework of the general programmes of the High Authority should lead to an exceptional reduction in labour requirements in the coal and steel industries, creating special difficulties in one or more areas for the re-employment of the workers released, the High Authority, on the request of the interested governments, (i) would consult the Consultative Com-mittee; (ii) might facilitate the financing of such programmes as it might approve for the creation, either in the industries subject to its jurisdiction or, with the concurrence of the Council, in any other industry, of 'new and economically sound' activities capable of assuring productive employment to the workers thus released; and (iii) would grant non-reimbursable assistance to contribute to: (*a*) the payment of grants to workers to tide them over until they could obtain new employment, (*b*) the granting of allowances to the workers for reinstallation expenses, (*c*) the financing of technical training for workers who were led to change their employment. The High Authority would grant non-reimbursable assistance, however, only on condition that the interested state paid a special contribution at least equal to such assistance, unless a two-thirds majority of the Council authorised an exception to this rule.

Production (Articles 57–9)   In the field of production the High Authority would give preference to the indirect means of action at its disposal (such as co-operation with governments) to regularise or influence general consumption, particularly that of the public services, or intervention on prices and commercial policy as provided for in the Treaty.

In case of decline in demand and if the High Authority deemed that the Community was faced with a 'period of manifest crisis' and that the action provided for above was not sufficient to cope with the situation, it should, with the concurrence of the Council, establish a system of production quotas on an equitable basis. It might, in particular, regulate the rate of operation of enterprises by appropriate levies on tonnages exceeding a reference level defined by a general decision, the amounts thus obtained being earmarked for the support of those enterprises whose production rate had dropped below the level envisaged, especially with a view to ensuring for them, as far as possible, the maintenance of employment.

The system of quotas would be terminated automatically on a proposal made to the Council by the High Authority after consultation with the Consultative Committee, or by the government of one of the member states, except in the case of a contrary decision of the Council; such a decision must be taken by unanimous vote if the proposal originated with the High Authority, or by simple majority if it originated with a government. The High Authority might impose upon enterprises violating the decisions taken by it in application of the present articles, fines not to exceed the sum equal to the value of the irregular production.

Prices (Articles 60–4) Pricing practices contrary to the provisions of Articles 2–4 were prohibited, particularly (i) unfair competitive practices (especially purely temporary or purely local reductions the purpose of which was to acquire a monopoly position within the Common Market) and (ii) 'discriminatory practices involving the application by a seller within the single market of unequal conditions to comparable transactions especially according to the nationality of the buyer'. For the above purposes:

(i) The price scales and conditions of sales to be applied by enterprises within the single market would be made public to the extent and in the form prescribed by the High Authority after consultation with the Consultative Committee; if the High Authority considered that an enterprise had chosen an abnormal base point for its price quotations, in particular one which made it possible to evade the provisions listed in (ii) below, it would make the appropriate recommendations to that enterprise;

(ii) The prices charged by an enterprise within the Common Market, calculated on the base of the point chosen for the enterprise's price scale, must not, as a result of the methods of quotation, (*a*) be higher than the price indicated by the price scale in question for a comparable transaction, or (*b*) be less than this price by a margin greater than either the margin which would make it possible to align the offer in question on that price scale, set up on the basis of another point, which procured for the buyer the lowest price at the place of delivery, or a limit fixed by the High Authority for each category of products, taking into account the origin and destination of such products.

The High Authority might also fix for one or more products subject to its jurisdiction, maximum and minimum prices within the Common Market, and maximum or minimum export prices. If the High Authority considered that such an action was appropriate 'in order to prevent the price of coal from being established at the level of the production costs of the most costly mine whose production was temporarily required to assure the accomplishment of the aims of Article 3', it might authorise compensations (i) among enterprises of the same coal basin to which the same price scales were applicable; and (ii) after consulting the Council, among enterprises situated in different coal basins.

Agreements and Concentrations (Articles 65–6)   All agreements among enterprises, all decisions of associations of enterprises, and all concerted practices which would tend, directly or indirectly, to prevent, restrict, or impede the normal operation of competition within the Common Market, were forbidden, especially those intended (i) to fix or influence prices; (ii) to restrict or control production, technical development, or investments; and (iii) to allocate markets, products, customers, or sources of supply.

Impairment of the Conditions Competition (Article 67)   Any action of a member state which might have noticeable repercussions on the conditions of competition in the coal and steel industries would be brought by the interested government to the attention of the High Authority. If such an action was liable to provoke a serious disequilibrium by increasing the differentials in costs of production otherwise than through variations in productivity, the High Authority, after consulting the Consultative Committee and the Council, might take the following measures:
(i) If the action of the state concerned produced harmful effects for coal or steel enterprises coming under its jurisdiction, the High Authority might authorise that state to grant to such enterprises assistance, the amount,

conditions, and duration of which would be determined in agreement with the High Authority;

(ii) If the action of that state produced harmful effects for coal or steel enterprises subject to the jurisdiction of other member states, the High Authority might address a recommendation to the state in question 'with a view to remedying such effects by such measures as that state may deem most compatible with its own economic equilibrium'.

Wages and Movement of Labour (Articles 68–9)   The methods of fixing wages and social benefits in force in the various member states should not, as regards the coal and steel industries, be affected by the application of the Treaty, subject to the following provisions:

(i) If the High Authority found that abnormally low prices practised by one or several enterprises were the result of wages fixed by those enterprises at an abnormally low level in comparison with the actual wage level in the same region, it should make the necessary recommendations to the interested enterprises after consulting the Consultative Committee:

(ii) If the High Authority found that a lowering of wages was leading to a drop in the standard of living of the labour force, and at the same time was being used as a means of permanent economic adjustment by enterprises or as a weapon of competition among enterprises, it should address to the enterprise or government concerned a recommendation intended to assure the labour force of compensatory benefits to be paid for by the enterprise in question. This provision should not apply, however, to (*a*) overall measures taken by a member state to re-establish its external equilibrium; (*b*) wage decreases resulting from the application of the sliding scale legally or contractually established; (*c*) wage decreases brought about by a decrease in the cost of living; (*d*) wage decreases to correct abnormal increases previously granted under exceptional circumstances no longer in existence.

If an enterprise failed to conform to a recommendation made to it in the above connection, the High Authority might impose on it fines and daily penalty payments not exceeding twice the amount of the savings in labour costs unjustifiably effected.

The member states further agreed to prohibit any discrimination in remuneration and working conditions between national workers and immigrant workers (without prejudice to special measures concerning frontier workers) and would work out among themselves any necessary arrangements so that social security measures did not stand in the way of the movement of labour.

Transport (Article 70) It was recognised that the establishment of the E.C.S.C. required the application of such transport rates for coal and steel as would 'make possible comparable price conditions to consumers in comparable positions'. Discriminations in transport rates, and conditions of any kind based on the country of origin or of destination of the products in question, were strictly forbidden for traffic among member states, whilst the application of special internal tariff measures in the interest of one or several coal- or steel-producing enterprises would be subject to the prior agreement of the High Authority.

Commercial Policy (Articles 71–5) Unless otherwise stipulated in the Treaty, the competence of the governments of the member states with respect to commercial policy would not be affected by the Treaty.

Minimum rates, below which the member states were bound not to lower their customs duties on coal and steel with regard to third countries, and maximum rates, above which they were bound not to raise such duties, might be fixed by unanimous decisions of the Council upon the proposal of the High Authority; between the limits thus fixed, each government could set its own tariffs according to its national procedure.

The administration of import and export licensing in relations with third Powers should be the responsibility of the government on whose territory was located the point of origin for exports, or the point of destination for imports, but the High Authority would be empowered to supervise the administration and control of such licensing where coal and steel were concerned.

The remaining clauses of the Treaty (Articles 76–100) provided, *inter alia*, that the Community should enjoy on the territory of the member states the privileges and immunities necessary to the exercise of its functions; that the seat of the institutions of the Community should be fixed by common agreement; and that the fiscal year of the Community should extend from 1 July to 30 June. The Treaty would apply to the European territories of the member states, but each bound itself to extend to the other member states the preferential measures which it enjoyed with respect to coal and steel in the non-European territories under its jurisdiction. It was expressly stated that the establishment of the Community in no way prejudiced the régime of ownership of the enterprises subject to the provisions of the Treaty (Articles 76–85).

The member states bound themselves to take all general and specific measures which would assure the execution of their obligations under the decisions and recommendations of the institutions of the Community, and to facilitate the accomplishment of the Community's purposes. They bound themselves to refrain from any measures compatible with the existence of the E.C.S.C., and agreed, to the extent of their competence, to take all appropriate measures to assure the international payments arising out of trade in coal and steel within the E.C.S.C., and to lend assistance to each other to facilitate such payments (Article 86).

The signatories also agreed 'not to avail themselves of any treaties, conventions, or agreements existing among them to submit any difference arising out of the interpretation or application of the present Treaty to a method of settlement other than those provided for therein' (Article 87).

Following the expiration of the transition period, amendments might be proposed by member states or by the High Authority; the Council, on a two-thirds majority vote, could then approve the calling of a conference of government representatives of the member states to consider such amendments (Article 96).

The Treaty would run for a period of fifty years from the date of its entry into force (Article 97) and other European States might accede to it by a unanimous vote of the Council (Article 98).

The Treaty would be ratified by all the member states (instruments of ratification being deposited with the French Government) and would enter into force on the date of deposit of the last instrument of ratification. If all the instruments of ratification had not been deposited six months after the signing of the Treaty, the governments of the states which had ratified would consult among themselves on the measures to be taken (Article 99).

Parliament, direct election to European

At the European Council meeting held in Brussels in July 1976 it was agreed that from 1978 the European Parliament would have a membership of 410. At their meeting in Sept. 1976 it was agreed that direct elections should be held, if possible in May or June of 1978. The national distribution of seats would be as follows:

	seats	% of seats
Belgium	24	5·85
Denmark	16	3·90
France	81	19·76
Federal German Republic	81	19·76
Irish Republic	15	3·66
Italy	81	19·76
Luxembourg	6	1·46
Netherlands	25	6·10
United Kingdom	81	19·76

Parliament, European

The European Parliament, referred to in the Treaties as the Assembly, consisted, in 1976, of 198 members nominated by the nine national Parliaments: thirty-six members each for France, the Federal German Republic, Italy and the United Kingdom, fourteen each for Belgium and the Netherlands, ten each for Denmark and the Irish Republic and six for Luxembourg. The Treaties, however, provide for the eventual direct election of the Parliament's members by universal suffrage; a draft Convention on the procedure for such elections was passed by the Parliament in 1960 but has not been acted upon by the Council. The Parliament is at present working on new proposals which will take account of the Community's enlargement in 1973.

Under the Treaties, the Council of Ministers is obliged to consult the Parliament on a wide range of legislative matters. Under its own rules the Parliament is also able to hold debates on whatever subjects it chooses, whether these are covered by the Treaties or not. The Parliament's twelve Standing Committes, Political, Legal, Economic and Monetary, Budgets, Social and Employment, Agriculture, Regional and Transport, Public Health and Environment, Energy and Technology, Cultural Affairs and Youth. External Economic Relations, and Development and Co-operation, work closely with the Commission in scrutinising and amending Community legislation. The Parliament has formal power to elicit information on policy from the Commission by written or oral questions, and has also acquired the informal power to question the Council of

Ministers. The Parliament can dismiss the Commission on a motion of censure approved by a two-thirds majority, but has as yet no power of appointment.

At present the Parliament exercises full budgetary control only over non-mandatory expenditure, *i.e.* expenditure not arising directly from the Treaties. Effectively this means control only over the administrative budget, about 3–4 % of the total. If the Community itself develops into the 'ever closer union of the peoples of Europe' that its founders envisaged, then greater powers for the Parliament, and its direct election, will be essential.

The members of the Parliament sit not in national delegations but in party groups, which together control the Parliament's business: arrangements for debates, appointment of *rapporteurs* to investigate Community legislation, etc.

Parliament, strength of political grouping in European

In April 1976, in the 198-seat European Parliament the membership of the various political groups was:

Socialists	66
Christian Democrats	51
Liberals	26
European Conservatives	17
European Progressive Democrats	17
Communists	15
Independent	6

passports
At the meeting of Heads of Government in Rome in Dec. 1975 agreement was reached on the introduction of a uniform passport for 1978. The colour will be deep lilac.

patents
The European Convention will achieve four objectives: (i) establish one set of patent procedures; (ii) enable patents to be granted from one central office; (iii) establish a common protection period of twenty years,

compared with the United Kingdom's protection of sixteen years, and (iv) give more geographic protection for a lower unit cost.

At the conclusion of a conference which had opened on 1·7 Nov. 1975, a Community Patent Convention was signed in Luxembourg on 15 Dec. by the member states of the European Community, providing for the harmonisation of the patent laws of the Nine with a view to creating a unitary corpus of patent law throughout the Community. Austria, Norway, Sweden, Switzerland and the Efta secretariat were represented at the conference as observers. The effect of this instrument established the E.E.C. as a uniform bloc within the framework of the broader European Patent Convention, officially the 'Convention on the Grant of European Patents' signed in Oct. 1973. Under the latter convention, twenty-year 'European patents' valid in all acceding states, but in most aspects subject to the patent laws of each state, would be obtainable from a European Patent Office in Munich.

The Community Patent Convention enters into force after ratification by all nine member states, while the European Patent Convention was expected to become effective at the end of 1976 for those states which had ratified it by that date. Of the twenty-one countries which had participated in the preparatory stages of the European Patent Convention, sixteen had completed ratification procedures by the end of 1975, namely, the nine Community member states, Austria, Greece, Liechtenstein, Monaco, Norway, Sweden and Switzerland.

P.C.I.J.
Permanent Court of International Justice.

political groups, strength within the European Parliament.
see Parliament, strength of political grouping in European

political union
Although political union was explicit in the Treaty of Rome little progress had been made by 1977.

Pompidou, Georges Jean Raymond
Born France, 1911, died 1974. Prime Minister of France, 1962–8. President
of France, 1969–74. Although a follower and close collaborator of
President de Gaulle, he reversed the veto on British membership of E.E.C.

population (1974)

country	total inhabitants	% women
Belgium	9,800,000	51·0
Denmark	5,000,000	50·4
France	52,500,000	51·0
Federal German Republic	62,100,000	52·1
Irish Republic	3,100,000	49·8
Italy	55,400,000	51·0
Luxembourg	360,000	50·4
Netherlands	13,500,000	50·2
United Kingdom	56,100,000	51·3
Total E.E.C.	257,800,000	

	% 0–14 years	% 15–64 years	% 65+ years
Belgium	22·6	63·6	13·8
Denmark	22·7	64·2	13·1
France	24·2	62·5	13·3
Federal German Republic			
Irish Republic	31·1	57·7	11·1
Italy	24·2	63·8	12·0
Luxembourg	20·2	66·8	13·0
Netherlands	25·6	63·7	10·7
United Kingdom	23·6	62·6	13·8

population, working (1973)

	Total population	Civil labour force
Belgium	9·7	3·8
Denmark	5·0	2·4
France	52·1	20·9
German Federal Republic	62·0	26·2
Irish Republic	3·0	1·1
Italy	54·9	18·3
Luxembourg	0·4	0·1
Netherlands	13·4	4·6
United Kingdom	56·0	24·6

Portugal

Portugal was a signatory of the Stockholm Convention (Efta) which came into force in 1960. In March 1977 Portugal lodged a formal application for membership of the E.E.C.

Economic profile: Area 92,100 sq. km. Population (1972) 8,590,000 (male (1970) 4,089,000) density 93 per sq. km. Births (per 1,000 of pop. 1973) 21.3; marriages, 9.4; deaths, 11.1. Infant mortality, 49.8.

Labour force (1972) 3,476,000; percentage in agriculture, 29.9; industry, 33.2; services, 36.9.

International trade (in millions of U.A.):

	1965	1970	1973
Imports	896	1,556	2,294
Exports	569	946	1,402

	per 1,000 of population
Standard of living:	
Motor vehicles (1973)	67
Televisions (1972)	49
Telephones (1972)	92

preference
A favour granted to the trade of a country or group of countries. This may be in terms of preferential tariff treatment or other charges, or other trade rules or formalities, *e.g.* import or export licensing.

prélevement
see levy

Presidents
of the High Authority of the European Coal and Steel Community

1952	Jean Monnet
1955	René Mayer
1958	Paul Finet
1959	Piero Malvestiti
1963	Dino Del Bo

of the Commission of the European Economic Community

1958	Walter Hallstein

of the Commission of the European Atomic Energy Community

1958	Louis Armand
1959	Etienne Hirsch
1962	Pierre Chatenet

The Institutions of the three Communities were merged on 1 July 1967.
of the Commission of the European Communities

1967	Jean Rey
1970	Franco-**Maria M**alfatti
1972	Sicco Mansholt
1973	François Xavier Ortoli
1977	Roy Harris Jenkins

Press Agencies, European Alliance of
The alliance was founded in 1957 and has a membership (1976) of twenty-three countries with headquarters in Brussels, Belgium.

primary product
Generally interpreted as any product of farm, forest or fishery, or any mineral, in its natural form or which has undergone such processing as is customarily required to prepare it for marketing in substantial volume in international trade.

Principles of the Treaty of Rome (Articles 1–8)
The High Contracting Parties would establish among themselves a European Economic Community.

The aim of the Community, by establishing a Common Market and progressively approximating the economic policies of member states, is to promote throughout the Community a harmonious development of economic activities, a continuous and balanced expansion, an increased stability, an accelerated raising of the standard of living and closer relations between its member states.

The activities of the Community shall include, under the conditions and with the timing provided for in the Treaty:
(i) The elimination, as between member states, of customs duties and of quantitative restrictions in regard to the importation and exportation of goods, as well as of all other measures with equivalent effect.
(ii) The establishment of a common customs tariff and a common commercial policy towards third countries.
(iii) The abolition, as between member states, of the obstacles to the free movement of persons, services and capital.
(iv) The inauguration of a common agricultural policy.
(v) The inauguration of a common transport policy.
(vi) The establishment of a system ensuring that competition shall not be distorted in the Common Market.
(vii) The application of procedures which shall make it possible to co-ordinate the economic policies of member states and to remedy disequilibria in their balances of payments.
(viii) The approximation of their respective muncipal law to the extent necessary for the functioning of the Common Market.
(ix) The creation of a European Social Fund in order to improve the possibilities of employment for workers and to contribute to the raising of their standard of living.
(x) The establishment of a European Investment Bank intended to

facilitate the economic expansion of the Community through the creation of new resources.

(xi) The association of overseas countries and territories with the Community with a view to increasing trade and to pursuing jointly their effort towards economic and social development.

The achievement of the tasks entrusted to the Community shall be ensured by: an Assembly, a Council, a Commission, and a Court of Justice.

The Council and the Commission shall be assisted by an Economic and Social Committee acting in a consultative capacity.

Member states shall take all general or particular measures which are appropriate for ensuring the carrying out of the obligations arising out of this Treaty, or resulting from the acts of the institutions of the Community. They shall facilitate the achievement of the Community's aims. They shall abstain from any measures likely to jeopardise the attainment of the objectives of this Treaty.

Member states, acting in close collaboration with the institutions of the Community, shall co-ordinate their respective economic policies to the extent that is necessary to attain the objectives of this Treaty.

The institutions of the Community shall take care not to prejudice the internal and external financial stability of member states.

Within the field of application of this Treaty, and without prejudice to the special provisions mentioned therein, any discrimination on the grounds of nationality shall hereby be prohibited.

The Common Market shall be progressively established in the course of a transitional period of twelve years. The transitional period shall be divided into three stages of four years each.

prix de base
see basic price

prix d'écluse
see sluicegate price

prix d'intervention
see intervention price

prix d'orientation
see guide price

prix de réference
see reference price

prix de seuil
see threshold price

prix indicatif
see target price

protective measures
The necessary 'protective measures' may be taken by a member state under Article 109, when a sudden balance of payments crisis occurs and where the Council has not given immediate assistance.

P.T.O.M.
Pays et Territoires d'Outre-Mer, Overseas Countries and Territories.

publications
Apart from the *Journal Officiel* the E.E.C. publish: *General Report on the activities of the Community* (annual, from 1958); *Bulletin of the E.E.C.* (monthly); *Bulletin Général de Statistiques* (monthly); *Statistique Mensuelle du Commerce Extérieur* (monthly); *Graphiques et Notes Rapides sur la conjoncture de la Communauté* (monthly, from 1959).

In addition the *European Community* (monthly) is obtainable from the United Kingdom office of the Commission of the European Communities, 20 Kensignton Palace Gardens, London, W8 4QQ.

publications, distribution of
E.E.C. publications are distributed by the following organisations:
BELGIUM, *Moniteur belge—Belgisch Staatsblad*, Rue de Louvain, 40–42,
1000 Brussels; DENMARK, *J. H. Schultz—Boghandel*, Møntergade 19, 1116
Copenhagen K; GERMAN FEDERAL REPUBLIC, *Verlag Bundesanzeiger*, 5
Köln 1—Breite Strasz; FRANCE, *Service de vente en France des publications
des Communautés européennes, Journal officiel*, 26, rue Desaix 75732
Paris—Cedex 15; IRISH REPUBLIC, *Stationary Office*, Beggar's Bush, Dublin
4; ITALY, *Libreria dello Stato*, Piazza G. Verdi 10, 00198 Rome;
LUXEMBOURG, *Office des publications officielles des Communautés euro-
péennes*, 5 rue du commerce, Luxembourg; THE NETHERLANDS,
Staatsdrukkerij- en uitgeverijbedriff, Christoffel Plantijnstraat, 's-
Gravenhage; UNITED KINGDOM, *H. M. Stationery Office*, Cornwall House,
P.O. Box 569, London SEI 9NH; UNITED STATES OF AMERICA, *European
Community Information Service*, 2100 M Street, N.W., Suite 707, Washing-
ton, D.C. 20037; SWITZERLAND, *Librairie Payot*, 6, rue Grenus, 1211
Geneva; SWEDEN, *Librairie C.E. Fritze*, 2, Fredsgatan, Stockholm 16;
SPAIN, *Libreria Mundi-Prensa*, Castelló 37, Madrid 1; OTHER COUNTRIES,
Office for Official Publications of the European Communities, 5, rue du
commerce, Boîte postale 1003, Luxembourg.
Efta publications are distributed by the following organisations:
AUSTRIA, Bundsministerium für Handel, Gewerbe und Industrie, Ab-
teilung 11/8, Stubenring 1, A–1011 Vienna; FINLAND, Suomen Efta-rhymä,
Liisankatu 14 B 58, SF—00170 Helsinki 17; ICELAND, Ministry of
Commerce, Arnarhvoli, Reykjavik; NORWAY, Utenriksdepartementet, 7
juniplassen 1, Postboks 8114 Oslo Dep., Oslo 1; PORTUGAL, Presidente da
Comissão, Executiva do Secretariado, para a Cooperacão Economica e
Tecnica Externa, Avenida da Republica 32, Lisbon 1; SWEDEN Handels-
departementet, Fack, 103 20 Stockholm 16; SWITZERLAND, Efta Information Service, 9–11, rue de Varembé, 1211 Geneva 20; BELGIUM, Librairie
européene S.A., 244, rue de la Loi, Bruxelles 4; DENMARK, Dansk
Informationskomité for Markedssørgsmål, Dronningens Tvaergade 28,
1302 Copenhagen K; FRANCE, Editions A. Pédone, 13, rue Soufflot, Paris
5ᵉ; GERMANY, Elwert & Meurer, Buchhandlung, Hauptstrasse 101, Berlin-
Schöneberg; ITALY, Libreria Commissionaria Sansoni, Via Gino Capponi
26, Casella Postale 552, Florence; NETHERLANDS, N. V. Martinus Nijhoff,
Lange Voorhout 9, The Hague; SPAIN, Libreria Mundi Prensa, Castello 37,
Apartado 1,223, Madrid (1); UNITED KINGDOM, Gothard House Publi-

cations Ltd., Gothard House, Henley, Oxon, RG9 1AJ.

Q

quota
A restricted volume of imports or exports, or of imports admitted at a particular tariff rate.

quotas in the E.E.C.
The establishment of the E.E.C. required the abolition of quantitative restrictions between member countries. No detailed provisions regarding quotas is made in the Treaty with respect to third countries, but Article 3 required that member states unify their lists of liberalised products as far as possible. The Council of Ministers allocates the share of quotas when they are applicable. By establishing tariff quotas, the Community does not fix quantitative restrictions as such but allows a certain quantity of a product to enter the Community duty-free, or with a reduced tariff. Quotas may be adopted either in the framework of preferential agreements or to meet the need of certain sectors in the Community.

R

real income
In order to make intertemporal or international comparisons of real purchasing power it is necessary to discount differences in price levels. This is done by dividing changes in money income by changes in the general price level; and the result gives a measure of differences in real income.

recommended price
A price recommended or suggested by a manufacturer, compliance with the recommendation being voluntary. Sometimes also known as guide price.

referendum, Denmark
Following the signing of the Treaty of Accession a vote was taken in the *Folketing* on 18 May 1972 and it was decided by 132 votes to twelve, with two abstentions, that the final decision on E.E.C. membership should be taken by popular vote. The voting was in favour of membership with 63·3% (1,958,115) of the total poll voting 'yes' and 36·7% (1,135,691) voting 'no'. This represented 90·1% of eligible voters.

referendum, Irish Republic
Following the signing of the Treaty of Accession, the Irish Republic decided to hold a referendum on membership of the E.E.C. Polling took place on 10 May 1972 and the voting was 83% (1,041,880) in favour of membership and 17% (211,888) against. This represented 71% of eligible voters.

referendum, Norway
Following the signing of the Treaty of Accession in Jan. 1972, Norway decided to hold a referendum. The 2·65m. eligible voters were asked to reply 'yes' or 'no' to the question 'Do you think Norway should join the European Economic Community?' 53·5% (1,099,389) of the total poll voted 'no' and 46·5% (956,043) voted 'yes'. This represented 77·6% of the eligible voters. Norway therefore did not ratify the Treaty of Accession.

referendum, United Kingdom
On 5 June 1975 a referendum, the first of its kind in history, was held in the United Kingdom. One simple question was asked, 'Do you think that the United Kingdom should stay in the European Economic Community?' This followed the completion of the renegotiations of the United Kingdom's entry terms at the Meeting of the E.E.C. Heads of Government in Dublin, 10–11 March.

The voting was as follows:

		%
'Yes' votes	17,378,581	67·2
'No' votes	8,470,073	32·8

'Yes' majority	8,908,508

(Spoilt papers, 54,540; total electorate including the service vote, 40,456,877.)

The geographical analysis of voting is given below:

	Yes	%	No	%	% Poll
ENGLAND					
Avon	310,145	67·8	147,024	32·2	68·7
Bedfordshire	154,338	69·4	67,969	30·6	67·9
Berkshire	215,184	72·6	81,221	27·4	66·4
Buckinghamshire	180,512	74·3	62,578	25·7	69·5
Cambridgeshire	177,789	74·1	62,143	25·9	62·9
Cheshire	290,714	70·1	123,839	29·9	65·5
Cleveland	158,982	67·3	77,079	32·7	60·2
Cornwall	137,828	68·5	63,478	31·5	66·8
Cumbria	162,545	71·9	63,564	28·1	64·8
Derbyshire	286,614	68·6	131,457	31·4	64·1
Devon	334,244	72·1	129,179	27·9	68·0
Dorset	217,432	73·3	78,239	26·5	68·3
Durham	175,284	64·2	97,724	35·8	61·5
Essex	463,505	67·7	222,085	32·4	67·7
Gloucestershire	170,931	71·7	67,465	28·3	68·4
Gr. London	2,201,031	66·7	1,100,185	33·3	60·8
Gr. Manchester	797,316	64·5	439,191	35·5	64·1
Hampshire	484,302	71·0	197,761	29·0	68·0
Hereford and Worcs.	203,128	72·8	75,779	27·2	66·4
Hertfordshire	326,943	70·4	137,266	29·6	70·2
Humberside	257,826	67·8	122,199	32·2	62·4
Isle of Wight	40,837	71·2	17,375	29·8	67·5
Isles of Scilly	802	74·5	275	25·5	75·0
Kent	493,407	70·4	207,358	29·6	67·4

213

	Yes	%	No	%	% Poll
ENGLAND					
Lancashire	455,170	68·6	208,821	31·4	67·2
Leicestershire	291,500	73·3	106,004	26·7	66·4
Lincolnshire	180,603	74·7	61,011	25·3	63·7
Merseyside	465,625	64·8	252,712	35·2	62·7
Norfolk	218,883	70·1	93,198	29·9	63·8
Northamptonshire	162,803	69·5	71,322	30·5	65·0
Northumberland	95,980	69·2	42,645	30·8	65·0
Nottinghamshire	297,191	66·8	147,461	33·2	67·7
Oxfordshire	179,938	73·6	64,643	26·4	67·7
Salop	113,044	72·3	43,329	27·7	62·0
Somerset	138,830	69·6	60,631	30·4	67·7
Staffordshire	306,518	67·4	148,252	32·6	64·3
Suffolk	187,484	72·2	72,251	27·8	64·9
Surrey	386,369	76·2	120,576	27·8	70·1
East Sussex	249,780	74·3	86,198	23·8	68·6
West Sussex	242,890	76·2	73,928	23·8	68·6
Tyne and Wear	344,069	62·9	202,511	37·1	62·7
Warwickshire	156,303	69·9	67,221	30·1	68·0
West Midlands	801,913	65·1	429,207	34·9	62·5
Wiltshire	172,791	71·7	68,113	28·3	67·8
North Yorkshire	234,040	76·3	72,805	23·7	64·3
South Yorkshire	377,916	63·4	217,792	36·6	62·4
West Yorkshire	616,730	65·4	326,993	34·6	63·6
WALES					
Clwyd	123,980	69·1	55,424	30·9	65·8
Dyfed	109,184	67·6	52,264	32·4	67·5
Mid Glamorgan	147,348	56·9	111,672	43·1	66·6
South Glamorgan	127,932	69·5	56,224	30·5	66·7
West Glamorgan	112,989	61·6	70,316	38·4	67·4
Gwent	132,557	62·1	80,992	37·9	68·2
Gwynedd	76,421	70·6	31,807	29·4	64·3
Powys	38,724	74·3	13,372	25·7	67·9
SCOTLAND					
Borders	34,092	72·3	13,053	27·7	63·2

	Yes	%	No	%	% Poll
SCOTLAND					
Central	71,986	59·7	48,568	40·3	64·1
Dumfries and Galloway	42,608	68·2	19,856	31·8	61·5
Fife	84,239	56·3	65,260	43·7	63·3
Grampian	108,520	58·2	78,071	41·8	57·4
Highland	40,802	54·6	33,979	45·4	58·7
Lothian	208,133	59·5	141,456	40·5	63·6
Orkney	3,911	61·8	2,419	38·2	48·2
Shetland*	2,815	43·7	3,631	56·3	47·1
Strathclyde	625,939	57·7	459,073	42·3	61·7
Tayside	105,728	58·6	74,567	41·4	63·8
Western Isles*	3,393	29·5	8,106	70·5	50·1
NORTHERN IRELAND					
Northern Ireland	259,251	52·1	237,911	47·9	47·4

* Returned majority votes against E.E.C. membership.

Regional Development Fund

The Regional Development Fund was established in Jan. 1975, in response to the difficulties of solving regional economic imbalance solely by domestic resources. Symptoms of the regional problems include (i) high unemployment; (ii) low average incomes; (iii) inadequate communications and amenities and (iv) net migration from these regions. Main regions requiring aid are fringe farming areas, traditional industrial centres depending on declining or obsolescent industries, and, of course, Greenland.

National maximum entitlements 1975–7 (£m.): Italy, 216·7; the United Kingdom, 150·4; France (including overseas departments), 80·5; Irish Republic, 35; Federal German Republic, 34·4; Netherlands, 9·1; Belgium, 8·1; Denmark (including Greenland), 7; Luxembourg, 0·5. Total E.E.C. fund, 541·7.

regional policy

The Treaty of Rome prescribes the arrangements for ensuring the

harmonious development of the member countries by strengthening their economies and reducing the difference between various regions. The following regions are considered to have special priority:
(i) Regions lagging behind in development, mainly because of the predominance of agricultural activities;
(ii) Frontier regions where the need to co-ordinate action of member countries is felt strongly;
(iii) Regions where there is structural unemployment;
(iv) Regions which are declining because of the trend of predominant economic activity.

The Council of Ministers agreed in 1975 to establish a Regional Development Fund and a Regional Policy Committee.

The Fund's allocation of resources for the period 1975–77 was as follows:

	%
Belgium	1·5
Denmark	1·3
France	15·0
German Federal Republic	6·4
Irish Republic	6·0
Italy	40·0
Luxembourg	0·1
Netherlands	6·4
United Kingdom	28·0

regions

In E.E.C. terms regions are areas of the member countries which, for reasons of national economic change, have obsolete, obsolescent or declining industries, and suffer from lack of investment and high unemployment. Individual member states have sought to solve their regional problems by a wide range of measures, such as preferential taxation rates, loans at preferential rates, development control in congested areas to promote movement of industry into the regions. The E.E.C., by establishing its Regional Development Fund and Regional Policy Committee in 1975, is seeking to co-ordinate the policies of the individual countries into a common regional policy.

Regulations
A Regulation is the legal instrument by which a decision of the Council of Ministers is enacted and joins the body of E.E.C. law. A Regulation is binding in its entirety and has the effect of law in each member state without the intervention of the national parliament of that state.

R.E.I.
Rat der Europäischen Industrieverbande, Council of European Industrial Federations.

resale price maintenance
The practice by a supplier of prescribing, and taking action to enforce, retail or wholesale prices for the resale of goods.

research (1975)
Public expenditure on research and development. Total expenditure in U.A. *per capita* at 1975 exchange rates.

Belgium	35·22
Denmark	33·36
France	51·52
Federal German Republic	63·88
Irish Republic	8·47
Italy	8·70
Luxembourg	—
Netherlands	42·93
United Kingdom	36·48

restitution payments
Payments on exports by E.E.C. member states to make up the difference between the world price and the (higher) domestic price in the exporting state. Such payments will be charged gradually to the E.E.C.'s Agriculture Guidance and Guarantee Funds so that by the end of the transitional period all exports of agricultural produce from the Community will be financed out of this central fund. (Also referred to as export refunds or

compensation payments.)

restrictive practices
see Competition Policy

Rey, Jean

Born Liège, Belgium 1902. Advocate, Liège court of Appeal since 1926. Deputy for Liège, 1939 and 1946–58. Founder member, *Entente Libérale Wallone*. Delegate to Consultative Assembly of Council of Europe, 1949–53. Minister of Reconstruction, 1949–50; Minister of Economic Affairs, 1954–8. Sectional President for External Relations, E.E.C. Commission, 1958–67. President of the E.E.C. Commission, 1967–70.

R.G.W.

Rat für gegenseitige Wirtschaftshilfe, Council for Mutual Economic Assistance (German).

Rippon, Geoffrey

Born England, 1924. Member of the British Parliament from 1955. Minister of Public Buildings and Works, 1962–4. President of the British section of the Council of European Municipalities since 1951. President of the British section of the European League for Economic Co-operation since 1969. Chancellor of the Duchy of Lancaster in charge of negotiations for British entry to E.E.C., 1970–2.

Roman Empire

The Roman Empire, at its fullest extent, covered all the countries of the E.E.C with the exception of Ireland, Denmark and parts of Britain and Germany. It included however, all of North Africa, the Middle East, most of Turkey and many of the countries now applying for E.E.C. membership, such as Portugal, Spain and Greece.

The Roman Empire fulfilled many of the dreams of European federalists: a common currency, free trade, a common legal system, though local laws were also permitted, a unified defence and foreign policy and a great deal of regional autonomy. The Roman Empire's collapse was brought about by a combination of factors, many of which are familiar to modern Europeans. The unpopularity of a military career led to small mercenary armies, an increasing bureaucracy brought about high taxation which in turn encouraged the flight from a large interdependent Empire to small, self-sufficient communities. The Barbarian invasions, to which Rome's fall is usually ascribed, merely pushed over an already decayed system and legitimised what had been happening for neary two centuries.

Rome Treaty

The Treaty of Rome establishing the European Economic Community came into force on 1 Jan. 1958. The final drafts of the Treaty had been completed by the inter-governmental committee in Brussels on 9 March 1957, and the Treaty was signed in Rome by Belgium, France, West Germany, Italy, Luxembourg, and the Netherlands on 25 March 1957. The signing ceremony took place at the Palazzo dei Conservatori on the Capitoline Hill. The signatories were Signor Segni (then Italian Prime Minister); Dr Adenauer (then Federal German Chancellor); the Foreign Ministers of Belgium (then M. Spaak); France (then M. Pincau); Italy (then Dr Martino); Luxembourg (then M. Bech); and the Netherlands (then Mr Luns); The West German State Secretary for Foreign Affairs (Professor Hallstein, representing the then Foreign Minister, Dr von Brentano, who was on a visit to Australia).

Between July and Dec. 1957 the Treaty was ratified by the Parliaments of all the six member countries.

The Treaty, which was concluded for an unlimited period, consists of 248 Articles, 15 Annexes, 4 declarations of intention, and 3 protocols.

In the preamble to the Treaty, the six signatory countries declared their intention of establishing 'the foundations of an enduring and closer union between European peoples' by gradually removing the economic effect of their political frontiers. It was agreed that a common market and a common external tariff (Customs Union) would be established for all goods; common policies would be devised for agriculture, transport, labour mobility, and important sectors of the economy; common institutions would be set up for economic development; and the overseas territories and possessions of member states would be associated with the new Community. All these measures had one 'essential aim' — the steady improvement in the conditions of life and work of the peoples of the member countries.

The tasks of the Community were defined in Article 1 of the Treaty as 'the achievement of a harmonious development of the economy within the whole Community, a continuous and balanced economic expansion, increased economic stability, a more rapid improvement in living-standards, and closer relations between the member-countries'. *(The table of contents of the Treaty are given below and readers should refer to the individual sections of the dictionary for fuller explanations of the various articles)*:

Rules of Competition

The Rules of Competition are contained in Articles 85–9 of the Treaty of Rome and in the implementing Regulations. They encompass the wide field of: restrictive trade practices; types of trade agreement prohibited and permitted; monopolies and the dominant position; and mergers. They may be said to represent the guidelines to the process of unifying the markets of the nine member states into a single Common Market.

Rwanda

Rwanda was a signatory of the Yaoundé Conventions of 1963 and 1969 and of the Lomé Convention of 1975.

S

S.A.

Société Anonyme, company with limited liability in Belgium and France. In

Safety, Hygiene and Health Protection at Work, Advisory Committee on
The Advisory Committee on Safety, Hygiene and Health Protection at Work, a Commission advisory committee on social policy, was created by Council decision in 1974. It has fifty-four members, two government, two employer and two trade union per country, and fifty-four substitutes. The members are appointed by governments. The Committee is serviced by the Commission.

São Tomé and Principe
São Tomé and Principe became a member of the Lomé Convention in 1977.

Scheel, Walter
Born Solingen, Germany, 1919. Member of the *Bundestag* of the Federal German Republic since 1953. Federal Minister for Economic Co-operation, 1961–6. Vice-President, 1967–9. Chairman of Free Democratic Party, 1968–74. Minister of Foreign Affairs, 1969–74. President of the Federal Democratic Republic, 1974–

Schumann, Maurice
Born Paris, France, 1911. Parliamentary Deputy, 1945–73. Chairman of the Popular Republican Movement, 1945–9. French delegate to the Council of Europe, 1949. Foreign Minister, 1951–4. President of the Foreign Affairs Commission of the National Assembly, 1959. Minister of State, 1962 and 1967–8. Minister of Social Affairs, 1968–9. Minister of Foreign Affairs, 1969–73.

Schuman Plan
The Schuman Plan consisted of proposals put forward by Robert Schuman of France on 9 May 1950. The main aim was to call for a conference to discuss the pooling of the coal and steel resources of Western Europe. The French invitation was accepted by the Benelux countries, Italy and the

Federal German Republic. Negotiations began in Paris in June 1950 and the Paris Treaty setting up a supranational authority, the European Coal and Steel Community, was signed in April 1951.

Schuman Prize
see awards

Schuman, Robert
Born Luxembourg, 1886, died 1963. Prime Minister of France, 1947 and 1948. Propounded the Schuman Plan for the pooling of European resources of coal and steel in 1950. President of the Strasbourg European Assembly in 1958. Signatory to the statute setting up the Council of Europe in 1949. Awarded the Charlemagne Prize, 1958.

'Five years, almost to the day, after Germany's unconditional surrender, France is taking the first decisive step in the construction of Europe, and is associating Germany with it. . . . Europe will not be made all at once, or as a single whole: it will be built of concrete achievements which first create *de facto* solidarity' (In a speech to a press conference at the Quai d'Orsay, 9 May 1950.)

s.d.r.
see special drawing rights

Senegal
Senegal was a signatory of the Yaoundé Conventions of 1963 and 1969 and of the Lomé Convention of 1975.

S.E.V.
Sovet Ekonomicheskoy Vzaimopomoshchi, Council for Mutual Economic Assistance, known in West as Comecon (U.S.S.R.)

Seychelles
The Seychelles became a member of the Lomé Convention in 1977.

Sierra Leone
Sierra Leone was a signatory of the Lomé Convention of 1975.

S.I.I.C.
Secrétariat international des groupements professionels des industries chimiques des pays de la C.E.E., International Secretariat of Professional Groups in the Chemical Industries of the E.E.C. countries.

S.I.T.C.
see Standard International Trade Classification.

site of the Institutions
At the merger of the executives of the Communities it was agreed that Brussels, Luxembourg and Strasbourg would remain the working seats of the Community as long as no final choice of a single capital had been made. Brussels would be the seat of the new single Community Executive and the consultative bodies attached to it; meetings of the Council of Ministers would be held there except in April, June and October when Luxembourg would be the meeting-place.

Luxembourg would retain the Secretariat of the European Parliament and the Court of Justice and would also become the seat of other legal and quasi-legal bodies which might be set up, including any body with legal jurisdiction in the patents field.

Strasbourg continued to be the meeting-place of the European Parliament.

Luxembourg became the seat of the financial institutions such as the European Investment Bank, which was formerly in Brussels.

Under the Treaty certain other services would be transferred to, or remain in, Luxembourg, such as the Community Statistical Offices which were divided between Brussels and Luxembourg, the joint publication office, services dealing with workers' health and the dissemination of scientific data from Euratom.

Sitpro
The United Committee for the *S*implification of *I*nternational *T*rade *Pro*cedures.

Six, The
The original countries in membership of the E.E.C. established on 1 Jan. 1958 by the signing of the Treaty of Rome on 25 March 1957. The signing ceremony of the Treaty took place at the Palazzo dei Conservatori on the Capitoline Hill in Rome. The signatories were Signor Segni (then Italian Prime Minister); Dr Adenauer (then Federal German Chancellor); the Foreign Ministers of Belgium (then M. Spaak); France (then M. Pincau); Italy (then Dr Martino); Luxembourg (then M. Bech); and the Netherlands (then Mr Luns); the Federal German State Secretary for Foreign Affairs (Professor Hallstein, representing the then Foreign Minister, Dr von Brentano, who was on a visit to Australia).

Between July and Dec. 1957 the Treaty was ratified by the Parliaments of all the six member countries.

sluice gate price
The minimum import price at which certain commodities, *e.g.* pigmeat, can be imported into the E.E.C. If payment of tariff, levies or other charges on these commodities does not bring the import price up to the 'sluice gate' level, an additional levy can be charged to bridge the gap. Under this arrangement it is open to an exporter to adjust his offer price so that no additional levy is chargeable.

snake
The 'snake' is a stable exchange rate parity club with 2·25% margins. Membership consists of the various member states of the E.E.C. except Italy (which left in Feb. 1973), the United Kingdom and the Irish Republic (who never joined on accession to the Communities in Jan. 1973) and France (which left in March 1976, having previously been out of the snake

between Jan. 1974 and July 1975). In addition Sweden and Norway are members.

After a long period of troubles on the foreign exchange markets, members of the International Monetary Fund had agreed at the Smithsonian Institute in 1971 to ensure their currencies did not fluctuate by more than 4·5% (2·25% for the U.S.$) from parities declared to the I.M.F. This band of 4·5% above or below, *i.e.* 9% total, the declared parities, which became known as the 'tunnel', was considered too wide by members of the E.E.C., who decided to limit the fluctuations of their currencies still further. They did this by agreeing to limit fluctuations of their own currencies so that the strongest and weakest currencies should not deviate from each other by more than 2·25% of the value of the strongest. This agreement came into effect in July 1972 and was known as the snake.

The snake in the tunnel is seen by many who support it as a step towards economic and monetary union, both because stabilised exchange rates would make possible the introduction of a European Currency, sometimes referred to by the name suggested for its unit, the Europa, and because stable exchange rates can only exist between states whose respective economies are advancing at the same rate. European Federalists, who saw the political impossibility of member states accepting direction of their various economies from Brussels, saw that the snake would achieve the same results.

The worm, or mini-snake, was the joint float between the Belgian/Luxembourg Franc and the Dutch Guilder, which kept to a 1·5% band. Instituted in 1971 it was dissolved in March 1976, at the same time as the French Franc left the snake.

snake in the tunnel
see snake

Soames, Sir Christopher
Born England, 1920. Member of the British Parliament, 1950–66. Secretary of State for War, 1958–60; Minister of Agriculture, Fisheries and Food, 1960–4. Ambassador to France, 1968–72. Vice-President of the Commission of European Communities, 1973–6.

Social Fund, European
The fund's budgetary allocation in 1976 was 441m. U.A. some of the allocations were as follows:

	U.A. (in millions)
Retraining workers leaving agriculture	66·1
Retraining textile workers	66·1
Retraining handicapped workers	28·9
Migrant workers	20·8

Social Fund Committee
The Social Fund Committee, a Commission advisory committee on social policy, was created in 1960, by Article 124 of the Rome Treaty. It advises the Commission on the administration of the European Social Fund, which exists to part-finance programmes for the training of workers, submitted through national governments.

S.O.E.C.
Statistical Office of European Communities.

soft terms
Aid is given on 'soft terms' when it is made available at less than the cost of its provision by the donor country.

Somalia
Somalia was a signatory of the Yaoundé Conventions of 1963 and 1969 and of the Lomé Convention of 1975.

Sonning Prize
see awards

S.p.A.
Società per Azioni, joint stock company in Italy.

Spaak, Paul-Henri
Born Belgium, 1899, died 1972. Parliamentary Deputy, 1932. First socialist Prime Minister of Belgium, 1938–9. Foreign Minister of the Government in exile, 1940–5. Prime Minister, 1946, and 1947–9. President of the first general assembly of the United Nations, 1946. President of the Consultative Assembly of the Council of Europe, 1949–51. Foreign Minister, 1954–7 and 1961–6. Chairman of the committee set up by the Messina Conference to draft the Treaty of Rome, 1956–7. Secretary General of Nato, 1957–61.

Spain
A six-year preferential trade agreement signed with the E.E.C. came into force on 1 Oct. 1970. Negotiations for an agreement with the Nine started in 1976. Spain aims at full membership of the E.E.C. by the early 1980s.
Economic profile: Area 504,800 sq. km. Population (1973) 34,857,000 (male (1971) 16,642,000) density 69 per sq. km. Births (per 1,000 of pop. 1973) 19·4; marriages, 7·6; deaths, 8·2. Infant mortality, 16.
Labour force (1972) 12,847,000; percentage in agriculture, 27·6; industry, 37·7; services, 34·6.
International trade (in millions of U.A.):

	1965	*1970*	*1973*
Imports	3,019	4,747	7,703
Exports	967	2,387	4,143

	per 1,000 of population
Standard of living:	
Motor vehicles (1973)	94
Televisions (1972)	132
Telephones (1972)	151

special drawing right
Special drawing rights (S.D.Rs.) are equivalent to the United States $ at par value in Dec. 1946.

Sri Lanka
Sri Lanka signed a five-year commercial co-operation agreement with the E.E.C. which came into force on 1 July 1975.

Stabex
Stabex, an *ex*port *stab*ilisation scheme, is part of the European Development Fund set up by the Lomé Convention of 1975 and is designed to stabilise the export earnings of the A.C.P. countries from sales of commodities.

The E.E.C. has set aside 75m. (basket) units of account per annum for five years for the benefit of the A.C.P. countries and a further 5m. units of account per annum for the benefit of the overseas territories of member states. Equivalent to about 4% of the value of A.C.P. countries' earnings from commodity exports to the E.E.C., the fund is financed by member states separately from the Budget.

The fund achieves its objects by making cash grants to those countries whose foreign exchange earnings have suffered from the deterioration of commodity markets. The operation of the fund is thus designed both to be a neutral influence on prices and to give beneficiary states' governments the maximum discretion in how the grant is to be used.

Table of the major commodity groups covered by Stabex, together with the value of total exports to the E.E.C. by the A.C.P. countries in 1973.

millions of units of account

Tropical wood	514
Coffee	350
Cocoa and products	341
Iron ore	276
Ground-nuts and products	185
Cotton	127

Sugar is the only major commodity not included in the list. Different arrangements based on guaranteed import quotas have been made in this case.

Most A.C.P. countries are very highly dependent on exports of commodities, a dependency made worse by the fact that often it is on only one product, as is the case of Burundi where coffee accounts for 86 % of all exports, or Liberia where iron ore accounts for 71 %. The danger of this high dependence on commodities is that prices tend to fall dramatically during periods of economic downturn when world demand is at a low level. Thus in periods of slump producer countries sell less commodities at lower prices, but this is not made good in periods of high economic activity, when the excess export earnings tend to be used for purchases of consumer products rather than laying down the basis for further economic develop-ment. This made the creation of a stabilisation fund such as Stabex highly desirable.

Breakdown by Product of Stabex Transfers for 1975

Product	Amount in EUA	%
Groundnuts	6,590,863	9·17
Bananas	1,296,907	1·80
Wood in the rough	31,139,508	43·35
Cocoa	276,978	0·39
Coffee	13,242,175	18·43
Cotton	9,077,108	12·64
Copra oil	615,410	0·86
Raw hides and skins	8,401,981	11·70
Oil cake	1,191,079	1·66
	71,832,009	100·00

Standard International Trade Classification (S.I.T.C.)
The Standard International Trade Classification was adopted by the United Nations in 1950 as a basis for reporting commodity detail in foreign trade statistics, and member countries were urged to make use of it. It was revised in 1960. Governments of countries accounting for about 80 % of

world trade compile statistics in accordance with this classification, which consists of ten sections.

standard quality
The level of production of a particular commodity to which the full United Kingdom guaranteed price applies.

standby
Standby usually means arranged in advance of need. Most commonly used of I.M.F. standby arrangements under which members can negotiate a drawing with the Fund in advance and then make the drawing immediately on demand without further consultation or Fund examination of their policies.

statistics published by the Statistical Office of the European Communities
Basic Statistics   Yearbook.
General Statistics Eleven issues a year.
Agricultural Statistics   Six issues a year.
Energy Statistics   Quarterly, and yearbook.
Foreign Trade: Monthly Statistics   Eleven issues a year.
Industrial Statistics   Quarterly, and yearbook.
Social Statistics   Six issues a year.
Iron and Steel Bulletin   Six issues a year. Yearbook produced every two years.
Balance of Payments   Annual balance of payments information, generally for an eleven-year period.
National Accounts   Annual national accounting data, generally covering the preceding eleven years.
Regional Statistics   Yearbook.
Tax Statistics   Annual.
Transport Statistics   Yearbook
    Part I—broadly comparable data about the infrastructure, mobile plant, industrial structure, technical operations and commercial operations of railways, inland navigation and road transport.
    Part II—data taken from national sources concerning sea and air

231

transport and oil pipelines.

Part III—record of results from studies or surveys conducted by the Community.

Stewart, R. Michael

Born England, 1906. Member of the British Parliament, 1945. Minister for Education and Science, 1964–5. First Secretary of State from 1966. Minister for Economic Affairs, 1966–7. Minister for Foreign Affairs, 1965–6 and 1968–70, with responsibility in the latter period for negotiating British entry to the E.E.C.

Stockholm Convention

The Stockholm Convention establishing the European Free Trade Association came into force on 3 May 1960 and its objectives are:

(i) to promote in the area of the Association and in each member state a sustained expansion of economic activity, full employment, increased productivity and the rational use of resources, financial stability and continuous improvement in living standards;

(ii) to ensure that trade between member states takes place in conditions of fair competition;

(iii) to avoid significant disparity between member states in the conditions of supply of raw materials produced within the area of Association; and

(iv) to contribute to the harmonious development and expansion of world trade and to the progressive removal of barriers to it.

The main provisions of the Convention are as follows:

Elimination of tariffs on industrial goods was originally to be achieved at the latest by Jan. 1970, but this date was brought forward to 31 Dec. 1966.

The Convention provides for the progressive reduction of quantitative restrictions on all imports from member states and their complete elimination by 1 Jan. 1970. This date was also brought forward to 31 Dec. 1966.

Member states do not have a common external tariff in relation to countries outside the area. 'Origin' rules have therefore been worked out to identify the products of member countries to which the tariff reductions will apply.

Member countries will be free to take action which they consider necessary for the protection of their essential security interests and, consistently with their other international obligations, their balance of payments. In certain circumstances a member state may also take special safeguarding action where the application of the Convention leads to serious difficulties in a particular sector of industry.

The Convention contains provisions to ensure that the benefits which are expected from the removal of tariffs and quotas are not nullified through the use of other measures by Governments, public undertakings or private industries. These include provisions about subsidies, restrictive business practices and discriminatory restrictions against nationals of member states wishing to establish business anywhere in the area.

Special arrangements have been made for agricultural goods and fish and other marine products. The objective is to facilitate reasonable reciprocity to those member states whose economies depend to a great extent on agricultural or fish exports. Arrangements have also been concluded between several member countries in respect of trade in agricultural goods.

Strasbourg
Strasbourg is capital of the Bas-Rhin department in eastern France situated on the Ill river and four miles from the west bank of the river Rhine. The European Parliament meets in this city. Population at the 1968 census, 249,369.

Streseman Prize
see awards

Sudan
Sudan was a signatory of the Lomé Convention of 1975.

sugar
One of the terms of the United Kingdom's entry to the E.E.C. was that the Government's contractual obligations to buy agreed quantities of sugar under the Commonwealth Sugar Agreement would be fulfilled until 1974,

and domestic beet sugar production continued to be limited until then. Thereafter it was agreed that the arrangements for sugar imports from developing Commonwealth sugar producers should be made within the framework of an association or trading agreement with the Nine.

summits
In July 1969 the E.E.C. Council of Ministers approved a proposal put forward by the French Government 'for convening a conference of Heads of State or Heads of Government at the Hague before the end of the year, in order to examine the problems of the Community . . .'. This was the first of the 'summits'.

Some important summits:

Dec. 1969	The Hague	The Six agreed to complete, enlarge and strengthen the Communities, *i.e.* the time was right for the accession of the four proposed new member states, Denmark, Irish Republic, Norway and the United Kingdom.
May 1971	Paris	The Prime Minister of the United Kingdom, Edward Heath, and President Pompidou of France prepared for agreement on entry to E.E.C. of the four new member states.
Oct. 1972	Paris	Plans were prepared for future development of the Communities.
Dec. 1973	Copenhagen	Heads of Government of Nine considered the energy and Near East crises. Unexpected arrival of Ministers from five Arab states led to Euro-Arab Dialogue.
Nov. 1975	Rambouillet	Heads of Government of France, Federal German Republic, Italy, Japan, United Kingdom, and the United States stressed the urgent need for economic recovery in industrialised countries. The smaller states, Belgium, Luxembourg and the Netherlands, complained that their voice was not heard at the meeting.
June 1976	Puerto Rico	Heads of Government of Canada, France, Fed-

eral German Republic, Italy, Japan, United Kingdom and the United States met to consider economic problems.

Suppression of Terrorism, European Convention on

The Committee of Foreign Ministers of the Council of Europe adopted a European Convention on the Suppression of Terrorism at their meeting in Strasbourg in Nov. 1976. The Irish Republic abstained. The sixteen-article Convention will require signature and ratification by member countries.

Surinam

Surinam became a member of the Lomé Convention in 1977.

Swaziland

Swaziland was a signatory of the Lomé Convention of 1975.

Sweden

Sweden signed the Stockholm Convention (Efta) which came into force in 1960.

Economic profile: Area 450,000 sq. km. Population (1973) 8,140,000 (male 4,051,000) density 18 per sq. km. Births (per 1,000 of pop. 1973) 13·8; marriages, 4·8; deaths, 10·4. Infant mortality, 10·8.

Labour force (1972) 3,970,000; percentage in agriculture, 7·4; industry, 36·8; services, 55·8.

International trade (in millions of U.A.):

	1965	1970	1973
Imports	4,378	7,005	8,462
Exports	3,973	6,782	9,696

	per 1,000 of population
Standard of living:	
Motor vehicles (1973)	302
Televisions (1972)	323
Telephones (1972)	557

switch dollar market
Investment in foreign securities by United Kingdom residents is not normally allowed by United Kingdom Exchange Control, but existing holdings may be realised and the proceeds switched into (*i.e.* used to buy) other securities, or sold, usually at a premium because of the limited supply available in relation to demand, to other United Kingdom residents who wish to purchase foreign securities. For convenience, such funds, whatever the currency, are expressed in terms of United States dollars called Switch, security or investment dollars.

Switzerland
Switzerland signed the Stockholm Convention (Efta) which came into force in 1960.
Economic profile: Area 41,300 sq. km. Population (1972) 6,282,000 (male 3,071,000) density 152 per sq. km. Births (per 1,000 of pop. 1973) 14·3; marriages, 6·7; deaths, 8·8. Infant mortality, 13·3.
  Labour force (1972) 3,078,000; percentage in agriculture, 7·1; industry, 46·8; services, 46·1.
  International trade (in millions of U.A.):

	1965	*1970*	*1973*	*1976*
Imports	3,706	6,467	9,293	
Exports	2,993	5,137	7,622	

	per 1,000 of *population*
Standard of living:	
Motor vehicles (1973)	250
Televisions (1972)	222
Telephones (1972)	509

Syria
Syria signed a co-operation agreement with the E.E.C. on 18 Jan. 1977.

T

Tanzania
Tanzania was a signatory of the original Arusha Convention of 1968, which was not ratified by all the E.E.C. countries before the expiry date, and also of the 1969 Arusha Convention. When the Arusha Convention expired in 1975 Tanzania was a signatory of the Lomé Convention.

target price
The wholesale price objective within the E.E.C. for certain products (*e.g.* wheat) which market management provisions are intended to achieve. It is linked with the intervention price.

T.E.E.
see Trans-Europ-Express.

Ten
The Ten would have consisted of the original Six E.E.C. countries plus the Four countries signing the Treaty of Accession. In the event Norway did

not ratify, and so it became the Nine.

territoriality

The principle of territoriality, deriving from the application of national law concerning intellectual, industrial and commercial property does not, in general terms, permit the partitioning of markets within the E.E.C. The application of territoriality has been called in question in the area of trade mark law in the E.E.C. on account of the conflict between the protection of industrial property on the one hand, and the free movement of goods within the E.E.C. on the other.

third world

see less developed countries

Thomson, George

Born Stirling, Scotland, 1921. Member of the British Parliament, 1952–72. Chairman of the Parliamentary Group for World Government, 1962–4. Chancellor of the Duchy of Lancaster and Deputy Foreign Secretary with special responsibility for European Affairs and Common Market negotiations, 1969–70. Chairman of the Labour Committee for Europe, 1972–3. Member of the E.E.C. Commission 1973–77.

Three

The Three consist of those countries ratifying the Treaty of Accession; Denmark, the Irish Republic and the United Kingdom.

threshold price

The minimum price for the import of certain commodities (*e.g.* cereals) into the Community. It is fixed in relation to the target price so that imports do not undermine the desired internal price level. In broad terms, where a threshold price system operates the rate of levy varies so as to bring the cheapest import on offer up to the threshold price. The rate of levy so determined is applied to all offers; thus an exporter who raises his offer price could price himself out of the market.

Tindeman's Report

At the Paris summit conference held 9–10 Dec. 1974 Leo Tindeman, Prime Minister of Belgium, was invited to submit a 'comprehensive report on an overall concept of European Union'. His report, published on 7 Jan. 1976, made the following main recommendations:

(i) Member states should accept an obligation to reach a common foreign policy on major issues, if ncessary by majority rather than unanimous voting. It was suggested that such a policy could begin with the less developed countries and the United States, defence, and crises affecting non-E.E.C. European countries.

(ii) There should be faster progress towards economic and monetary union, with economically stronger member states possibly moving towards closer integration at a faster rate initially than the weaker countries, although the latter would be expected to catch up eventually. The 'snake' of linked currencies should be consolidated by joint action on monetary, budgetary, and short-term economic policy, but member states not yet belonging to the 'snake' should be brought into these discussions. Machinery for short- and medium-term support, the European Monetary Co-operation Fund, should be made automatic and strengthened. The 'snake' countries should gradually abolish the remaining barriers to capital movements between them, and 'non-snake' countries should be helped to join it.

(iii) The development of common policies in important fields such as industry, energy and research should be regarded as a priority.

(iv) Community institutions, particularly the European Parliament, should be strengthened in a number of ways. Direct elections would give the European Parliament a new political authority. The European Council should immediately undertake to consider the resolutions which the Parliament addresses to it, and the Parliament should at once be empowered to consider all questions within the scope of the Union, whether deriving from the Treaties or not. A Treaty amendment should give the Parliament a real right of initiative. Once a year, it should hold a State of the Union debate. In this and in other important debates, the President of the European Council and other leading non-members of the Parliament should be invited to take part.

The European Council should make coherent general policy statements. On Community matters it should follow the Treaties' procedures, with the Commission present. In other fields it should draw up guidelines, appoint an institution or other organisation to apply them, and where necessary set deadlines. Its meetings should be prepared by the Council of Foreign Ministers.

The Council of Ministers may be given competence outside the Treaties on the authority of the European Council. The Foreign Affairs Council should co-ordinate specialist Councils. Majority voting in the Council should become normal practice and, outside the field of the Treaties, the minority should rally to the majority's view at the end of the discussion. The presidency of the Council should be extended from six months to a full year. The Commission, a single country, a person, or a group of persons, could be entrusted with special tasks.

The Commission should reassert its freedom and be given more mandates. Its President should be appointed by the European Council; he should make a policy statement to the European Parliament, and be confirmed by its vote; he should then appoint his colleagues in consultation with the Council.

The Court of Justice should have jurisdiction over the new fields covered by the Union. Other existing Community bodies should continue and develop, and administrative decentralisation should also be taken into account.

(v) All citizens of member countries should be guaranteed certain fundamental rights and have the right of appeal to the European Court of justice in the case of apparent violation.

T.I.R.

Transport International Rontier is a carnet issued to international vehicle operators which allows loaded vehicles to cross international borders with minimum formalities.

Togo

Togo was a signatory of the Yaoundé Conventions of 1963 and 1969 and of the Lomé Convention of 1975.

Tokyo Round

A ministerial meeting of Gatt was held in Tokyo in Sept. 1973 and attended by over one hundred contracting and other countries to initiate the process of obtaining an agreement on a new set of tariff cuts and other barriers to world trade. It has subsequently been called the 'Tokyo Round' Other 'Rounds' have included the 'Dillon Round 1960–62' and the 'Kennedy Round 1964–67'.

Tonga

Tonga was a signatory of the Lomé Convention of 1975.

tourism (1975)

	overseas earnings millions	*as percentage of overseas earnings*	*as percentage of invisible earnings*
Belgium/Luxem-bourg	32,400 francs	2·4	6·8
Denmark	4,291 kroner	6·0	17·9[1]
Federal German Republic	7,014 marks	2·4	15·2[1]
France	14,879 francs	5·0	12·5[1]
Irish Republic	103 £s	7·1	21·5[1]
Italy	1,684,000 lira	5·8	25·1
Netherlands	2,803 guilders	2·5	9·4
United Kingdom	1,114 £s	3·7	10·1

[1] 1974.

towns, largest in Western Europe
(last census figures)

city	*population*	*agglomeration*
1. London	7,418,000	12,762,000
2. Madrid	3,146,000	—
3. Rome	2,731,000	—

city	*population*	*agglomeration*
4. Paris	2,591,000	8,197,000
5. Berlin	2,134,000	–
6. Hamburg	1,817,000	–
7. Barcelona	1,745,000	–
8. Milan	1,702,000	–
9. Vienna	1,603,000	–
10. Munich	1,326,000	–
11. Naples	1,277,000	–
12. Turin	1,177,000	–
13. Brussels	1,071,000	1,071,000
14. Birmingham	1,013,000	2,369,000
15. Glasgow	894,000	1,723,000
16. Marseilles	889,000	964,000
17. Athens	867,000	2,540,000
18. Cologne	866,000	–
19. Genoa	842,000	–
20. Amsterdam	831,000	1,040,000
21. Lisbon	782,000	1,651,000
22. Stockholm	740,000	1,345,000
23. Essen	705,000	–
24. Rotterdam	687,000	1,061,000
25. Düsseldorf	681,000	–
26. Frankfurt on Main	660,000	–
27. Palermo	659,000	–
28. Valencia	654,000	–
29. Dortmund	647,000	–
30. Copenhagen	630,000	1,383,000
31. Stuttgart	628,000	–
32. Bremen	607,000	–
33. Liverpool	603,000	1,263,000
34. Dublin	566,000	670,000
35. The Hague	551,000	719,000
36. Seville	548,000	–
37. Manchester	542,000	2,394,000
38. Helsinki	533,000	804,000
39. Lyon	528,000	1,075,000
40. Hanover	518,000	–

city	population	trade marks agglomeration
41. Sheffield	516,000	—
42. Leeds	501,000	1,736,000
43. Bologna	491,000	—
44. Oslo	487,000	579,000
45. Zaragoza	480,000	—
46. Nürenberg	477,000	—
47. Florence	459,000	—
48. Duisburg	458,000	—
49. Edinburgh	453,000	—
50. Göteborg	452,000	678,000

trade marks

In a memorandum on the creation of an E.E.C. trade mark published in 1976 the Commission said 'It is clearly in the interests of manufacturers, distributors and consumers in the Common Market that a Community trade mark should be created enjoying protection on a uniform basis throughout E.E.C. territory.'

A Community trade mark would enable branded goods, now restricted because of national trade marks, to move freely with proper protection throughout the member states.

The need for a system of Community trade mark law was not, the Commission argued, diminished by the Madrid Agreement of 1891 or the more recent Trade Mark Registration Treaty (T.R.T.) signed in Vienna in 1973. The idea of a Community system emerged in 1959 when the Commission began work on the harmonisation or unification of industrial property law. The Trade Mark Working Group, then set up, produced a preliminary draft of a Convention for a European Trade Mark in 1964, but work on this was suspended during the wider international negotiations which led to the signing of the Trade Mark Registration Treaty in 1973. The Commission then decided that it was time to follow up the 1964 draft Convention. The 1976 memorandum contains a number of new proposals for dicsussion.

There are thought to be more than 1·5m. trade marks at present in use in the Community governed by seven different systems of law. Some approximation of national laws is desirable, therefore, both to encourage the freer movement of branded goods and to reduce conflict over confusing or similar national trade marks. **Approximation** cannot resolve conflicts arising from co-existence of identical or similar trade marks owned by undertakings which are legally independent and economically unconnected.

This could only be done by a Community system of Trade Mark Law and the establishment of an E.E.C. Trade Mark Office, adequately equipped with staff and research facilities. Its object would be to ensure 'a forward looking, balanced and attractive system of protection . . . which reflects the most recent developments in international trade mark law, . . . and international systems.' This would require a simple, flexible and inexpensive registration procedure which gives firms, within a reasonable time, effective and easily enforceable trade mark protection.

The Commission favoured a registration system whereby an E.E.C. trade mark could be registered only if a prior examination had shown it to be eligible for protection, subject to optional third party opposition proceedings. This is a compromise between systems operated nationally by member states. Protection would last ten years and registration would be renewable provided there was proof that the trade mark was still in use. To avoid conflict between E.E.C. and national trade marks the Commission proposed the establishment of a Conciliation Board at the E.E.C. Trade Mark Office, which would hear and seek to resolve cases by consent.

Trade Union Institute, European
At a meeting of Heads of State and Government in Oct. 1972 it was agreed, as part of the Community Social Action Programme, to set up such an Institute. Talks were still proceeding in 1976 between the E.E.C. Commission and the European Trade Union Confederation.

trade union membership (1975)

country	Percentage of employees who are members of trade unions
Belgium	66
Denmark	70–75
France	22

country	Percentage of employees who are members of trade unions
Federal German Republic	38
Irish Republic	49
Italy	50–55
Luxembourg	55
Netherlands	41
United Kingdom	47

trade unions

International trade union co-operation is organised through the three major 'Internationals', the Democratic International Confederation of Free Trade Unions (I.C.F.T.U.), the Communist-directed World Federation of Trade Unions (W.F.T.U.) and the World Confederation of Labour (W.C.L.). In addition, federations of specific trades or industries protect their special interests by organising on an international level and are associated to a varying degree with their corresponding 'Internationals'. The International Trade Secretariats (I.T.S.) are completely autonomous but seek to co-ordinate their policies and activities with those of the I.C.F.T.U.: the International Trade Federations (I.T.F.s) are very closely integrated with the W.C.L.; the Trade Union Internationals (T.U.I.s) are completely subservient to W.F.T.U.

The first general trade union International, the International Federation of Trade Unions (I.F.T.U.), was set up in 1913, but no real achievement was possible until its post-war reconstitution in 1919. Some trade union movements, seeking to implement the social precepts of the Christian faith, established the International Federation of Christian Trade Unions (I.F.C.T.U.) in 1920. The name was changed to the World Confederation of Labour in 1968.

During the Second World War moves to establish universal trade unionism resulted in the formation of the World Federation of Trade Unions (W.F.T.U.) in 1945. The Christian trade unions refused to join the new association and reconstituted the I.F.C.T.U. Attempts by the Communists to impose their own ideology within the W.F.T.U. led to the eventual secession of the democratic elements, which reconstituted themselves in the I.C.F.T.U. in 1949.

Trans-Europ-Express (T.E.E.)

Trans-Europ-Expresses connect major cities in nine European countries by a network of very fast and comfortable trains for which frontier formalities have been reduced to a minimum. The routes are, with name of train in brackets: Amsterdam-Munich (Rembrandt); Amsterdam-Zürich (Edelweiss); Avignon-Milan (Ligure); Basel-Milan (Gottardo); Bremen-Milan (Roland); Bremen-Vienna (Prinz Eugen); Brussels-Hanover (Diamant); Frankfurt-Amsterdam (van Beethoven); Geneva-Barcelona (Catalan-Talgo); Geneva-Milan (Lemano); Hamburg-Klagenfurt (Blauer Enzian); Hamburg-Zürich (Helvetia); Hook of Holland-Geneva (Rheingold); Munich-Milan (Mediolanum); Munich-Zürich (Bavaria); Nürnberg-Brussels (Saphir); Paris-Amsterdam (L'Etoile du Nord); Paris-Bordeaux (Aquitaine); Paris-Brussels (Brabant); Paris-Düsseldorf (Paris-Ruhr); Paris-Frankfurt (Goethe); Paris-Hamburg (Parsifal); Paris-Milan (Le Cisalphin); Paris-Nice (Le Mistral); Paris-Strasbourg (Stanislas); Paris-Toulouse (Le Capitole); Paris-Zürich (L'Arbalète); Zürich-Milan (Ticino).

transitional period

When the E.E.C. was first established, some of the provisions of the Treaty of Rome were applied in stages covering several years. This was known as the transitional period. The adaptation of the new member states to the Treaty was made similarly in stages over a transitional period. In the case of these new members the transitional period is still in operation, *e.g.* over tariff reductions.

Treaty of Brussels
see Accession, Treaty of

Treaty of Paris
see Paris Treaty

Treaty of Rome
see Rome Treaty

Trinidad and Tobago
Trinidad and Tobago signed the Lomé Convention of 1975.

Truman, Harry S.
Born Missouri, U.S.A., 1884, died 1972. Senator for Missouri in the United States from 1934. Chairman of the special committee on defence (especially defence expenditure), 1940. Vice-President of the United States of America, 1944. President, 1945–52. Supported the Committee of European Co-operation (Marshall Aid) plan for European recovery which was passed by Congress under his presidency.

In a message to Congress on 19 Dec. 1947, President Truman presented a draft of the Economic Co-operation Act which was designed to implement the Marshall Plan, or European Recovery Programme, as it was now called. 'The funds we make available will enable the countries of Europe to purchase goods which will achieve two purposes, to lift the standard of living in Europe closer to a decent level, and at the same time enlarge European capacity for production. Our funds will enable them to import grain for current consumption, and fertilisers and agricultural machinery to increase their food production. They will import fuel for current use, and mining machinery to increase their coal output. In addition, they will obtain raw materials, such as cotton, for current production, and some manufacturing and transportation equipment, to increase their productive capacity . . . The fundamental objective of further United States aid to European countries is to help them achieve economic self-support and to contribute their full share to a peaceful and prosperous world. Our aid must be adequate to this end. If we provide only half-hearted and half-way help, our efforts will be dissipated and the chances for political and economic stability in Europe are likely to be lost.'

Tunisia
Tunisia signed a preferential trade agreement with the E.E.C. which came into force on 1 July 1976 and which is part of the E.E.C. Mediterranean Policy.

tunnel

tunnel
see snake

Turkey
Turkey applied for association with the E.E.C. on 31 Oct. 1959 and the association agreement was signed in Ankara on 12 Sept. 1963. The aim of the first stage of five years was to speed up industrialisation, modernise agriculture and improve infrastructures before planning any mutual reduction of customs duties leading to a customs union. The second stage, which could last for a period of up to twelve years, was for the gradual establishment of a customs union, and in the third stage there would be a full customs union between the E.E.C. and Turkey. When this had been achieved Turkey would be eligible to apply for full membership of the E.E.C. Progress was slower than expected but an agreement came into force on 1 Jan. 1973 for implementing the Customs union. Turkey is eliminating duties on imports from the E.E.C. according to two time-tables – one of twelve years ending in 1985 and one of twenty-two years ending in 1995.

Economic profile: Area 780,600 sq. km. Population (1973) 37,933,000 (male (1970) 18,063,000) density 49 per sq. km. Births (per 1,000 of pop. 1973) 40.1; deaths, 13.6.

Labour force (1972) 14,438,000; percentage in agriculture, 67.4; industry, 13.1; services, 19.5.

International trade (in millions of U.A.):

	1965	*1970*	*1973*
Imports	577	885	1,680
Exports	459	589	1,056

	per 1,000 of population
Standard of living:	
Motor vehicles (1973)	4
Televisions (1972)	3
Telephones (1972)	18

two-tier tariff
A two-tier tariff consists of two sets of rates for the same goods in the tariff. The United Kingdom has a full rate and a preferential rate for the Commonwealth and, when a member of Efta, had a three-tier tariff.

U

U.A.
unit of account.

U.D.E.A.C.
Union douanière et économique de l'Afrique centrale, Central African Customs and Economic Union.

U.E.B.
Union Économique Benelux, Benelux Economic Union.

U.E.F.
Union européenne des fédéralistes, European Union of Federalists.

U.E.P.
Union européenne de paiements, European Payments Union.

Uganda
Uganda was a signatory of the Arusha Convention in July 1968 and, because this Convention was not ratified in time, of the second Arusha Convention of Sept. 1969. Uganda also signed the Lomé Convention of 1975.

U.N.C.T.A.D.

U.N.C.T.A.D.
The United Nations Conference on Trade and Development was established in 1964 and is concerned with the fundamental problems affecting the trade of developing countries. The headquarters are in Geneva, Switzerland.

undeveloped countries
see less developed countries

Unemployment benefits

Country	*Payments System*
Belgium	(1) Unemployment benefits.
	(2) Short-time employment benefits.
Denmark	(1) Voluntary insurance run by trade unions.
	(2) Short-time employment benefits.

unemployment (seasonally adjusted figures)

	1975	1977
Belgium	251,000	283,500
Denmark	146,600	138,500
France	974,600	950,200
German Federal Republic	1,179,700	1,002,400
Irish Republic	108,200	108,500
Italy	1,163,500	1,214,800[1]
Luxembourg	600	700
Netherlands	214,300	197,800
United Kingdom	1,235,500	1,422,400

[1]1976

Conditions of Payment

(1) 75 days at work out of the last 10 months or 600 days out of the last 36 months according to age. Payment for an unlimited period with few exceptions.

(2) Maximum: 1 year.

(1) 26 weeks employment out of the last 3 years and 12 months insurance with a Fund. Payment limited to 2½ years.

(2) Maximum of 130 weeks.

Benefits

(1) 60% of previous pay for the first year, 40% for those who are not heads of household.

(2) 60% of gross income plus fixed supplements ranging from approx. £1·34–£3·93 per day, and an extra 25p–£1·17 per day in some sectors.

(1) Normal rate is 90% of average pay in the last 5 weeks though each Fund fixes maximum for a year ahead (current year maximum=£12 per day approx.).

(2) 90% of wages up to a maximum of £77·95 per week approx.

251

Unemployment benefits

Country	Payment System
France	(1) Two-tier system of unemployment benefits and supplementary benefit schemes. (2) Short-time employment benefits.
Federal German Republic	(1) Two tier system of unemployment benefits and unemployment assistance. (2) Short-time employment benefits.
Irish Republic	(1) Unemployment insurance. (2) Unemployment assistance. (3) Short-time unemployment benefits.

Conditions of Payment

(1) After three months basic benefit is subject to a maximum on other income. It is also cut by 10 % for each year unemployed.

(2) 12 weeks per year.

(1) Unemployment benefits: minimum of 6 months insured employment in the last 3 years. Maximum pay period of 1 year.
Unemployment assistance: 10 weeks insured employment and stringent means test.
(2) 6 months renewable up to 12 months.

(1) 26–48 contributions paid or credited during preceding year. Maximum of 312 days in most cases.
(2) Means test, unlimited payment period.

(3) Unlimited.

Benefits

(1) Basic benefit = £1·30 per day approx. Maximum for combined benefit under both schemes is 90 %–95 % of previous pay. Those unemployed since Dec. 1974 for economic reasons entitled to 90 % of previous pay up to 1 year.
(2) 63p per hour approx. plus a supplement to reach £123 per month approx.

(1) Unemployment benefits: Approx. 70 % of previous earnings plus family allowances.
Unemployment assistance: Approx. 60 % of net pay.

(2) 68 % of net income and supplements in some sectors to reach 93 % of net income.

(1) Basic: £9·40 plus dependants' allowance plus 40 % of taxable weekly earnings between £14–£50.

(2) Maximum in urban areas £7·70 per week. £5·35 elsewhere plus dependants' allowance.

(3) 25 %–80 % of wage based on worker's family situation.

Unemployment benefits

Country	Payment System
Italy	(1) Unemployment benefits.
	(2) Short-time unemployment benefit.
Luxembourg	(1) Unemployment benefits.
Netherlands	(1) Waiting allowance.
	(2) Unemployment insurance.
	(3) Unemployment assistance.
	(4) Short-time unemployment benefit.
United Kingdom	(1) Flat rate contributions plus earnings related supplement.
	(2) Short-time unemployment benefits.

Conditions of Payment

Benefits

(1) At least 52 weeks contributions to the insurance fund in the past 2 years and at least 2 years in the insurance fund. Maximum of 180 days per year.
(2) 3 months renewable.

(1) Normal rate: Approx. 56p per day for a 26 day month. Workers made redundant for 'economic reasons' entitled to 66% of normal pay.

(2) 80% of gross income.

(1) 200 days employment during the previous year. Benefit limited to 26 weeks a year.

(1) 60% of normal pay.

(1) At least 130 days paid employment during last year. Maximum of 40 days per year.
(2) 65 days paid employment in the past year. Maximum benefit for unemployment insurance is 130 days per year and 2 years for unemployment assistance.
(3) Benefits under assistance are reduced according to claimants' other sources of income.
(4) 130 days.

(1) 80% of daily pay.

(2) Minimum of 75% of salary.

(3) Maximum of £23.50 per day approx.

(4) 100% of wages lost through short-time working.

(1) 26 contributions paid in previous year. Earnings related supplement requires 50 contributions during previous year. Flat rate benefits maximum period 312 days. Earnings related benefit maximum period 156 days.
(2) 60 hours in 6 months.

(1) Flat rate benefit £9·80 per week for single person plus allowances for dependants.

(2) 75% of wages lost through short-time working.

255

U.N.E.S.E.M.

U.N.E.S.E.M.
Union européenne des sources d'eaux minérales naturelles du Marché Commun, European Union of Natural Mineral Water Sources of the Common Market.

U.N.I.C.E.
Union des industries de la communauté européenne, Union of Industries of the European Community. This organisation brings together national federation of employers' associations. The Union holds regular meetings with the President and other members of the E.E.C. Commission and also has regular contacts with individual departments of the Commission.

U.N.I.D.O.
The United Nations Industrial Development Organisation was created in 1967 to assist in the industrialisation of the developing countries through direct assistance and mobilisation of national and international resources. The headquarters are in Vienna, Austria.

unification, previous attempts at European
Europe, as a concept, begins after the fall of the Roman Empire, which was in effect a world empire. The only portions of the world known to the Romans and not subject to them were the Parthian Empire and the tribes of Africa, Germany, Russia, Arabia and Asia who had no recognisable social systems. When the Roman Empire fell it split into two distinct parts: the homogenous Eastern Empire covering Balkan Europe and the Near East, and the Western Empire which was subjected to an almost complete extinction of civilised life.

Rome remained as a symbol; not only of civilisation but of unity. During the Dark Ages it was the Church of Rome which kept learning and religion alive. It was a Pope who invested Charlemagne with the title of Holy Roman Emperor on Christmas Day 800. A united Europe was not conceived of in those days. Charlemagne, as the most renowned warrior and most powerful monarch in the West, became the Papal champion in a dispute with the Eastern Empire. At the most he represented a sentimental longing for the return of civilisation; at the least, a convenient military support for a universalist Papacy. His Empire, which comprised most of France, Western Germany, the Low Countries and Northern Italy, was formally divided into three at the Treaty of Verdun in A.D. 843.

The conquests of Islam destroyed the Eastern Roman Empire, and as a result Western Europe became the sole heir of Rome and the sole repository of Christianity but there was no revival of a move towards a united Europe. The Holy Roman Empire, revived about A.D. 1000, came to be the title given to Habsburg possessions which included, by the sixteenth century, Spain, Austria, Bohemia, Northern Italy, parts of Hungary, the Low Countries and the Spanish Overseas Empire. The Habsburgs were also nominal heads of the German Confederation whose electors voted for the Holy Roman Emperor. However, the extent of Imperial power in Germany was strictly limited and France was a hereditary foe. With the death of the Habsburg Emperor Charles V in A.D. 1558 even this fragile unity disappeared and Spain and the Low Countries and Spanish America became a separate Habsburg monarchy. The rise of Protestantism at this time split the German Confederation and, more significantly, destroyed the one European survival from Rome, a unitary Church. Henceforth Europe was divided increasingly into national and religious blocs, many of them mutually antagonistic.

The French Revolution with its universalist ideas was brought to the rest of Europe on French bayonets. So far from uniting Europe, Napoleon actually revived dormant nationalist feelings in Spain, Holland, Prussia, Poland, Austria and Russia. For, just as France had always resisted inclusion into a Europe defined by the Holy Roman Empire, so the states of that Empire, which Napoleon abolished in 1806, resisted inclusion in a French Europe. To make their states better able to resist France the monarchs of the Old Regime borrowed from France legal and adminis-trative reforms and military ideas, and certain new attitudes to government did follow in Napoleon's wake, but after 1815 Europe was as fiercely national as ever.

Hitler was the last conqueror who gilded his actions with the tincture of European unity. He brought even fewer benefits than Napoleon, since his idea was openly racist. He sought a slave continent over which the superior Germans would rule, and from his rule the other nations derived neither material nor administrative benefits.

Thus the four previous attempts to unify Europe were hardly attempts at all. They tried to harness European power to combat, in each case, an

257

extra-European phenomenon. Charlemagne lent his strength to the Pope's battle against the Eastern Empire. Charles V lent the Church his soldiers to fight Islam and to convert American Indians. Napoleon needed Europe's goods and soldiers to fight England. Hitler claimed to be marshalling Europe to fight Russian Communism. The presence of this extra-European factor has lent colour to subsequent efforts to call these men the fathers of a united Europe.

Union of Soviet Socialist Republics

The U.S.S.R. attempts to negotiate with the E.E.C. through the Council for Mutual Economic Assistance (Comecon). In Sept. 1974 the secretary of Comecon invited the President of the E.E.C. Commission to visit Moscow. The invitation was accepted and contact was established in Dec. 1974. The meeting was not successful because the Commission's view was that Comecon was not of the same stature as the E.E.C. and therefore could not expect to conduct negotiations as equals. It was pointed out that the Community was a supranational organisation whereas Comecon was an intergovernmental agency and its secretariat had only a limited policy-making role and no authority to conclude trade agreements.

Economic profile: Area 22,402,200 sq. km. Population (1972) 247,459,000 (male (1971) 113,163,000) density 11 per sq. km. Births (per 1,000 of pop. 1973) 18.0; marriages, 9.4; deaths, 8.5. Infant mortality, 24.3.

International trade (in millions of U.A.):

	1965	*1970*
Imports	8,059	11,739
Exports	8,174	12,800

	per 1,000 of population
Standard of living:	
Motor vehicles (1973)	7
Televisions (1972)	160
Telephones (1972)	49

United Kingdom
The United Kingdom signed the Stockholm Convention (Efta) on 20 Nov.
1959. On 10 Aug. 1961 she requested that negotiations aiming at
membership of E.E.C. should start and these negotiations failed on 29 Jan.
1963 following President de Gaulle's statement on 14 Jan. that the United
Kingdom was not ready for Community membership. A further application was made on 11 May 1967 and on 22 Jan. 1972 the United Kingdom
signed the Treaty of Accession. On 31 Dec. 1972 she withdrew from Efta,
and joined the E.E.C. on 1 Jan. 1973. On 4 June 1974 details of the
renegotiation of the conditions of entry to the E.E.C. were published and
on 5 June 1975 the United Kingdom held its first referendum and the
electorate voted by a two-to-one majority to remain in the E.E.C.
Economic profile: Area 244,000 sq. km. Population (1973) 56,021,000
(male 27,271,000) density 230 per sq. km. Births (per 1,000 of pop. 1973)
14.0; marriages, 8.1; deaths, 12.0. Infant mortality, 17.2.

Labour force (1972) 24,816,000; percentage in agriculture, 3; industry,
42.9; services, 54.1.

International trade (in millions of U.A.):

	1965	*1970*	*1973*	*1976*
Imports	16,103	21,723	31,026	44,211
Exports	13,722	19,351	24,374	36,512

E.E.C. trade (in £1m.)

	1973	*1974*	*1975*	*1976*
Imports	5,197	7,722	8,802	11,396
Exports	4,030	5,508	6,389	9,174

	per 1,000 of population
Standard of living:	
Motor vehicles (1973)	234
Televisions (1972)	298
Telephones (1972)	289

United Kingdom, relative shares of international trade by area

Imports (percentage of world total)
Exports

	1970	1971	1972	1973	1974
E.E.C. (eight)	27·0	29·7	31·5	32·8	33·4
	29·2	29·0	30·2	32·4	33·4
Commonwealth	23·9	22·3	19·3	17·5	14·2
	21·0	21·9	18·9	16·6	16·4
Efta	12·6	13·0	14·5	15·0	13·0
	13·2	12·6	13·8	14·0	13·6
U.S.A.	13·0	11·1	10·5	10·2	9·7
	11·6	11·7	12·4	12·2	10·6
Soviet Eastern Europe	3·9	3·5	3·5	3·5	2·9
	3·2	2·7	2·8	2·6	2·6
Rest of World	19·6	20·4	20·7	21·0	26·8
	21·8	22·1	21·9	22·2	23·4

United Kingdom, Renegotiation of terms of Accession
On 1 April 1974 the British Labour Government demanded the re-negotiation of the terms of British accession to the Treaty of Rome. The Prime Minister announced in Parliament on 18 March that the Cabinet had decided to recommend that in the forthcoming referendum the British people should vote for continued membership of the E.E.C. The announcement was made after the conclusion of the British renegotiation process at the Dublin meeting of the E.E.C. Heads of Government.

The renegotiations covered a number of areas including the Community budget, New Zealand dairy produce, agriculture, regional aid and industrial policy and development co-operation.

United Kingdom, Terms of entry into the E.E.C.

The main points of agreement for the United Kingdom's entry into the E.E.C. were:

(i) *Transitional Period*   Five years from 1 Jan. 1973.

(ii) *Industrial Tariffs*   The removal of tariffs on goods traded amongst the Ten (later Nine) would be made in five stages each of 20 %, the first on 1 April 1973 and the last on 1 July 1977.

The Common External Tariff would be adopted in four stages, the first being an alignment of 40 % of the differences on 1 Jan. 1974 followed by three further moves each of 20 % of 1 Jan. 1975, 1 Jan. 1976 and 1 July 1977 respectively. For thirteen products (twelve industrial raw materials and tea) the United Kingdom would continue to import more than 90 % of her requirements duty-free. (The Common External Tariff would apply, with certain exceptions, to the United Kingdom's imports of Commonwealth manufactures.)

(iii) *Agriculture*   The United Kingdom would adopt the Community system of support, but not Community prices, in the first year of membership. Thereafter the United Kingdom would increase her threshold and intervention prices to full Community levels by six stages over the five-year transitional period. Tariffs on Horticulture would be dismantled in five equal stages of 20 % at the end of Dec. 1973 and ending in 1977.

(iv) *Community Finance*   The United Kingdom accepted the Community 'own resources' system of finance. From its inception until 1970 the Community's expenditure was financed by a combination of the proceeds from levies on agricultural imports which were made over to the Community and financial contributions from the member states.

On 21 April 1970 the Council of Ministers adopted a new system designed to make the Community self-financing and to bring its expenditure into one central budget. Between 1971 and 1977 the Community is phasing in the provision of its funds by payment from member countries of 90 % of the import levies they collect on imported farm produce and of the import duties on all other goods and the proceeds of up to a 1 % value added tax.

It was necessary to find a method to enable the United Kingdom gradually to adopt the Community system over a period of years without placing an undue burden on her economy.

A percentage of *key* has been set, broadly corresponding to the United Kingdom's share of the total gross national product (G.N.P.) in the ten

261

countries of the enlarged Community. This represents the proportion of the budget which the United Kingdom would nominally be expected to pay in the first year of membership. This key would then increase marginally in each of the four subsequent years under similar arrangements to those agreed by the Six for themselves.

However, the United Kingdom would pay only a proportion of her nominal contribution for the first five years. The proportion would increase in annual stages.

The effect of these arrangements is shown in the following table.

Column 2 sets out the nominal key.

   3 shows the proportion which the United Kingdom would, in practice, be required to pay.

   4 gives the United Kingdom's resulting share of the Community budget in each year.

(1) Year	(2) U.K. Percentage of Community budget	(3) Percentage of key to be paid	(4) U.K. contribution as percentage of Community budget
1973	19·19	45·0	8·64
1974	19·38	56·0	10·85
1975	19·77	67·5	13·34
1976	20·16	79·5	16·03
1977	20·56	92·0	18·92

After the first five years there would be a further period of two years, during which the size of the United Kingdom's contribution would be limited by reference to the previous year's contribution.

In 1980 and subsequent years the United Kingdom would be required to pay 90% of her agricultural levy and customs duties and such value added tax (V.A.T.) (not exceeding the yield of a 1% V.A.T.) as is necessary to close any gap between Community expenditure and Community revenue.

This gap cannot be estimated, but it is important to note that in common with other members the United Kingdom is entitled to receive payments from the Community budget, as well as to make contributions to it.

If Community expenditure moves away from agricultural subsidies and assistance towards industrial and regional activities, as seems likely in the course of time, the United Kingdom could expect to enjoy larger receipts from the Community budget for her needs under a wider regional policy.

(v) *Institutions* The United Kingdom would have the same representation and voting weight in the enlarged Community as the other three large countries, Federal German Republic, France and Italy. Most decisions of the Council of Ministers are taken on the basis of a proposal by the Commission. For certain Council decisions unanimity is required. In cases where qualified voting with weighting of votes is provided in the Treaty, the members of the Council have the following weightings: Federal German Republic 10, Italy 10, France 10, the United Kingdom 10, Belgium 5, the Netherlands 5, Denmark 3, Norway 3, Irish Republic 3, Luxembourg 2. Total 61.

In those cases where the Council decision follows a proposal by the Commission, the decisions of the Council are to be effective only if at least forty-three votes are cast in favour out of sixty-one.

Where the decision is one on which the Commission has not made a proposal, it is approved only if forty-three votes are cast in favour by at least six members. In cases in which a simple majority is required, a majority will, of course, be six out of the ten states.

(vi) *Sugar* The United Kingdom Government's contractual obligations to buy agreed quantities of sugar under the Commonwealth Sugar Agreement would be fulfilled until 1974, and domestic beet sugar production continued to be limited until then.

Thereafter it has been agreed that the arrangements for sugar imports from developing Commonwealth sugar producers should be made within the framework of an association or trading agreement with the enlarged Community.

(vii) *New Zealand* The quantities of New Zealand butter and cheese on which import levies would not be payable would be run down to a figure of 80% of New Zealand's current butter exports to the United Kingdom and 20% of her cheese exports by the end of five years. The butter situation would be reviewed in the third year of the United Kingdom's membership and the enlarged Council of Ministers would decide on measures for assuring the exceptional treatment granted to New Zealand to be continued after 1977.

(viii) *Sterling* The United Kingdom has agreed to an orderly and gradual rundown of sterling balances after joining the Community and in the meantime they would be stabilised. No time-table has been set for the

263

dismantling of sterling's reserve role.

(ix) *Coal and Steel*   The United Kingdom needs no transitional period for applying the rules of the European Coal and Steel Community, but the alignment of tariffs on steel products would be made at the same rate as the alignment of tariffs on industrial goods generally.

(x) *Fiscal Harmonisation*   Britain would adopt the various measures of fiscal harmonisation. Her use of Value Added Tax would be in advance of membership of the Community and she would also adopt other harmonisation measures according to her terms of membership. She would convert customs duties at present levied on hydro-carbon oils, beer, spirits and tobacco into internal taxes similar to V.A.T. to allow free movement of these commodities in accordance with the Treaty.

(xi) *Channel Islands and Isle of Man*   There would be free trade in agricultural and industrial goods between the islands and the members of the Community, but the islands would be exempt from other Community rules and regulations, including Value Added Tax, free movement of labour, freedom of establishment and competition policy.

(xii) *Export Credits*   The United Kingdom's present system of export credits operated by the Export Credits Guarantee Department requires adjustment to comply with the Community's rules and would be changed during a two-year transitional period.

(xiii) *Independent Commonwealth Countries* in Africa, the Caribbean, the Indian Ocean and the Pacific would be able to choose between (*a*) association under a renewed Yaoundé Convention (which became the Lomé Convention); (*b*) some other form of association exemplified by the Arusha Convention, or (*c*) a commercial agreement.

(xiv) *All British dependent territories*, except Gibraltar and Hong Kong, would be offered association under Part iv of the Treaty of Rome.

(xv) *Gibraltar*   The Treaty provisions would apply to Gibraltar as a European Territory for whose external relations a member state is responsible. Gibraltar would not, however, be included in the customs area of the enlarged Community as she is not part of the United Kingdom customs territory.

(xvi) *Hong Kong* is included in the Community scheme of generalised preferences.

(xvii) *India, Pakistan, Sri Lanka, Malaysia and Singapore* are also included in the generalised system of tariff preferences. After enlargement, the Community would examine trade problems, including Indian exports of sugar and textiles. The Community tariff on tea, as stated elsewhere, has also been suspended.

(xviii) *Malta and Cyprus*   Association agreements for preferential trading arrangements.

(xix) *Fisheries*   Notwithstanding the policy of the Community to limit restrictions on fishing to within six miles of the coast of member states, the limit would be extended to twelve miles for certain coastal waters of Denmark, France, Irish Republic and the United Kingdom for a period of five years after accession. At the end of five years, the Council, acting on a proposal from the Commission, would determine conditions for fishing to ensure protection of fishing grounds and the conservation of resources.

United Nations Development Programme
see International Bank for Reconstruction and Development

United States of America, attitude to the E.E.C. of
President Carter stated, on 8 May 1977, that 'I see no way that we can have a successful resolution of East-West problems without the full understanding and participation of our allies and friends in Europe', and again, 'I strongly favour, perhaps more than my predecessors, a close inter-relationship among the nations of Europe, the European Community in particular'.

In presenting his annual report on foreign policy on 25 Feb. 1971, the then President stated 'The European Community is on the threshold of a momentous advance. Last year the Commission of the Community began negotiating with Great Britain, Norway, Denmark and Ireland for their full membership. It opened talks with Sweden, Austria, Switzerland and other members of the European Free Trade Association looking toward some form of relationship. The prospect of an expanded Community . . . makes the Community a potential economic giant. . . .

   The United States has always supported the strengthening and enlargement of the European Community. We welcome cohesion in Europe because it makes Europe a sturdier pillar of the structure of peace. Regional cohesion contributes to world stability and America's and Western

Europe's fundamental interests are parallel in most areas of policy. . . . Ultimately we may see a single entity making policy for Western Europe in all fields, including diplomacy and defence. We would welcome this, because we believe that Western European and American interests in defence and foreign policy are complementary. . . .'

Economic profile: Area 9,363,100 sq. km. Population (1973) 210,400,000 (male (1972) 102,053,000) density 23 per sq. km. Births (per 1,000 of pop. 1973) 15.6; marriages, 10.9; deaths, 9.4. Infant mortality, 18.5.

Labour force (1972) 86,542,000; percentage in agriculture, 4.2; industry, 31; services, 64.8.

	per 1,000 of population
Standard of living:	
Motor vehicles (1973)	460
Televisions (1972)	449
Telephones (1972)	604

Trade with E.E.C. (US$1m.):

	Imports	*Exports and re-exports*
1960	2,263	3,437
1970	6,612	8,423
1974	19,206	22,068
1975	16,732	22,862

Trade with Efta (US$1m.)

	Imports	*Exports and re-exports*
1960	1,608	2,277
1970	3,854	4,517
1974	7,344	8,045
1975	7,040	8,458

Trade with the Soviet bloc (US$1m.):

	Imports	Exports and re-exports
1960	81	193
1970	225	168
1974	526	1,801
1975	891	1,432

unit of account

The unit of account is a common concept of value, independent of national currencies but linked to them by conversion rates. It also enables single common prices to be established for the whole of the Community. The unit of account can fulfil these two functions satisfactorily, however, only if the conversion rates reflect market exchange rates.

For a long time the gold-parity unit of account was the only one used by the Community and it fulfilled the above functions admirably until 1971. Then, however, it ceased to reflect market relationships and its use led to distortions, so that the Communities had to make many adaptations. The situation with regard to units has now become extremely complicated, and the Commission is working towards substituting a unit of account that can be used generally for those used at present.

The following table shows the main areas of use of the different units of account in the Community institutions:

Agriculture	agricultural U.A.
Budget	gold parity U.A.
Customs Tariff	gold parity U.A.
E.C.S.C.	E.U.A.
E.D.F.	E.U.A.
E.I.B.	E.U.A.
E.M.C.F.	E.M.U.A.
S.O.E.C.	E.U.R.

Gold-parity unit of account has a reference weight of 0.88867088 grams of fine gold. The conversion rate of a currency into parity units is the ratio between the reference weight in gold of the unit of account and the last parity of the currency as declared to the International Monetary Fund.

267

This conversion rate remains unchanged, therefore, unless the legal I.M.F. parity is changed. As long as I.M.F. gold parities stayed close to market exchange rates, currency exchange relationships deriving from conversion rates of the gold-parity unit continued to reflect market exchange relationships.

As the member states of the Community have not changed their currency gold parities since 1969, whereas market exchange rates have altered considerably, the gold-parity unit of account no longer accurately reflects exchange relationships between the different currencies.

The gold-parity unit of account is used in the general budget of the European Communities. The financial contributions to the budget by member states are worked out in gold-parity units and the equivalent in national currency is given by the gold-parity unit conversion rate for that currency.

This unit of account is also used in many other areas of Community activity, for example, for fixing common maximum amounts or common prices, including the specific duties in the Common Customs Tariff and fines imposed for breaches of competition policy.

Agricultural unit of account is officially defined as the value of 0.88867088 grams of fine gold, like the gold-parity unit, but representative conversion rates have gradually been substituted for gold-parity conversion rates for converting the common prices, which are fixed in agricultural units of account, into amounts expressed in member states' currencies. From time to time these conversion rates are changed by Council decision to bring them into line with market exchange rates. These rates are known as the 'green' pound, the 'green' lira, etc.

European Monetary Unit of Account (E.M.U.A.) is defined as equal in value to 0.88867088 grams of fine gold. The rates for converting E.M.U.A.s into national currencies are the same as the central rates, established in accordance with Article XXI, Section 2, of the I.M.F. Articles of Agreement. In theory the E.M.U.A. should have a rate of conversion only into those currencies which are still within the European limited banks of fluctuation, 'the snake'. However, the European Monetary Co-operation Fund fixes a conversion rate for the E.M.U.A. into U.S. dollars.

The E.M.U.A. is used by the E.M.C.F. to settle claims and liabilities between central banks, arising from their intervention operations on the exchanges designed to keep their currencies within the maximum margin of 2.25% at any given time. The fact that the E.M.C.F. calculates these amounts in E.M.U.A. constitutes an exchange guarantee and enables the credit and debit positions *vis-à-vis* the Fund to be settled on a multilateral basis.

European Unit of Account has the same gold reference weight as the E.M.U.A. and is converted in the same way for those currencies within the European exchange rate system. However, unlike the E.M.U.A. conversion rates are also calculated for all other floating currencies. This unit of account is used by the Statistical Office of the European Communities.

The E.U.A. is a composite basket of fixed amounts of currencies of the nine member states. Its value in various currencies is calculated daily by reference to the market exchange rates of the component currencies. It varies according to the variations of the rates of each of the currencies in the basket, the influence of each currency in the variation being a function of the weighting assigned to it at the outset.

To establish the value of the composite basket in any given currency, whether it be Community currency or not, the going market exchange rates are used so that the exchange relationships between the various currencies, derived from the E.U.A. conversion rate, always accurately reflect the market situation.

The E.U.A. is used by the European Development Fund and by the European Coal and Steel Community for their respective budgets and also to express most expenditure and revenue items. The E.U.A. is also used by the European Investment Bank for its accounts. It is now being introduced for agreements with non-Community countries and for fixing ceilings previously calculated in gold-parity units.

The Commission was (1977) in the process of harmonising the units of account in use. Instead of the unit of account being valued by reference to a single currency or gold the aim is for a gradual and widespread adoption of a 'currency basket' or collection of currencies unit of account.

University Institute, European

The Convention setting up the European University Institute by the E.E.C. came into effect on 19 April 1972. The institute is situated at Villa Tolomei, Florence, Italy. It had 70 post-graduate students in 1976 and it is planned to house a library of 150,000 volumes.

Principal: Max Kohnstamm.

U.P.E.
Union Parlementaire Européenne, European Parliamentary Union.

Upper Volta
Upper Volta was a signatory of the Yaoundé Conventions of 1963 and 1969 and of the Lomé Convention of 1975.

urban population (1970)

country	% of total population
Austria	51
Belgium	67
Denmark	45
Finland	51
France	70
Federal German Republic	70
Greece	53
Iceland	69
Irish Republic	49
Italy	64
Luxembourg	62
Netherlands	80
Norway	43
Portugal	24
Spain	51
Sweden	67
Switzerland	59
United Kingdom	77

Uruguay
Uruguay signed a non-preferential trade agreement, for a period of three years, with the E.E.C. under Article 113 of the Treaty of Rome on 2 April 1973, which came into force on 1 Aug 1974.

U.S.S.R.
see Union of Soviet Socialist Republics

V

value added tax
The first aim of the E.E.C. in the field of indirect taxation harmonisation was for each member country to abandon its particular form of turnover taxation in favour of value added tax (V.A.T.), and the aim is to adopt later a level of V.A.T. common to all member countries.

The arguments for adopting V.A.T. as the common system of turnover taxation in the E.E.C. have been stated by the Commission as:
(i) V.A.T. is competitively neutral. At equal prices the same kind of goods carry the same amount of tax;
(ii) V.A.T. encourages productivity and modernisation, tax already paid on investment goods being deductible.
(iii) The fiscal burden is not affected by the number of intermediate stages or intermediaries involved in the production and marketing of the goods. Integrated businesses are, in spite of their apparent suppression of one or several stages, put on the same footing as non-integrated businesses;
(iv) V.A.T. encourages specialisation, since an increase in the number of stages to achieve greater specialisation does not lead to an increase in the tax burden;
(vi) It adapts to the pursuit of the economic and social objectives of the Community, in particular because it allows the application of reduced rates at any stage.

The characteristics of V.A.T. as a method of imposing a general tax on the use of goods and services by the final consumer lie, firstly, in the fact that it is charged at each stage in production and distribution on the value that has been added to the product, by processing costs and profit in the

271

case of manufacture or by profit in the case of re-sale; and, secondly, that tax paid at earlier stages is deductible at each stage so that it is only at the final stage, that of final consumption, that the tax becomes a fiscal charge which is no longer deductible.

The following table shows that V.A.T. rates applicable in the member countries:

	Standard rate	Reduced rates (foodstuffs and other essential goods)	Increased rates (luxury goods)
Belgium	18	6	25
Denmark	15	9·25	–
France	20	7	33
German Federal Republic	11	5·5	–
Irish Republic	20	10	40
Italy	14	9	35
Luxembourg	10	2	–
Netherlands	18	4	–
United Kingdom	8	–	12·5

van Zeeland, Paul

Born Belgium, 1893. Belgian delegate to the conference setting up the Council of Europe, 1949. Belgian Foreign Minister, 1950–4. Belgian delegate to the Council of Europe Consultative Assembly. Leader of the European Union League which joined the International Committee of Movements for European Unity, sponsor of the Hague Congress of Europe, in 1948.

variable import levy

A charge levied on certain agricultural products, *e.g.* some cereals, which is varied so as to raise the price of imports into the Community broadly to the price level which it is desired to maintain within the E.E.C. During the transitional stage such levels will be applied to trade between member states so that Community suppliers will enjoy a preference over other sources of supply. The intra-E.E.C. levies will be eliminated when the full Common Market stage is reached.

Varoni Plan

The Varoni Plan was a ten-year plan for industrial expansion in Italy and a protocol of the Treaty of Rome stipulated that this plan should be taken into account in the policy of the E.E.C.

V.D.I.

Verein Deutscher Ingenieure, Association of German Engineers, issues *Richtlinien*, recommendations, similar to the British Standards Institution's Code of Practice.

Vedel, Georges

Born France, 1910. Professor of Law at the University of Paris. Technical counsellor to French Foreign Minister, 1956–8. Associate of *Le Monde* since 1966. President of an independent commission of the E.E.C. 1971–2.

Vedel Report

In April 1972 the E.E.C. Commission drew up a report, known as the Vedel Report, which advocated a change in the rôle and power of the European Parliament.

The report argued that under existing conditions the Parliament, while democratically reflecting the political patterns of the member states, was working 'in a vacuum', and its debates had 'almost no impact on the Press, public opinion and the life of the political parties'; the root cause of this general indifference was the lack of legislative power, to the extent that 'the rôle of the assembly is something less than that of a Parliament, and Community decisions acquire democratic legitimacy almost exclusively through national channels.' The report also pointed out that a serious imbalance existed between the Council, the Commission and the Parliament. While the Treaty of Rome gave the Council a predominant rôle in the Commission's decision-making process, practice had 'served only to increase this preponderance to such a point that the Council...has become the sole effective centre of power in the system.' Through lack of powers, the Commission was prevented from playing a full part and was regarded as being seriously hampered by its lack of political influence in its relations with the Council. The balance between the three institutions had been further upset, the report continued, by the practice of taking most decisions only on the basis of unanimous agreement within the Council, whereby the Commission's freedom to make innovatory proposals had been restricted and it had been forced to make compromise solutions to receive unanimous support.

To replace the form of 'diplomatic-style negotiations' which the decison-making process had assumed, by an effective system subject at all times to political arbitration, and in which Parliament could play a genuine rôle, the report made a number of specific proposals designed to give the Parliament powers of co-decision with the Council and rights of veto over its decisions by means of modifications to the Treaties of Rome. This would mean that a Council decision could not come into force without prior approval by the Parliament. During the first stage of the progressive implementation of the proposals, the Parliament would be given greater powers of consultation, consisting of the right to ask the Council to reconsider a decision. The report suggested that the Parliament should be consulted in the preparation of medium-term economic policy programmes, and that all three institutions should work together to prepare Community budget estimates.

veto

The Treaties do not indicate that member states of the European Communities can exercise a veto in the Council, except of course by implication where a Treaty specifies that a vote on a particular subject must be unanimous.

The French government, however, recorded their view in the Accords of Luxembourg in Jan. 1966, that 'where very important interests are at stake the discussion must be continued until unanimous agreement is reached.'

The practical result is that since 1966 almost all Council acts have been the result of unanimous agreement.

Vocational Training, Advisory Committee on
The Advisory Committee on Vocational Training, an E.E.C. Commission advisory committee on social policy, was created by Council decision in 1963. It has fifty-four members, two government and two trade union representatives and two employers per country. The members are appointed by governments. The Committee is serviced by the Commission.

Vocational Training, European Centre for
The European Centre for Vocational Training, established by the Council of Ministers in 1975 and opened in West Berlin on 9 March 1977, is an institute of a new kind. It has a quadripartite administrative board with thirty members: nine representatives of the Governments of member states, nine representatives of the trade union organisations, nine representatives of the employers and three representatives of the Commission. The Centre has the task of encouraging, at E.E.C. level, the development of vocational training. Through its scientific and technical activities it aims to contribute to the implementation of a common vocational training policy, mentioned in Article 128 of the E.E.C. treaty. It has the particular duty of encouraging the exchange of information and the comparison of experience.

voting procedures and majorities
see majorities

W

Warsaw Pact
The Warsaw Treaty Organisation was created on 14 May 1955 as a mutual defence alliance of Albania, Bulgaria, Czechoslovakia, the German Democratic Republic, Hungary, Poland, Romania and the U.S.S.R., Albania was barred from meetings in 1962 and withdrew in 1968.

W.C.L.
see World Confederation of Labour

Werner, Pierre
Born Luxembourg, 1913. Luxembourg lawyer and politician.Prime Minister, 1959–74. Chairman of the Committee on Monetary Union. The Committee reported in 1970 leading to the adoption by the Council of Ministers of various measures for economic co-operation including the creation of the 'snake'.

Werner Report
The first Werner Report was presented to the E.E.C. Council of Ministers in May 1970 and discussions took place on this document in June when a second report was called for. This second report was completed in Oct. 1970. The report reiterated the objectives of the economic and monetary union agreed at the Hague summit conference in Dec. 1969, and emphasised that decisions on economic policy would be taken at Community level rather than at national level and that this in turn would inevitably lead to political union. Such a monetary union would lead to 'the total and irreversible convertibility of currencies, the elimination of margins of fluctuation in rates of exchange, the irrevocable fixing of parity ratios and the total liberation of movements of capital'.

In Dec. 1970 the Council of Ministers agreed on the first stage of the Werner Report but could reach no agreement on the final stages of the report.

Western European Union (W.E.U.)
On 17 March 1948 a 50-year treaty 'for collaboration in economic, social and cultural matters and for collective self-defence' was signed in Brussels by the Foreign Ministers of the United Kingdom, France, the Netherlands, Belgium and Luxembourg.

On 20 Dec. 1950 the functions of the Western Union defence organisation were transferred to the North Atlantic Treaty command and the Western Union command ceased to exist.

After the rejection by France of the European Defence Community on

30 Aug. 1954, attended by Belgium, Canada, France, Federal German Republic, Italy, the Netherlands, Luxembourg, the United Kingdom and the U.S.A., it was decided to invite the Federal German Republic and Italy to accede to the Brussels Treaty, to end the occupation of Western Germany and to invite the latter to accede to the North Atlantic Treaty; the Federal Republic agreed that it would voluntarily limit its arms production, and provision was made for the setting up of an agency to control the armaments of the seven Brussels Treaty powers; the United Kingdom undertook not to withdraw from the Continent her four divisions and the Tactical Air Force assigned to the Supreme Allied Commander against the wishes of a majority, *i.e.* four of the Brussels Treaty powers, except in the event of an acute overseas emergency.

At a Conference of Ministers held in Paris from 20 to 23 Oct. 1954 these decisions were put into effect. The Union was formally inaugurated on 6 May 1955.

The Council of W.E.U. consists of the Foreign Ministers of the seven powers or their representatives. An Assembly, composed of the W.E.U. delegates to the Consultative Assembly of the Council of Europe, meets twice a year, usually in Paris. An Agency for the Control of Armaments and a Standing Armaments Committee have been set up in Paris. The social and cultural activities were transferred to the Council of Europe on 1 June 1960.

After the breakdown of the negotiations for the United Kingdom entry into the Common Market in 1963, the six E.E.C. countries proposed to the United Kingdom that the W.E.U. Council (the Six and the United Kingdom) should meet every three months 'to take stock of the political and economic situation in Europe'. The United Kingdom welcomed this proposal and regular meetings took place. While political consultation continues, discussion of the economic situation has been suspended since June 1970 when negotiations for the enlargement of the E.E.C. began.

Western Samoa

Western Samoa was a signatory of the Lomé Convention of 1975.

W.E.U.

see Western European Union.

W.F.T.U.
see World Federation of Trade Unions.

W.H.O.
World Health Organisation

Wilson, Sir Harold
Born Huddersfield, England, 1916. Elected member of Parliament, 1945. President of the Board of Trade, 1947–51. Leader of the Parliamentary Labour Party, 1963. Prime Minister, 1964–70 and 1974–6. Proposed British entry to the E.E.C. in 1967–8; and a referendum on continued British membership 1975.

wine
Annual wine consumption in litres per head in E.E.C. countries for year ended 31 Aug. 1975:

Belgium	15
Denmark	11
France	103
German Federal Republic	23
Irish Republic	2
Italy	103
Luxembourg	40
Netherlands	9
United Kingdom	6

wine, 'lake'
see 'lake'

working groups
see committees

World Bank

see International Bank for Reconstruction and Development.

World Confederation of Labour

The first congress of the International Federation of Christian Trade Unions (I.F.C.T.U.), as the W.C.L. was then called, met in 1920; but a large proportion of its 3·4m. members were in Italy and Germany, where affiliated unions were suppressed by the Fascist and Nazi regimes, and in 1940 I.F.C.T.U. went out of existence. It was reconstituted in 1945, and declined to merge with W.F.T.U. and, later, with I.C.F.T.U. The policy of I.F.C.T.U. was based on the papal encyclicals *Rerum novarum* (1891) and *Quadragesimo anno* (1931), but in 1968, when the Federation became the W.C.L., it was broadened to include other concepts. The W.C.L. now has Protestant, Buddhist and Moslem members as well as its mainly Roman Catholic members.

The W.C.L. is organised on a federative basis which leaves wide discretion to its autonomous constituent unions. Its governing body is the Congress, which meets every four years. The Congress appoints, or reappoints, the Secretary-General at each four-yearly meeting. The General Council which meets at least once a year, is composed of the members of the Confederal Board, at least twenty-two members, elected by the Congress, and representatives of national confederations, international trade federations, and trade union organisations where there is no confederation affiliated to the W.C.L. The Confederal Board is responsible for the general leadership of the W.C.L., in accordance with the decisions and directives of the Council and Congress. The headquarters are in Brussels.

There are regional organisations in Latin America (office in Caracas), Africa (office in Banjul, Gambia) and Asia (office in Manila). There is also a liaison centre in Montreal.

A total membership of 14m. in about ninety countries is claimed. The biggest groups are the French Democratic Confederation of Labour (800,000), the Confederation of Christian Trade Unions of Belgium (1m.), the Netherlands Catholic Workers' Movement (340,000). (*see also* trade unions.)

World Federation of Trade Unions

The W.F.T.U. formally came into existence on 3 Oct. 1945, representing trade union organisations in more than fifty countries of the world, both Communist and non-Communist, excluding Germany and Japan, as well as a number of lesser and colonial territories. Representation from the U.S.A. was limited to the Congress of Industrial Organisations, as the American Federation of Labor declined to participate.

In Jan. 1949 the British, U.S.A. and Netherlands trade unions withdrew from W.F.T.U., which had come under complete Communist control; and by June 1951 all non-Communist trade unions, including the Yugoslavian Federation, had left W.F.T.U.

The Congress meets every four years. In between, the General Council, of 134 members including deputies, is the governing body, meeting in theory at least once a year. The Bureau controls the activities of W.F.T.U. between meetings of the General Council; it consists of the President, the General Secretary and members from different continents, the total number being decided at each Congress. The Bureau is elected by the General Council.

In 1972 a total membership of 150m. was claimed. The biggest groups are the Soviet All-Union Central Council of Trade Unions (89m.), the East-German Free German Trade Union Federation (7·3m.), the Polish Central Council of Trade Unions (6·9m.), the Czechoslovak Central Council of Trade Unions (5·4m.), the Italian General Confederation of Labour (G.C.I.L., 3·8m.), the Romanian General Confederation of Labour (3·2m.), the Hungarian Central Council of Trade Unions (2·8m.) and the French Confederation of Labour (C.G.T., 1·5m.); the General Federation of Iraqi Trades Unions was affiliated in 1967. (*see also* trade unions.)

worm
see snake

Y

Yaoundé, Cameroon
Capital situated on railway to Douala. Commercial centre for the Central African Republic. Manufactures include cigarettes and soap. The first E.E.C. Yaoundé Convention was signed there is 1963 and the second in 1969. Population was estimated at 274,399 in 1975.

Yaoundé Conventions
The first Yaoundé Convention on the Association of Overseas Territories with the E.E.C. expired on 31 Dec. 1962. A number of independent African states which had formerly been French, Belgian or Italian colonies had expressed a wish to continue the association under a new agreement. After protracted negotiations the Convention of Association between the E.E.C. and associated African states and Madagascar was signed at Yaoundé, Cameroon, on 20 July 1963, and the Yaoundé Convention, as it was known, entered into force on 1 June 1964. The eighteen associated African states were Benin (then Dahomey), Burundi, Cameroon, Central African Republic, Chad, Congo, Gabon, Ivory Coast, Madagascar, Mali, Mauritania, Niger, Rwanda, Senegal, Somalia, Togo, Upper Volta and Zaïre.
    The main provisions of the Yaoundé Convention were as follows:
(i) Exports from the associated states to the E.E.C. member countries would be subject to the same gradual elimination of duties and expansion of quotas as applied within the Community. Certain tropical products would enter Common Market countries duty-free, and the common external tariff would operate at reduced rates for these products.
(ii) Not later than six months after the Convention's entry into force, the associated states would extend the same tariff treatment to products originating in all E.E.C. countries, and would gradually abolish quantitative restrictions. In certain cases, however, duties might still be applied by associated states to products from the Community, when such duties corresponded to the requirements of their development, industrialisation or budget.
(iii) The object of the Convention—to foster the economic and social development of the associated states—would be achieved through the

281

European Development Fund and the European Investment Bank.
(iv) The provisions on establishment, service, payments and capital were
based on the principle of reciprocal non-discrimination against individuals
and companies.

The Convention was to be valid for five years, but could be terminated at
six months' notice by any of the associated states with respect to the
Community or vice versa.

The institutions of association, set up under the Convention, are:
(i) the Council of Association, composed of members of the Community's
Council of Ministers and Commission, and a member of the Government
of each associated state;
(ii) the Parliamentary Conference of the Association, consisting of
members of the European Parliament and of the Parliaments of the
associated states;
(iii) the Association Committee, made up of one representative of each of
the Community countries and the associated states, and
(iv) the five-member Court of Arbitration of the Association.

The 'Second Yaoundé Convention', renewing the Convention of 1963
with modifications, was signed on 29 July 1969, again after protracted
negotiations.

Difficulties had arisen through criticism by the African states of the
divergent results of the first Convention; they pointed out that their exports
to the E.E.C. had risen by less than 1% between 1964 and 1966 and had
fallen by 1% in 1967, whereas E.E.C. exports to the African countries had
increased by some 10% in 1966–7. The associated states also expressed
dissatisfaction with the allocation of aid from the European Development
Fund, which had shown only a small increase in genuine aid against a high
relative increase in loans.

The second Convention, which expired on 31 Jan. 1975, provided:
(i) that the E.E.C. would grant to agricultural imports from the associated
states a more favourable treatment than before, while continuing the
complete exemption from customs duty of imports of non-agricultural
products from these states;
(ii) that aid of $918m. (to be supplied through the European Development
Fund in the form of grants totalling $748m. and loans on favourable terms
of $80m., and through the European Investment Bank as loans totalling
$90m.) would be provided to the associated states for the five-year period of
the new Convention—the associated states having previously requested a

total of $1,500m.;

(iii) that of the total grants, from $65m. to $80m. should be set aside as a 'disaster fund' to be used in emergencies, including severe falls in exports prices; and

(iv) that African companies should have a 15 % advantage in tendering for certain E.E.C.-financed projects.

An agreement providing for the accession of Mauritius to the Yaoundé Convention was signed in Port Louis on 12 May 1972, and came into effect on 1 June 1973.

The second Yaoundé Convention was replaced by the Lomé Convention of 1975.

Yugoslavia
Yugoslavia signed a non-preferential trade agreement under Article 113 which came into force on 1 Sept. 1973 for a period of five years. Yugoslavia is the only Communist country with such relations with the E.E.C.

Z

Zaire
Zaire was signatory of the Yaoundé Conventions of 1963 and 1969 and of the Lomé Convention of 1975.

Zambia
Zambia was a signatory of the Lomé Convention of 1975.

Zoja Laboratories
The United States Commercial Solvents Corporation holds a world-wide monopoly for the production of a chemical compound which is essential for the production of a drug used against tuberculosis. One of the principal buyers in Europe was the Zoja Laboratories, who bought the compound

from the Instituto Chemiterapeutico Italiano, a subsidiary of Commercial Solvents. After failing in an attempt to take over Zoja, Commercial Solvents Corporation ordered its subsidiary to cease delivering to Zoja and to produce the drug itself. The E.E.C. Commission fined Commercial Solvents Corporation and its Italian subsidiary and ruled that the cut-off of the traditional deliveries by a firm holding a dominant position constitutes an abuse under Article 86 of the Rome Treaty. It also ordered the firms to immediately supply Zoja with the chemical compound.

Zollverein

Zoll, customs and *Verein*, union. The word is generally applied to the German union formed in 1833 instigated by Prussia. The *Zollverein* created the economic unification of Germany. It allowed the expansion of commerce and industry, the improvement of transport and building of railways and prepared the way for the alignment of commercial and industrial law.

Select Bibliography

POST-WAR EUROPE AND GENERAL BOOKS ON THE E.E.C.:

Hallstein, W., *United Europe: Challenge and Opportunity*, 1962.
Der Unvollendete Bundesstaat, 1969. *Europe in the Making*, 1972.
Gimbel, J., *The Origins of the Marshall Plan* (Stanford Univ. Press, 1976).
Henderson, W. O., *The Genesis of the Common Market* (London, 1962).
General Report on the Activities of the Communities (Annual from 1958).
Paxton, J., *The Developing Common Market* (London, 1976).

THE TERMS OF BRITAIN'S ENTRY INTO THE E.E.C.:

Butler, D., and Kitzinger, U., *The 1975 Referendum* (London, 1976).
Kitzinger, U., *Diplomacy and Persuasion* (London, 1973).
Krag, J. O., *Le Danemark à l'heure du marché commun: Bloc-notes, 1971–1972* (Paris, 1974).
Northern Ireland and the European Communities (Cmnd 563, H.M.S.O., 1971).
Pisani, E., and others, *Problems of British Entry into the E.E.C.* (London, 1969).
Treaty concerning the Accession of the Kingdom of Denmark, Ireland, the Kingdom of Norway and the United Kingdom of Great Britain and Northern Ireland to the European Economic Community and the European Atomic Energy Community, and Decision of the Council of the European Communities concerning the Accession of the said States to the European Coal and Steel Community (Two parts. Cmnd 4862–I and 4862–II, 1972).
The United Kingdom and the European Communities (Cmnd 4715, H.M.S.O., 1971).
Young, S. Z., *Terms of Entry* (London, 1974).

THE TREATIES OF PARIS, ROME AND THE TREATY OF ACCESSION (BRUSSELS):

Calmann, J., *The Rome Treaty—the Common Market Explained* (London, 1967).
Treaty establishing The European Coal and Steel Community (Cmnd 4863, H.M.S.O., 1972).

Treaty establishing the European Economic Community (Cmnd 4864, H.M.S.O., 1972).
Treaty establishing the European Atomic Energy Community (Cmnd 4865, H.M.S.O., 1972).
THE INSTITUTIONS OF THE EUROPEAN COMMUNITIES:
Mayne, R., *The Institutions of the European Community* (London, 1968).
Oudenhove, G. van, *The Political Parties in the European Parliament* (Leyden, 1965).
THE TARIFF STRUCTURE OF THE COMMON MARKET:
Walsh, A. E., and Paxton, J., *Trade in the Common Market Countries* (London, 1968). *Trade and Industrial Resources of the Common Market and EFTA Countries* (London, 1971).
COMMUNITY LAW IN THE MEMBER STATES:
Bebr, G., *Judicial Control of the European Communities* (London, 1962).
Scheingold, S. A., *The Rule of Law in European Interaction: The Path of the Schuman Plan* (Yale Univ. Press, 1965).
Schmitthoff, C. M., *The Harmonisation of European Company Law* (London, 1973).
AGRICULTURE AND FISHERIES:
Agricultural Policy of the European Economic Community (O.E.C.D., Paris, 1974).
Butterwick, M., and Neville-Rolfe, E., *Agricultural Marketing in the E.E.C.* (London, 1971).
The Common Agricultural Policy of the European Community (Cmnd 3274, H.M.S.O., 1967).
Farmers' and Growers' Guide to the E.E.C. (London, 1972).
Marsh, J., and Josling, T., *Agricultural Policy and the Common Market* (London, 1971).
Rogers, S. J., and Davey, B. H., *The Common Agricultural Policy and Britain* (London, 1973).
Tracey, M., *Agriculture in Western Europe* (London, 1964).
SALES AND TURNOVER TAXATION:
Dosser, D., *British Taxation and the E.E.C.* (London, 1973).
Report of the Committee on Turnover Taxation (H.M.S.O., 1971).
Value-added Tax, Report of the National Economic Development Office (H.M.S.O., 1971).
THE RULES OF COMPETITION:
Dyas, G. P., and Thanheiser, H. T., *The Emerging European Enterprise*

Bibliography

(London, 1976).

Love, J., (ed.) *Jane's Major Companies of Europe* (London, annual).

Swann, D., and McLachlan, D. L., *Competition Policy of the European Community* (London, 1967).

Walsh, A. E., and Paxton, J., *Competition Policy: European and International Trends and Practices* (London, 1975).

INDUSTRIAL PROPERTY: PATENTS AND TRADE MARKS:

Second Preliminary Draft of a Convention Establishing a European System for the Grant of Patents, 2 vols (Brussels, 1971).

TRADE UNIONS IN THE E.E.C.:

Beever, R. C., *European Unity and the Trade Union Movement* (Leyden, 1960).

Kendall, W., and Marx, E., *Unions in Europe* (London, 1972).

Stewart, M., *Employment Conditions in Europe* (London, 1973).

Williams, M., *Directory of Unions in the European Economic Community* (London, 1974).

COMMON TRANSPORT POLICY:

Despicht, N., *The Transport Policy of the European Community* (London, 1969).

REGIONAL POLICY:

Barzanti, S., *The Underdeveloped Areas within the Common Market* (Princeton Univ. Press, 1968).

Holland, S., *The Regional Problem* (London, 1976).

Lilly, W. G., *Plant Location in Europe* (London, 1974).

AGREEMENTS OF ASSOCIATION AND TRADE:

Coffey, P., *The External Economic Relations of the E.E.C.* (London, 1976).

Morgan, E. V., and Harrington, R., *Capital Markets and the E.E.C.* (London, 1977).

Okigbo, P. N. C., *Africa and the Common Market* (London, 1967).

Zartman, I. W., *The Politics of Trade Negotiations between Africa and the E.E.C.* (London, 1971).